With Liberty and Justice for All

The Story of the Bill of Rights

Student Text

Center for Civic Education 5146 Douglas Fir Road • Calabasas, CA 91302 • (818) 591-9321

Directed by the
Center for Civic Education
and
Funded by the
U.S. Department of Education by act of Congress
Established 1987 under the
Commission on the Bicentennial of the United States Constitution

CURR
JK
38
.W41
1994

Copyright © **Center for Civic Education** 1991
Fourth Printing 1994

ISBN 0-89818-144-5

Acknowledgments

The following staff and consultants have contributed to the development of this text.

Editorial Directors
Charles N. Quigley
Duane E. Smith

Editorial Associates
Judith A. Matz
Lorenca Rosal

Art Director and Illustrator
Richard Stein

Staff Associates
Elaine Craig
Wilson Jordan
Alita Letwin
Mark Molli
Kenneth Rodriguez
Jane Sure

Photo Research
Lisa Hartjens/Imagefinders

Production
Roslyn Danberg
Michael Geller
David Hargrove
Lisa Mathwig
Pat Mathwig
Theresa Richard
Jan Ruyle
Valerie Stephens
Dan Wojcik

Outline Preparation
Howard Gillman, Assistant Professor, Dept. of Political Science, University of Southern California

Unit Resource Papers and Reviews
Jack Coogan, Consultant
Michelle Dye, Honors Research Associate, Dept. of Political Science, University of Colorado
Howard Gillman, Assistant Professor, Dept. of Political Science, University of Southern California

Calvin Jillson, Professor, Dept. of Political Science, University of Colorado
Donald Nieman, Professor, Dept. of History, Clemson University
Thomas Pangle, Professor, Dept. of Political Science, University of Toronto
Melvin Urofsky, Professor, Dept. of History, Virginia Commonwealth University
Tinsley Yarbrough, Professor, Dept. of Political Science, East Carolina University

The Center wants to express special appreciation for their assistance to **Chairman Warren E. Burger** and the **staff of the Commission on the Bicentennial of the United States Constitution**. In particular, we have enjoyed the insight and thoughtful suggestions during the preparation of this manuscript from **Herbert Atherton**, Staff Director; **Jackson Barlow**, Associate Director of Education for Higher Education; and **Steven Sorensen**, Program Officer. Appreciation is also owed to **Anne Fickling**, Associate Director of Education for Grants, who has provided support to the Center in all aspects of this project.

The Center is also grateful for the many helpful comments and suggestions that have been received from the following persons who have reviewed the manuscript in its various stages. The Center has attempted to be responsive to all the many valuable suggestions for improvement in the text. However, the final product is the responsibility of the Center and does not necessarily reflect the views of those who have contributed their thoughts and ideas.

Field Review and Critique

Herbert Atherton, Staff Director
and Director of Education,
Commission on the Bicentennial
of the United States Constitution
William Baker, Governor's Task
Force on Citizenship Education, Indiana
Jack Barlow, Assistant Professor
of Political Science, Juniata College,
Huntingdon, PA - formerly
Associate Director of Education
for Higher Education,
Commission on the Bicentennial
of the United States Constitution

Alvin Bell, Teacher,
Findlay High School,
Findlay, Ohio
Margaret Branson, Administrator,
Division of Instructional
Services of the Kern County
Superintendent of Schools Office,
Bakersfield, California
R. Freeman Butts, William F. Russell
Professor Emeritus in the
Foundation of Education,
Teachers College,
Columbia University, New York

John Calimano, Teacher,
East Brunswick High School,
East Brunswick, New Jersey
Jim Creighton, Teacher,
Alden Central High School,
Alden, New York
Michael Fischer, Associate,
Bureau of Social Studies Education,
Albany, New York
Carter Hart, Jr., Consultant,
New Hampshire Department
of Education,
Concord, New Hampshire

Martha de la Houssaye, Teacher, Academy of the Sacred Heart, New Orleans, Louisiana
Pat Hussein, Teacher, Fremont High School, Los Angeles, California
Leon Letwin, Professor, School of Law, University of California at Los Angeles
Herbert Morris, Dean, Division of Humanities, University of California at Los Angeles

Ron Morris, Teacher, Arcadia High School, Arcadia, California
Arthur Pease, Social Studies Coordinator, Lebanon, New Hampshire
Cruz Reynoso, Professor, School of Law, University of California at Los Angeles
Constance Slaughter-Harvey, Assistant Secretary of State and General Counsel, Jackson, Mississippi

Deborah Snow, Teacher, East Kenwood High School, Grand Rapids, Michigan
Steven Sorensen, Program Officer, Commission on the Bicentennial of the United States Constitution
Richard Wasserstrom, Professor, Department of Philosophy, University of California, Santa Cruz

Table of Contents

Introduction

The Bicentennial of the Bill of Rights provides us an opportunity to reflect on the unique heritage of freedom we enjoy and the important role citizens have played in preserving that heritage. The vitality of the Bill of Rights reflects the human urge for freedom, the wisdom and experience of the Founders, and the commitment of Americans throughout our history to make the promise of freedom and equality a reality for all people.

Our government derives all its power from the people who created it. Its purpose, as enshrined in the Constitution and Bill of Rights, is to protect the freedom of every individual. The role of the judiciary has always been to preserve these constitutional protections.

But the preservation of individual rights is not, and cannot be, the sole responsibility of the judiciary. All branches of government and citizens alike share this responsibility. We must all develop an understanding of the principles and values of the Bill of Rights and make the commitment necessary to promote liberty, justice, and equality.

by

Warren E. Burger, Chairman

Commission on the Bicentennial of the United States Constitution

Chief Justice of the United States, 1969-1986

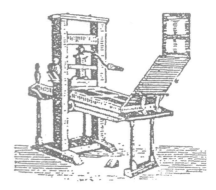

Preface

The first ten amendments to the Constitution are known as the Bill of Rights. They contain some of the basic rights of individuals that the government is prohibited from violating. For example, the government may not interfere with your freedom to believe what you wish. The government may not stop you from practicing your beliefs unless your doing so clearly endangers others.

When the Framers wrote our Constitution and Bill of Rights, they were careful to include written protections of what they thought were many of the basic rights of a free people. They intended to prevent such violations of rights as they had experienced under the British government and, in some cases, by their own state governments. In the eighteenth century, however, these rights were not thought to be possessed equally by everyone. Generally speaking, they were the rights of free, white men. The history of the Bill of Rights is the history of the evolution of our thinking about rights: what rights we have, why they are important, and how they were extended to people denied them in the past.

Today we often take our rights for granted. They are so much a part of our everyday lives, we rarely think what it would be like not to have them. If you were told that the government would not allow you to read or write what you wanted or to criticize the government, you would probably say, "They can't do that!" or "This is America! I have a perfect right to say that I think our mayor or governor is doing a terrible job."

Most Americans would agree with you. Americans have been talking about their rights for over two hundred years. In fact, some people say we Americans talk so much about our rights that we fail to pay enough attention to our responsibilities. As you study this text, you will learn why it is important we understand both our rights and our responsibilities in order to promote liberty and justice for all people.

This book is not like most history books which focus upon the story of the people and events of the past. This book is a **history of ideas** that have influenced the development of our Bill of Rights and its application to the events of today. Throughout the book we will use the term **Framers** to refer to the people who drafted our Constitution and Bill of Rights. We will use the term **Founders** to refer to all of the men and women who were influential in creating our government. We will also use the term **federal government** to refer to the national government as opposed to state and local governments.

At the beginning of each lesson, you will find a list of the most important ideas and terms discussed in that lesson. These ideas and terms are defined in the lesson itself or in the glossary at the end of the book. Each lesson also begins with a statement of its purpose to guide your reading and understanding.

We hope this book will help you develop an understanding and appreciation for the rights you have inherited and the constant need to protect and insure them for all people.

An Introduction to the Study of the Bill of Rights

American colonist James Otis argues before a British judge against searches and seizures by the king's officials (1761).

Purpose of Introduction

During the period before the Revolution, Americans constantly complained that the British were violating their rights. In response, the British said Americans were obsessed with the idea of rights—which they did not understand—and were claiming rights no British subject had.

The idea of rights was a difficult one. Even the most educated Americans debated the subject constantly, and the average person was often confused. In 1780, townspeople in Massachusetts begged the delegates who were writing their state constitution to talk about rights in a language they could understand.

Even today confusion and disagreement still exist. Although Americans feel as strongly as ever about their rights, a recent survey indicated that only 47% of the adults polled knew that the Bill of Rights is the first ten amendments to the Constitution. Other polls have also shown an alarming ignorance among citizens of their rights and the purposes of the Constitution and Bill of Rights.

The lessons in this introduction begin by giving you an opportunity to test your own understanding of the Bill of Rights. You will also explore other legal protections for your rights and consider the relationship between rights and responsibilities. These lessons will demonstrate the importance of understanding the history of rights and will introduce a way to analyze rights in relation to contemporary issues.

LESSON 1

What Do You Know About the Bill of Rights?

Purpose of Lesson

This lesson consists of three critical thinking exercises that will help to clarify your understanding of the Bill of Rights and its purposes. First we will begin by examining what you already know about the subject. Then we will look closely at the First Amendment to see what it appears to do. Finally, we will look at the entire Bill of Rights to identify its purposes and then provide you an opportunity to revise and extend your answers to the first exercise.

When you have completed this lesson, you should be able to explain some of the basic purposes of the Bill of Rights. Before you begin, you may wish to look at the glossary at the end of this text for definitions of the following terms: amendment, bill of rights, federal government, state and local government.

What is the importance of freedom of the press?

Critical Thinking Exercise I
EXAMINING YOUR KNOWLEDGE OF THE BILL OF RIGHTS

Write your answers to the following questions based upon what you already know about the Bill of Rights. Do not refer to the Bill of Rights itself or any other references. Be prepared to discuss your answers with the class.

1. What rights are protected by the Bill of Rights?

2. From whom does the Bill of Rights protect you?

3. Does the Bill of Rights provide all the protections you need for your lives, liberty, and property? Explain your answer.

Now that you have thought generally about the Bill of Rights, perhaps it will help you if we examine in more depth one of its amendments.

Critical Thinking Exercise II
EXAMINING THE FIRST AMENDMENT

Let's examine the First Amendment of the Bill of Rights to see what it appears to do. Work in small groups to review the amendment. Each group should develop and record its answers to the questions that follow and be prepared to discuss them with the entire class.

Amendment I: *Congress shall make no law respecting an establishment of religion, or prohibiting the free exercise thereof; or abridging freedom of speech, or of the press; or the right of the people peaceably to assemble, and to petition the Government for a redress of grievances.*

1. The powers of which branches of government are limited by this amendment?

2. Does this amendment appear to limit the powers of your state or local governments?

3. From whom does the amendment protect you?

4. Does the amendment appear to require the federal government to protect your rights from violations by private individuals? From violations by state or local governments? Explain your answer.

5. What appear to be the purposes of each limitation of power contained in the First Amendment?

6. Does the First Amendment provide all the protections you need for your rights to freedom of religion and expression? Explain your answer.

How does freedom of assembly enable people to influence government policy?

Now that you have examined and discussed the First Amendment, the following exercise provides you an opportunity to reconsider some of your original ideas about the Bill of Rights.

Critical Thinking Exercise III
REVISING YOUR ANSWERS TO THE FIRST EXERCISE

Complete this lesson by revising your answers to the first exercise in light of what you have learned. Follow these steps:

1. Refer to the Bill of Rights in the Appendix. Find at least three rights it contains that you did not list in response to Question 1 in the first exercise. What appear to be the purposes of the additional rights you have identified?

2. Review your answers to the other questions in the first exercise and make any changes or additions to them you think should be made. How, if at all, do your answers in Exercise II differ from your answers in Exercise I?

Using the Lesson

1. What arguments can you make for having a written Bill of Rights containing amendments such as those you have just examined?

2. What might be the advantages and disadvantages of having a list of rights the government cannot violate?

3. Can you think of any laws that might protect your rights from violations by private individuals? Who do you think would enforce these laws?

LESSON 2

Where Are Legal Protections of Your Rights Found?

Purpose of Lesson

The exercises in Lesson 1 should have helped clarify your understanding of the Bill of Rights and its purposes. It is important to understand that there are also other laws that protect your rights. This lesson will help you learn where various legal protections of your rights may be found. It will also provide you an opportunity to discuss the relationship between rights and responsibilities.

When you have finished this lesson, you should be able to identify various sources of legal protections of individual rights. You should also be able to explain the importance of the relationship between rights and responsibilities.

Terms to Know

federal government
state and local government
state constitution
criminal law
civil law
civil rights law

Critical Thinking Exercise
IDENTIFYING LAWS THAT PROTECT YOUR RIGHTS

Each of the following imaginary situations involves a possible violation of a legal right. Work individually or with a study partner to review each situation and to answer the questions that follow. Then be prepared to discuss your answers with the class.

- You buy a stereo set that fails to work after a week. Although it has a one-year warranty, the store from which you bought it claims you were responsible for breaking it. Despite the warranty, the store refuses to repair the stereo or to give you a new one. You claim you have a right to have the stereo repaired free of charge or to be given a new one.

- Your bike is stolen. You learn from a friend the identity of the person who has stolen it. You want the bike returned and the person arrested and punished.

- You participate in a demonstration that becomes violent. Although you are not involved in the

violence, you are arrested and jailed. The police fail to inform you of your right to a lawyer and question you about all the people you know who were involved in the demonstration.

What laws protect your rights?

1. In which of these situations might your rights be protected by the Bill of Rights? From whom would they be protected? Explain your answer.

2. In which situations might the Bill of Rights not protect you? What laws might protect you in those situations? Explain your answer.

Where can you find legal protections for your rights?

The Bill of Rights was adopted to protect you from violations of your rights by people serving in the **federal government**. Later amendments to the Constitution have extended most of its provisions to protect you from the actions of **state** and **local governments**.

Your rights are also protected by other laws. These are found in the body of the Constitution itself, in your state constitutions, in laws passed by Congress and your state and local legislatures, and in court decisions. These different legal protections of rights are explained below.

1. **The Constitution, Bill of Rights, and other amendments.** The Constitution, the Bill of Rights, and subsequent amendments to the Constitution contain protections of individual rights from actions by the government. They prohibit members of government from violating such rights as freedom of religion and speech. They also protect the rights of persons accused of crimes to a fair hearing in a court of law.

If the government violates the rights of an individual, that person may write to his or her member of Congress or to the local newspaper. Individuals whose rights are violated also have the right to complain in court. If the court finds the government has violated the person's rights, the judge will order the government to stop doing so. The court may also order that the person be compensated and it may even punish the member of government who violated the right.

If you look at the Bill of Rights, you will see it contains a list of things the government may not do. For example, it may not take private property for public use without just compensation. In this way, it limits the powers of government.

In some cases, the limits on the government's power also require the government to do certain things. For example, the right to a fair hearing for someone accused of a crime means the government must provide courtrooms, judges, and juries. It must also provide the opportunity for the testimony and presentation of evidence that is required for a fair hearing.

A person accused of a serious crime has the right to have a lawyer in his or her defense. This right has been interpreted by the courts to mean that the government must provide a lawyer free of charge to persons accused of serious crimes who cannot afford to pay for one themselves.

What rights would you want if you were accused of a crime?

2. **State constitutions and bills of rights.** Each state also has a constitution that establishes the state government. These **state constitutions** contain bills of rights that limit the powers of state and local governments in order to protect your rights.

If a member of a state or local government violates any of these rights, people may be able to get help by appealing to public officials or by writing to their local newspapers. There are also organizations that will assist people who think their rights are being violated by the government.

If all else fails, you can ask a state court for protection. In some cases, you can ask a federal court for help. We will talk more about state constitutions in Unit Three.

3. **Civil and criminal laws.** You also have numerous rights not protected under constitutions that are protected by criminal and civil laws passed by your state and local legislatures, by Congress, and by court decisions. For example, some of these laws protect your right to property. Suppose a person steals something from you or destroys your home. You typically would have rights under both the criminal and civil law in your state.

The **criminal law** protects your right to property and to be secure in your home. It makes violations of these rights crimes. Your state and local governments provide police departments to prevent such crimes and to find and arrest persons who commit them. They also provide courts in which to try the accused person.

The **civil law** would give you the right to sue the person to make him or her pay for your property and any other damages for which that person is held responsible.

Some laws passed by Congress or your state legislatures are designed to protect your right to fair treatment by private persons, groups, organizations, or businesses, as well as by your government. These are often called **civil rights laws**. For example, some of these laws prevent businesses from refusing to hire qualified people because of their race, sex, or age.

Are laws enough to protect rights?

Many nations have statements of rights that claim to protect their citizens. In many of these societies, these rights are only paid lip service and are violated continually.

The existence of a written constitution or a bill of rights does not mean that citizens actually have the rights they contain. Nor does the existence of civil and criminal laws guarantee that citizens will actually receive the rights the laws are supposed to protect.

People who have observed the common violations of individual rights in our own society and others have argued that the most important protection of rights lies in the hearts and minds of the people of a nation. The following exercise contains a statement Judge Learned Hand made to the graduating class at Yale University in 1941.

Critical Thinking Exercise
ANALYZING JUDGE HAND'S STATEMENT

Work in small groups to read the following quotation and answer the questions that follow it. Be prepared to discuss your answers with your class.

I often wonder whether we do not rest our hopes too much upon constitutions, upon laws and courts. These are false hopes; believe me, these are false hopes. Liberty lies in the hearts of men; when it dies there, no constitution, no law, no court can save it; no constitution, no law, no court can even do much to help it. While it lies there it needs no constitution, no law, no court to save it.

1. What are the major points in Judge Hand's argument?

2. What responsibilities of citizens are implied by his position?

3. **What do *you* think?**

   a. Do you agree with Judge Hand's position? Explain your answer.

   b. In view of Judge Hand's statement about where liberty lies, do you think that constitutions and bills of rights are unnecessary? Explain your position.

Americans' historical emphasis upon rights

The United States Constitution and Bill of Rights are based on the belief that the major purpose of government is to provide citizens with security and safety. This makes it possible for people to live their lives generally as they wish so long as they don't interfere with the rights of others to live as they wish. Americans have also believed that individuals possess certain basic rights. These are the rights to life, liberty, property, and the pursuit of happiness.

The Founders thought that while government was necessary, it was also the greatest threat to individual rights. This is why the Constitution and Bill of Rights contain so many ways to limit the powers of government. The Bill of Rights is intended to prevent majorities from using government to violate the rights of individuals. Men such as James Madison thought that in a democracy, the greatest threat came from majorities who would use the power of the government to oppress minorities. We also now know that it is sometimes possible for powerful minorities using money, advertising skills, and political organization to present the same kind of danger. The limits imposed on government by the Constitution and Bill of Rights serve to protect our rights from both majorities and powerful minorities.

Some people have argued that Americans are so concerned with their individual rights that they tend to forget about individual duties to society. One of the most frequent criticisms of Americans is that their emphasis on individual rights and their own self-interest prevents them from working together effectively to find common solutions to common problems.

When you have finished your study of the history, philosophy, and development of the Bill of Rights, you will be in a better position to respond to this criticism.

Using the Lesson

1. What examples can you give of rights protected by civil and criminal law that are not protected by the Bill of Rights?

2. Select a particular right and explain what you think is the greatest threat to it.

3. What do you think is important for the preservation of our rights besides the Constitution and Bill of Rights?

4. What responsibility should be taken by the schools in promoting an understanding and respect for individual rights? How might schools fulfill this responsibility?

LESSON 3

How Can Studying the History of Rights Help You Deal with Contemporary Issues?

Purpose of Lesson

This lesson will help you understand why it is important to study the history of rights. It provides a brief review of the historical background and contemporary relevance of freedom of the press. The lesson will discuss the importance of freedom of the press, the consequences of its suppression, and common threats to this right. It will also identify conflicts between this right and other important rights and interests.

When you have finished this lesson, you should be able to explain how studying the history of a right can help you deal with contemporary issues. You should also be able to take and defend positions on issues involving freedom of the press.

Terms to Know

freedom of conscience
censorship
prior restraint
seditious libel
right to know
freedom of expression

Examining the history of specific rights

The first eight amendments of the Bill of Rights contain a listing of specific rights the government is prohibited from violating. To understand why the first Congress considered these rights so important, it is useful to look at their history. By doing so, you will learn that certain basic rights have been violated by governments throughout history, usually in order to maintain power at the expense of the people. You will also learn that issues regarding these rights exist today. This understanding should help you learn to take and defend reasoned positions on such issues.

To illustrate the usefulness of knowing the history of rights, we will examine briefly the history of freedom of the press and look at a contemporary issue regarding this right. But before doing so, we need to discuss the question of limitations upon rights.

When should rights be limited?

One of the few rights that most people would argue should not be limited is **freedom of conscience** or belief. People should be free to hold their own beliefs about what is right and wrong. Many consider this an absolute right, one that has no limitations.

Apart from freedom of conscience, people usually take the position that other rights may be limited in specific situations when it is necessary to balance their importance against other rights, values, or interests with which they may conflict. For example, the right to freedom of the press does not protect a person who has published military secrets that cause the loss of American lives. Even the right to life itself may be limited in a situation where the only way for a police officer to save an innocent person's life is to take the life of someone threatening to kill that person.

Generally, limitations are placed upon rights in order to

- **protect the rights of other individuals.** Your right to speak at a public meeting, for example, might be limited by the need to provide other people an equal right to speak.

- **protect the welfare of the community**. Your right to use your property as you wish, for example to have a party with loud music, might be limited by laws against disturbing the peace.

How to make fair and reasonable decisions about the proper limits of rights is a subject that will be dealt with throughout this text. We will begin this study by dealing with the question of placing limitations on freedom of the press.

The right to freedom of the press

Ever since the printing press was invented, governments have tried to control what was printed and distributed to the people of their nations. This control was usually intended to prevent the publication and distribution of information that was critical of government, its policies, or its leaders. Controlling the press was seen as an important way to control the minds and thoughts of the people.

The following is a brief account of the history of the attempts by the British government to control the press in the seventeenth and eighteenth centuries. Since the Founders were

British subjects, they were familiar with this history, and it influenced their ideas about freedom of the press.

Printing presses were first used in England at the end of the fifteenth century. For many years, the ownership and use of printing presses were controlled by acts of the British king, the Parliament, and the Star Chamber. The licensing act passed in Parliament is an example of such control. Under this act, nothing could be published in England without first being approved by an official of the government or the Church of England. Further, no books could be imported or sold without such approval. This type of control or **censorship** is called **prior restraint**. A government restrains (controls) the press prior to (before) publication of materials to which it objects.

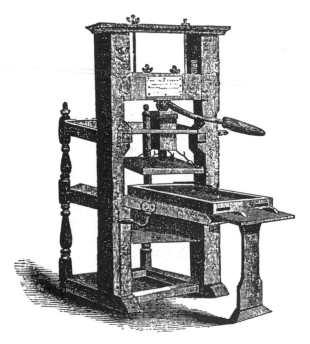

Why would a government want to limit freedom of the press?

The attitude of many government leaders toward the press can be seen in an account of events in the Virginia colony in the seventeenth century. The English governor outlawed all printing presses in the colony. He claimed that learning made people disobey and gather together with others who were critical of the government. Printing encouraged people to learn and criticize even the best governments. He concluded by asking God to safeguard Virginia from ever having free schools and printing presses and hoped they would not have them for a hundred years.

England's licensing act expired in 1695. After that time, there was no direct government censorship of the press in England or in the American colonies. However, the government estab-

lished another, perhaps more effective, way of controlling the press. This was the law of **seditious libel**. The law said that anyone who wrote or published anything that criticized the government or its leaders, or that made people dissatisfied with them, could be arrested and tried in court. Anyone found guilty could be punished according to the law. In some instances, people were imprisoned and even executed. The laws of seditious libel were an effective means of controlling criticism of the government.

Even after the American Revolution, some state governments had laws of seditious libel. Under these laws, editors were prosecuted for printing criticisms of the government. Critics of President John Adams, for example, were fined and imprisoned, sometimes for relatively minor offenses. When President Adams visited New Jersey, cannons were fired in a ceremony honoring him. Luther Baldwin was overheard to say he hoped the cotton wadding behind the powder would hit the President in the seat of his pants. Baldwin was fined $100.

For more than a hundred years, state governments sometimes violated freedom of the press. It was not until after World War I that the Supreme Court began to expand the protection of freedom of the press to the level found today.

Critical Thinking Exercise
EXAMINING THE RIGHT TO FREEDOM OF THE PRESS

1. What means did the British government use to control the press?

2. Why would leaders of a government want to control the press? What kinds of ideas would they want to suppress? Whose interests might they be protecting?

3. What arguments can you make for protecting freedom of the press?

4. What values and interests, such as freedom of conscience, privacy, or intellectual growth, might be endangered if there were no limits placed on the press?

5. What limits, if any, should your government be able to place on freedom of the press? Explain your position.

Why should citizens have the right to know what their government is doing?

Under our Constitution, the people are the ultimate source of the authority of the government. The government is the servant, not the master, of the people. The people have the right to tell officials in the government what they want them to do and how they should do it. They have the right to participate in their government by such means as voting, joining political parties and interest groups, supporting candidates, and running for office themselves.

The people also have the **right to know** how well the members of their government are doing their jobs. Citizens must have access to information on how the government is fulfilling its responsibilities to make sure it is fulfilling them properly. Therefore, some people claim that the government has no right to control what may be said or heard by citizens. Others have difficulty with this position. They claim that, in certain situations, the right to know and freedom of expression can conflict with other important values and interests.

The First Amendment protects the rights to freedom of speech, the press, assembly, and petition. These rights have been interpreted to guarantee **freedom of expression** to all Americans. Freedom of expression is essential in communicating information, ideas, and opinions. The First Amendment is also considered to protect the people's right to know. This right means that the

- press has the right to investigate situations, and the
- public has a right to that information. Most important, the public has the right to know how the government is doing its job. Despite the importance of the public's right to know, it may be necessary sometimes to place limitations on this right. Suppose your government is conducting a war. What issues would this situation raise regarding the public's right to know?

Should the government be the public's only source of information during wartime?

What issues of rights were involved during the Persian Gulf War?

During the war in the Persian Gulf, a number of reporters complained that the Department of Defense was placing too many restrictions on the news media. As a result, members of Congress decided to hold a hearing to investigate these accusations. The meeting was held by the Committee on Government Affairs of the United States Senate. Witnesses from the Department of Defense and the news media testified.

What limits should be placed upon the press during wartime?

Representatives of the Department of Defense explained the procedures they had established to handle reporters in the battlefield area. Reporters were assigned to small groups or "pools" which had to be escorted by military officers at all times. They could only go where they were taken by the military. Reporters had to submit their stories to military officers for review before publication. If the military officers found information they thought might aid the enemy, it was cut out of the stories. The Department representative admitted that some of the military escorts had been overly strict in supervising the reporters.

Walter Cronkite, a famous reporter and commentator, testified for the news media. He said that during World War II, reporters had been free to travel anywhere and see anything. Then they wrote their stories and submitted them to the military censor. The censor took out any information that might be helpful to the enemy; the rest was published.

Cronkite complained that during the Persian Gulf War reporters were not free to travel wherever and whenever they wanted. Reporters were told what they could not see, not what they could not report. According to Cronkite and others, such a system did not allow reporters to gather information and report it properly. Limitations on access to information was a form of censorship. It made it far more difficult for the American public to decide whether the news they were receiving was accurate and could be trusted.

An independent expert testified that the press had sent too many reporters to the region to be handled effectively. He also claimed that the reporters often asked questions during televised briefings that the military should not answer in order to protect the troops. Other people argued that because of the modern technologies involved in newsgathering, it is not possible to allow reporters the freedom they enjoyed in the pre-television days of World War II.

How much should you have the right to know when your government is conducting a war?

Most Americans agree that during a war it may be necessary to place some limits on the public's right to know. The difficulty is deciding what these limits should be. The situation raises the following important questions:

- **Access to information.** Should the government be required to allow reporters to know everything it is doing? For example, how far should the government be able to go in limiting a reporter's knowledge of how it is conducting the war?

- **Reporting information.** Should reporters be allowed to broadcast on television or publish whatever they may find out about the conduct of the war? How far should the government be able to go in limiting what reporters tell the public about how the war is being conducted? For example, should the government be given the power to review what reporters are planning to say or write from the battlefield and censor information that might endanger the lives of our troops?

These questions highlight the need to find a reasonable balance between the

- **right to know**, that is, the public's right to know how the government is conducting a war, and the

- **welfare of the nation**, that is, the government's responsibility to control the release of information that may endanger the troops in the field, national security, or the welfare of the nation.

Critical Thinking Exercise
ANALYZING ISSUES OF RIGHTS

The following questions will help you analyze some of the issues of rights that emerged during the Persian Gulf War. These questions may be used to analyze a wide variety of rights you will encounter as you explore the Bill of Rights.

Work in small groups to develop your answers to the following questions. Then be prepared to share and discuss your answers with the entire class.

1. **Describe the rights.** What rights are involved in this situation?

2. **Purposes.** What are the purposes of the rights you have identified? What arguments are used to support them?

3. **History.** What have you learned from history about why governments have often abused the rights you have identified?

4. **Limits.** Under what conditions have these rights been limited? What conflicts did these limitations raise? When do you think these rights should be limited?

5. **What do *you* think?** What position would you take on the issue of the public's right to know and the government's responsibility to protect national security during the Persian Gulf War? Be prepared to discuss and defend your positions.

Using the Lesson

1. What is the importance, in a free society, of the citizen's right to know how the government is doing its job?

2. What responsibility does a government in a free society have to make information available to the public?

3. What criteria should be used to determine how much control over information a government should have?

4. Who should settle conflicts over whether the people in the government are controlling information in order to serve the national interests or to promote their own interests?

Unit One: What Did the Founders Learn About Rights from History and Their Own Experiences?

What is the importance of the idea that your home is your castle?

Purpose of Unit

Americans in the seventeenth and eighteenth centuries believed that each individual has certain rights just because he or she is a human being. They also believed that while government is necessary, it is the greatest threat to people's rights. This fear of government came from the Founders' study of history and political philosophy, and from their own experiences. Because of this fear, the Founders thought the most important thing the Constitution should do is to limit the powers of government in order to protect individual rights.

Unit One will help you understand how the Founders developed their ideas on rights. They were influenced by their study of philosophy and their understanding of history from ancient times to their own time.

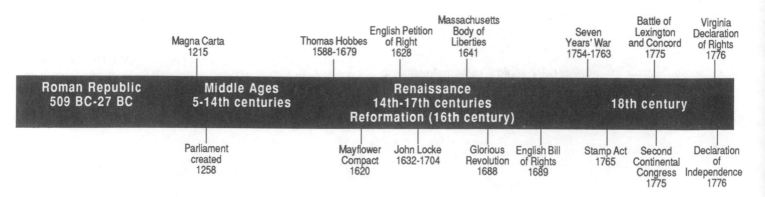

LESSON 4

How Did Our Ideas About Individual Rights Develop?

Purpose of Lesson

Our basic ideas today about individual rights and government are similar to those of the Founders. However, their ideas were very different from those commonly held throughout much of the history of Western Europe. This lesson will help you understand how the Founders' ideas about individual rights developed from earlier ideas about rights. We will focus upon ideas about rights that were held during the Greek and Roman Republics, the Middle Ages, the Renaissance, and the Reformation.

When you have finished this lesson, you should be able to explain the ideas about rights that predominated during the historical periods discussed. You should also be able to explain the special influence of the Renaissance and the Reformation on ideas about individual rights.

Terms to Know

individual rights
rights of groups
Roman Republic
common welfare
classical republicanism
civic virtue
moral education
diversity

factions
established religion
Middle Ages
feudalism
Renaissance
capitalism
Reformation

What is meant by the rights of groups?

The emphasis on **individual rights** is relatively recent in Western history, dating from the early sixteenth century. In ancient Greece and Rome and during the Middle Ages, individual rights were not thought to be as important as they are now. People emphasized the duties imposed on citizens by law, by God, or by society—not their rights.

Rights and duties were usually spoken of as belonging to members of various groups in society. The emphasis was upon the **rights of groups**, not the rights of individuals. For example, people spoke of the rights of royalty and the nobility,

the rights of the clergy, and the rights of tradesmen and craftsmen in groups called guilds. Any rights and duties individuals might have were usually related to their membership in such groups.

What ideas about rights are found in classical republicanism?

The Founders had studied the history of the classical periods of ancient Greece and Rome. The society that had the greatest influence on their ideas was that of the **Roman Republic**. This republic lasted for almost 500 years, from 509 B.C. to 27 B.C. Many philosophers and historians believed the Roman Republic had provided Roman citizens with the greatest amount of liberty under government that the world had ever known. It was also widely believed that the Roman Republic promoted the **common welfare**, that is, what was best for the entire society. The theory based on this form of society became known as **classical republicanism**.

Should the common welfare be the most important purpose of government?

Classical republicanism is a theory that the best kind of society is one that promotes the common welfare instead of the interests of only one class of citizens. In a classical republic, citizens are supposed to work cooperatively to achieve the common welfare rather than their own personal or selfish interests. The Roman Republic was thought to be one of the best examples of this type of society. Americans in the eighteenth century shared the view that citizens should work to promote the common welfare. They also believed that a republican government was the best type to serve this purpose. They thought that for a republican government to work, a society had to have the following characteristics:

1. **Civic virtue.** The classical republics demanded that their citizens have a high degree of civic virtue. A person with civic virtue was one who set aside personal interests to promote the common welfare.

Citizens were expected to participate fully in their government to promote the common welfare. They were not to be left free to devote themselves to their personal interests. They were discouraged from spending much time doing such things as making money or caring for their families. They were also discouraged from traveling or reading and thinking about things that had nothing to do with their government. If citizens had the freedom to do such things, it was feared, they might stop being reliable and fully dedicated to the common welfare.

To make sure citizens participated in their government, the classical republics often drastically limited individual rights. There was little concern with protecting an individual's family privacy, freedom of conscience or religion, or non-political speech or expression.

There were certain rights, however, that it was important for citizens to have in order to participate in governing themselves. These were political rights such as the right to vote, to express ideas and opinions about government, and to serve in public office.

2. **Moral education.** People who believed in classical republicanism were convinced that civic virtue is not something that comes automatically to people. Citizens must be reared and taught to be virtuous by moral education based on a civic religion consisting of gods, goddesses, and their rituals.

The classical republicans believed that young citizens must be raised to develop the right habits. They should learn to admire people with civic virtue who were described in literature, poetry, and music. Children as well as adults should be encouraged—partly by the belief in a watchful god or gods— to practice virtues such as generosity, courage, self-control, and fairness. They should learn the importance of their responsibility to take part in political debate and military service. The whole community must therefore closely supervise the upbringing of the next generation of citizens and the daily lives of one another.

3. **Small, uniform communities.** The classical republicans also believed that a republican government would only work in a small community. A small community is necessary if people are to know and care for each other and their common welfare. The classical republicans believed that people must

Why did the classical republicans want to limit diversity?

be very much alike and that a great degree of **diversity** should not be tolerated. They did not believe, for example, that people should be very different in their property ownership and wealth, religious or moral beliefs, or ways of life.

The classical republicans believed that if people differed greatly in such things, they would not be concerned with each other's welfare. Instead, they would begin to divide into **factions** or interest groups competing to dominate each other, rather than working together for the common welfare. To prevent this from happening, the classical republicans believed citizens should be supervised to avoid the development of great differences among them in their ownership of property, religion, and way of life.

Their fear of diversity led the classical republicans to be wary of money-making and economic growth. Since only a few people can ever be wealthy, it is better for all to be somewhat poor but equal. To prevent diversity in religious beliefs and lifestyles, the community needs to have one official, **established religion** and one set of family and moral customs to which all conform.

How did ideas about group rights and individual rights change?

The classical periods of ancient Greece and Rome had an important influence on the ideas of the Founders. There were three other periods of history that were also critical in the development of ideas about rights. These periods are described below.

1. **The Middle Ages.** The Middle Ages lasted from the fifth century, when the Roman Empire ended, to the fourteenth century. The political and military structure of medieval society was characterized by **feudalism**.

This was a system in which all land was considered to belong to the king and queen and everyone was subject to their rule. The king gave the land to his nobles in exchange for military or other service. The most important characteristics of feudalism that affected the way in which people thought about rights included the following:

- Society was divided into different classes and groups such as royalty, nobility, the clergy, tradesmen, craftsmen, and serfs. Some of these classes and groups had special privileges. There was no notion of rights possessed equally by everyone.

- If you were born into one of these groups, you had little chance of changing the group to which you belonged.

- Any rights and duties you had were usually spoken of in terms of the group to which you belonged. They were not commonly thought of as belonging to you as an individual member of society.

Feudalism was brought to England by William the Conqueror in the eleventh century. The three classes of English society were the

- **royalty**, which included the king, queen, and their family.

- **nobility**, which were the lords and ladies, the major followers of the king, who held such titles as earl or baron.

- **commons**, which consisted of different groups such as knights, merchants, craftsmen, and large land owners who were not members of the nobility. It did not include the serfs.

Each of these classes had certain rights and responsibilities. For example, the king gave land to the nobility and the right to collect rents from the common people living on their land. The nobility, in return, were responsible for supplying a certain number of knights to serve in the king's army.

It was during the Middle Ages, in 1215, that the English barons forced King John to sign the Magna Carta. Among other things, the Magna Carta protected the rights of the nobility from the king. This feudal contract, which set forth the rights and obligations of the nobility and the king, contained basic ideas that influenced our system of constitutional government. The importance of this document in the history of rights and government will be examined in a later lesson.

2. **The Renaissance.** The Renaissance began in Western Europe in the fourteenth century and lasted until the seventeenth century. The term Renaissance means rebirth. It refers to a renewed interest in classical Greece and Rome. People began to study history, science, literature, art, and philosophy. They expanded their knowledge and view of the world. This led to an increased interest in the rights of individuals and their relationship to religion and government.

As a result, people in Europe began to develop new ideas about the world in which they lived. These ideas were stimulated by a new economic system called **capitalism**. Capitalism is an economic system in which the means of producing and distributing goods are privately owned and operated for profit in a competitive market, rather than being owned or controlled by the government. Under capitalism people gained more freedom to choose their occupations, start their own businesses, and own personal property. More people had a greater

What was the importance of the Renaissance in the development of ideas about individual rights?

degree of control over their lives and how they made their living than had been possible under feudalism in the Middle Ages. This new economic system led people to pay more attention to their private interests in gaining property than to the common welfare.

In all areas of life, greater importance was placed on the individual, rather than the group into which he or she was born. People could work to improve their position in society. As a result, a middle class of successful citizens developed which gained political and economic power.

3. **The Protestant Reformation.** Early in the sixteenth century the Protestant Reformation, a religious reform movement, resulted in the development of new ideas about religion and government. Up to this time, Christianity in Western Europe had been dominated by the Church of Rome (the Roman Catholic Church). Many of the governments of Europe had also been closely tied to the Church.

During the Reformation, other Christian religious groups challenged the authority of the Church of Rome. Protestant churches were established which began to question the relationship between church and government. John Calvin, Martin Luther, and other Protestant reformers also questioned what authority religious institutions should have over the lives of individuals. A number of the European

governments became independent of the Church and a limited amount of religious freedom developed.

The printing press was developed and books that formerly only a few people could own became more available. The Bible was one of the most important of these books. For centuries the Bible had been printed in Latin, which few people other than priests could read. Christians relied upon the Church to convey the word of God to them. During the Reformation, Bibles were printed in English, German, French, Italian, and Spanish. Individuals were encouraged to read the Bible in their own language to determine for themselves what it meant.

Protestant religious doctrine emphasized the direct relationship between the individual believer and God. The result was to reduce the importance of the Church and to increase the importance of the individual. All individuals were seen as equal in the eyes of God. Each individual was to be respected and to be held accountable by God as an individual.

However, the new religious beliefs continued to emphasize the importance of working for the common welfare as had the classical republicans. For example, it was during the Reformation that the Puritans settled in New England. They emphasized the duty of each individual church member to be virtuous and work for the common welfare of the entire church and community.

How did the experiences of the Puritans influence ideas about individual rights?

The Puritans believed that every person was called upon by God to do a particular job. Whatever the task, the good Christian was expected to work hard at his or her calling. The practical result was that by the 1700s, the Puritans in the Massachusetts Bay Colony had prospered. They lived well and had gained a considerable amount of property.

With their newly gained wealth and prosperity, people became less concerned with working for the common welfare and more interested in pursuing their own personal interests. This change brought about a new way of looking at the relationship between individual rights and the common welfare.

How did the Renaissance and Reformation contribute to the growth of individual rights?

The Renaissance and Reformation led to a greater emphasis on the importance of the individual than had existed in the Middle Ages or in classical Greece and Rome. The ideas and opinions of individuals were thought to be more important than before. As the Renaissance emphasized individual economic activity and creativity, the followers of the Protestant Reformation emphasized the relationship between the individual believer and God. Both developments contributed to an increased emphasis on individual rights.

In this lesson, you were introduced to a few of the important developments in the history of thinking about rights. In the next lesson, you will learn about some important philosophical ideas that arose during the seventeenth century. Americans were greatly influenced by these new philosophical ideas as well as the historical developments you have studied.

Critical Thinking Exercise
UNDERSTANDING THE EFFECTS OF THE RENAISSANCE AND REFORMATION ON IDEAS ABOUT RIGHTS

Work individually or with two or three other students to develop responses to the following questions. Be prepared to share your answers with the class.

1. What changes occurred in the way people thought about rights from the time of the classical republics to the Reformation?

2. How did the economic changes during the Renaissance appear to affect people's ideas about rights?

3. How did the religious beliefs of the Reformation appear to affect people's ideas about rights?

4. **What do *you* think?**

   a. If the ideas about rights during the Middle Ages were dominant today, how would they affect your life?

   b. What conflicts might arise in a society that emphasizes both the importance of individual rights and of the common welfare? What evidence, if any, do you see of such conflicts in your own experiences?

Using the Lesson

1. What is meant by the rights of groups as opposed to the rights of individuals? What might be some of the advantages and disadvantages of thinking about rights in terms of groups?

2. What is meant by civic virtue and the common welfare?

3. What dangers did the classical republicans see if a society contained too much diversity? What dangers might result from suppressing diversity in a society?

4. What problems might classical republicans see in trying to establish their type of republican government in the United States today?

LESSON 5

What Influence Did the Ideas of the Natural Rights Philosophers Have on the Founders?

Purpose of Lesson

In the last lesson, you learned about some of the ideas and events of the past that shaped the thinking of the Founders about government and the rights of citizens. However, the most important influence on the ideas of the Founders came from the natural rights philosophers of the seventeenth century. These philosophers believed that individuals have certain basic rights just because they are human beings and the purpose of government should be to protect those rights.

When you have finished this lesson, you should be able to explain the major ideas of the natural rights philosophy and why they were so attractive to Americans.

Terms to Know

> natural rights
> unalienable rights
> state of nature
> consent of the governed
> social contract
> Mayflower Compact

What trends in history influenced the natural rights philosophy?

You have learned some of the major changes that took place in European history from the period of the Roman Republic to the time of the Founders. These changes included increased economic opportunities and the growth of a prosperous middle class that gained political power. New religious beliefs led to different ideas about the relationships among individuals, the church, and government. One of the most important results of these developments was an increased emphasis upon the rights of the individual.

With new ways of thinking about politics, government, and the role of citizens, came greater opportunities for individuals. The class or group into which you were born became less important than what you made of your life. People became more interested in pursuing their private interests and improving their standard of living than in promoting the common welfare. The ideas of the classical republicans gave way to the ideas of the natural rights philosophers. These philosophers explained and justified the changes that were taking place in society.

What did the natural rights philosophers say about individual rights?

The natural rights philosophy was developed most fully in the writings of the English philosophers Thomas Hobbes (1588-1679) and John Locke (1632-1704). The natural rights philosophers rejected many of the ideas of feudal society. They did not believe people's opportunities should be limited by the groups into which they were born. They did not agree with the limitations on people's rights imposed by the feudal system. Instead they saw society as a collection of individuals, each with a basic right to pursue his or her own interests in order to improve his or her life.

The natural rights philosophers justified the desire of individuals to accumulate money and other forms of property. They believed this economic activity would lead to greater

How did John Locke's ideas about the purposes of government differ from those of the classical republicans?

wealth for the entire society as well as encourage the development of science and technology.

These ideas about the rights of individuals were very different from older beliefs. They justified each person's right to live as he or she pleased. The older classical republican ideas emphasized the responsibility of individuals to fulfill themselves by participating in their government so as to promote the common welfare. On the other hand, the natural rights philosophers argued that what is important is the protection of individual rights. The purpose of government should be limited to the protection of these rights so people can be free to pursue their own interests. Participation in government is only important when it is necessary to make sure the government will protect rather than violate people's rights.

What rights would you have
in a state of nature?

The natural rights philosophers thought that all people are born with certain **natural rights.** This point of view provided the basis for the arguments of Hobbes, Locke, and others. To determine what our natural rights are, they asked themselves: "What are the things that all people always need and seek, no matter what they believe, no matter where and when they live?" Their answer to this question was the identification of the following natural rights:

- **Life.** People want to survive and they want their lives to be as free as possible from threats to their security.

- **Liberty.** People want to be as free as possible from the domination of others, to be able to make their own decisions, and to live as they please.

- **Property.** People want the freedom to work and gain economic goods such as land, property, tools, and money.

The natural rights philosophers argued that these rights are **unalienable,** that is, they are so much a part of human nature that they cannot be taken away or given up. These rights are established by nature. They are different from other rights that may be established by custom or law or gained by being a member of a group. For example, they are different from the right to obtain a driver's license upon reaching a certain age.

Ideas of the natural rights philosophers

In answering the questions you have just discussed, the natural rights philosophers argued that people would be free in a state of nature. But what would happen if everyone tried to pursue his or her own rights and there was no government with the authority to settle disagreements? Life might be dangerous and full of fear and insecurity. The strong might dominate the weak or the weak might work together to overcome the strong. In such a situation, how could people enjoy their natural rights?

The natural rights philosophers believed there will always be people who will try to take advantage of others or who may be carried away by passions of greed or anger or a desire for glory. People may also be confused by foolish beliefs or theories. So a government is needed to enforce rules and punish violations. But how are we to decide who should govern?

Why should government be based on consent?

The natural rights philosophers argued that no one had a right to govern the people unless the people had consented to be governed by that person. They insisted that while people differed from one another, no one was so intellectually and morally superior that he or she could claim the right to govern other people. Therefore, all legitimate government must rest on the **consent of the governed**.

What is the importance of a social contract?

The natural rights philosophers believed that government should be based on an agreement among the people to form a society. Once people have given their consent to be governed in a certain way, they are obligated to support and abide by the laws of the government they have created. This agreement among the people to live together in society and establish a government is called a **social contract**.

In this sense, the natural rights philosophers shared a similar point of view with the Puritans. The idea of a covenant or agreement with God was an important part of the Puritans' religious beliefs. One of the first documents written in the American colonies is an example of a covenant or social contract. The Pilgrims, a group of Puritans, had been given a charter that gave them permission to begin a colony in Virginia. However, their ships were blown off course and they landed on the coast of New England. They did not have permission to begin a colony where no British government authority yet existed. So they turned to the familiar idea of a covenant to create their new society. In November 1620, anchored offshore, they wrote and signed a social contract called the **Mayflower Compact** in which they consented to be ruled by the government they created.

What limits should be placed on the powers of government?

The natural rights philosophers believed that government should be the representative and the servant of the people, not their master. This view of government is stated in the Declaration of Independence. It is a view that requires the powers of government to be limited so those in government cannot abuse their power and violate the rights of the people.

According to the natural rights philosophers, government should be limited to protecting those rights with which we are born. For example, government has no business dictating to you what religion you should practice so long as you do not harm others. Government may not interfere with your rights so long as your exercise of those rights does not prevent other citizens from living their lives as they see fit.

Why was the natural rights philosophy so attractive to Americans?

Most Americans living in the English colonies enjoyed unusual opportunities compared with Europeans of the time. They did not live in a society dominated by a hereditary nobility. They had far greater economic opportunities than Europeans. By hard work they could gain private property and a better standard of living than most Europeans had. Their religious beliefs emphasized the dignity, worth, and independence of the individual. For these reasons, the natural rights philosophy appealed to them. It emphasized their right to lead their own lives and prosper under a government responsible for protecting their rights.

Using the Lesson

1. What are natural rights, according to Hobbes and Locke, and what is their source? What arguments can you make for and against the source you have identified?

2. According to the natural rights philosophers, what should be the main purpose of government? Why should its powers be limited? Do you agree? Why or why not?

3. How are the ideas of consent and social contract related to the origin and purpose of government?

4. Why was the natural rights philosophy attractive to Americans of the eighteenth century?

5. What changes in European society influenced the development of the natural rights philosophy and the emphasis on individual rights?

6. Which ideas of the natural rights philosophy, if any, are evident in your daily lives? In your local, state, or national government?

LESSON 6

What Did the Founders Learn About Rights from Studying British History?

Purpose of Lesson

This lesson will examine some of the early legal documents that protected rights in England. You will see how these listings of rights, and the struggles from which they emerged, contributed to the new American understanding of the need for a bill of rights. You also will see some of the important differences between the English idea of rights and the American Bill of Rights that was written in 1789.

From this point on in the text we will sometimes refer to England and other times to Great Britain. This is because in 1707, England and Scotland agreed to join together along with Wales to create the kingdom of Great Britain. Therefore, England is referred to as Great Britain for events occuring after that date.

When you have finished this lesson, you should be able to explain how rights were established in English history and the influence of this history on the Founders. You should also be able to explain what values and interests those rights protected and how they limited the powers of the English government.

Terms to Know

rights of Englishmen	Petition of Right
common law	Glorious Revolution
British constitution	English Bill of Rights
Magna Carta	ratified
rule of law	*habeas corpus*

What is meant by the "rights of Englishmen"?

The **rights of Englishmen** were established slowly over centuries of British history. They were certain basic rights that all subjects of the English king were understood to have. Some of the earliest of these rights were the right not to be kept in prison without a trial and the right to a trial by a jury.

The historical sources of these rights are custom and law. Evidence of these rights may be found in the literature of the times and in written documents such as various government papers. These rights also may be found in the **common law**. The common law is the collection of decisions or opinions of English judges that have developed over the centuries as they have made decisions in specific cases.

What is the British constitution?

The constitution of Great Britain is not a single written document. Instead it is made up of the common law, acts of Parliament, and political customs and traditions.

Three great historical documents are important in the development of the British constitution and the rights of the English people. These are the Magna Carta (1215), the Petition of Rights (1628), and the English Bill of Rights (1689).

These documents were written during times of great conflict. Much of English history is the story of a bloody struggle for power between the most important groups in society. These groups were the royalty, nobility, and the church. By the thirteenth century, the struggle was mainly between royalty and the Parliament. Parliament was originally a council of nobles created to advise the king. It soon became the branch of government that represented the most powerful groups in the kingdom.

For hundreds of years, Parliament and the king struggled for power. During these conflicts, English subjects were jailed, tortured, and executed. Kings and queens defeated in battle were imprisoned and beheaded. Because of these conflicts, several important legal documents were written that limited the power of the monarch (king or queen) in order to protect the rights of other groups. These documents were important not only in English history, but they also had a great influence on the Founders. Three of the most important of these documents are described below.

What is the importance of the Magna Carta?

The **Magna Carta** was signed by King John in 1215. It is the first important document describing the rights of Englishmen. Magna Carta means great or large charter. Originally, the term referred to the large size of the document, not to its importance.

It was not until the seventeenth century that the Magna Carta acquired its present importance in the history of constitutional government.

How did the Magna Carta limit the power of the king?

As you learned in Lesson 4, different groups in feudal society had certain rights and responsibilities. But the monarch had most of the political power. Over the years it had become a custom in England for the kings and queens to share some of their powers with the nobility. Struggles over these powers had led from time to time to the practice of writing documents that limited the king's powers and protected the rights of the nobility.

In 1215, King John tried to take back some of the rights and powers that the nobles had grown accustomed to having. A war resulted between the nobles and the king, a war that the nobles won. They were powerful enough to force King John to sign the Magna Carta.

The Magna Carta was perhaps the most important early example of a written statement of law limiting the power of the king and listing some of the rights of the nobility. It must,

however, be seen within the context of the history of the Middle Ages. Most of the provisions of the Magna Carta dealt with feudal practices that have little meaning in modern times. The rights it protected were those of the nobility, the upper classes of the time. The men who wrote the Magna Carta had no intention of changing feudal society or increasing the rights of the common people. They were interested in protecting their own rights within the feudal system. However, the following ideas in the Magna Carta were very important in the development of constitutional government in Great Britain and America:

- **Government should be based on the rule of law.** The Magna Carta stated that no one could be imprisoned nor any action taken against any freed man "except by the lawful judgment of his peers and by the law of the land." Although "judgment of his peers" did not mean trial by jury as we understand it today, the requirement that proceedings must follow the "law of the land" was basic to the development of the **rule of law.** It meant that no one, not even the king, was above the law.

- **Government should be based on an agreement or contract between the ruler and the people to be ruled.** In the Magna Carta, the agreement was between the king and the nobles and did not include the majority of the English people. It laid the foundation, however, for the idea of a social contract. Furthermore, government by contract meant that if either side broke the contract, it would no longer be valid.

- **Certain basic rights may not be denied by government.** While, at first, important rights were only granted to the nobility, they gradually were applied to all British subjects. These rights included freedom from imprisonment without trial, freedom from excessive fines, and freedom to travel for purposes of trade.

- **Representatives of the people should take part in government.** By denying the king the power to levy taxes without the consent of a "Great Council of the Realm," the Magna Carta laid the foundation for establishing Parliament and for parliamentary government.

As you have just read, people have fought and died to establish such rights as those described above. It is often difficult, however, to understand their importance from merely reading about them in a textbook. By examining specific rights more closely and discussing your opinions about them, you may be able to gain a greater appreciation of their meaning and importance. Let's examine more closely some of the rights in the Magna Carta.

Critical Thinking Exercise
ANALYZING AND EVALUATING SPECIFIC RIGHTS

Work in small groups to read the following excerpts from the Magna Carta that place important limitations on the powers of the king in order to protect the rights of English subjects. Develop responses to the questions that follow and be prepared to explain your answers to the class.

No freed man shall be taken, imprisoned, disseised [dispossessed], outlawed, banished, or in any way destroyed, nor will We proceed against or prosecute him, except by the lawful judgment of his peers and by the LAW OF THE LAND. (Magna Carta, Chapter 39)

To no one will We sell, to none will We deny or delay, right or justice. (Magna Carta, Chapter 40)

1. What rights are contained in the above statements?

2. How do these rights limit the power of the king?

3. Why would the English nobility want to place such limits on the power of the king?

4. What values and interests are protected by these statements?

5. What events in the United States or other nations can you identify in which one or more of the above rights have been upheld or violated?

6. **What do *you* think?**

   a. In what ways might the rights contained in the above statements be relevant to you today?

   b. Do you think these rights alone are enough to protect individuals from unfair and unreasonable treatment by their government? Why or why not?

What was the Petition of Right?

Even though rights may be established in custom or law, they may still be violated in practice. After the Magna Carta, English history continued to be filled with conflicts among different groups over their rights and powers.

More than four hundred years after the Magna Carta, the struggle for power between King Charles I and Parliament led to the **Petition of Right** (1628). This document limited the king's power to tax people without the consent of Parliament. It also guaranteed English subjects certain rights such as the protection of *habeas corpus* and the prohibition against forcing people to quarter (keep) troops in their homes.

We will examine the meaning and importance of the right to *habeas corpus* at the end of this lesson. The Petition of Right

strengthened the idea that English subjects enjoyed certain fundamental rights that no government could violate.

DRAWN BY GRAVELOT   HOUSE of COMMONS.   ENGRAVED BY W.J.WHITE.

What rights were established by Parliament to limit royal power?

Why was the Glorious Revolution important?

During the seventeenth century, England suffered from lengthy civil and religious wars. These wars involved, among other things, conflicts between Protestants and Catholics over which religion was to be the official, established religion of England. The wars ended with a Protestant victory known as the **Glorious Revolution** of 1688. The leaders of this bloodless revolution overthrew King James II who was suspected of trying to make Roman Catholicism the established religion of England.

The Protestant victory over James II resulted in the law that English rulers must be members of the Church of England. It also established the Church of England, which was Protestant, as the official religion of the country. These arrangements were written in the **English Bill of Rights** of 1689. This bill set forth the rights and liberties of English subjects.

The English Bill of Rights did not pretend to be a list of all the basic rights of Englishmen. Its purpose was to

- justify the Glorious Revolution by explaining the political and religious crimes of the ousted king

- establish a government in which the power of the king was checked and balanced

By far the greatest concerns of the English Bill of Rights were to limit the power of the king, place the dominant power of the government in Parliament, and insure the establishment of the Church of England. With regard to religion, the document was motivated by a deep fear of the Roman Catholic Church and the threat of a counter-revolution to reinstate King James II or his descendants.

What protections were included in the English Bill of Rights?

The first half of the English Bill of Rights spells out the ways the former king overstepped the limits of his power. He was accused, for example, of violating the rule of law and levying taxes without the consent of Parliament. The English Bill of Rights was intended to provide specific and lasting remedies for the actions of a tyrannical king. It contains many of the ideas about rights and government that were later included in the American Declaration of Independence, Constitution, and Bill of Rights.

The English Bill of Rights includes protections of such traditional rights of Englishmen as trial by jury, the prohibition against cruel and unusual punishments, and the right to keep arms for personal defense. However, the right to keep arms was only given to Protestants. The English Bill of Rights does not contain any reference to freedom of religion for all people. It also does not refer to freedom of the press or to freedom of speech outside of Parliament.

The Act of Toleration, passed shortly after the Glorious Revolution, gave freedom of worship to Protestant dissenters. Catholics were granted no such protection, although in the decades that followed they, too, were generally left alone to practice their faith. This toleration was not, however, the same as complete freedom of religion. Neither Protestant dissenters nor Catholics enjoyed all the political and civil rights granted to members of the established church.

Several of the basic ideas contained in the English Bill of Rights influenced our Constitution and Bill of Rights. These are as follows:

- **Rule of law.** The English Bill of Rights restated the ancient idea that all people, including their rulers, must obey the laws of the land.

- **Parliamentary supremacy.** The powers of Parliament, a representative legislature, are superior to those of the king.

- **Government by contract and consent.** Government is based upon a contract between the rulers and those ruled, which can be broken if the rulers violate the terms of the contract.

- **Balance of powers.** A balance of powers was established between the legislative and executive branches of government, and judges were made independent of both. This balance of powers was a first step toward the ideas of separation of powers and checks and balances contained in our Constitution.

How does the American Bill of Rights differ from the English Bill of Rights?

The English Bill of Rights was one of the main examples Americans had of a bill of rights. It is important to remember, however, that it differed from the American Bill of Rights in two significant ways:

- The English Bill of Rights was a law passed by Parliament and it could be changed by Parliament. The American Bill of Rights was adopted by Congress and **ratified** (approved) by the people. It can only be changed with the consent of the people through the process established by the Constitution.

- The English Bill of Rights was primarily intended to limit the power of the king and increase the power of Parliament. It prohibited the monarch from violating the rights of Parliament. The American Bill of Rights is intended to prohibit the government from violating the individual rights of all people and to protect the rights of minorities from majorities.

Nonetheless, the English Bill of Rights provided Americans with a powerful example of how to protect rights by limiting the powers of government. And, as in the Magna Carta and the Petition of Right, the rights of Englishmen were stated in a written, legal document.

Why are the rights to *habeas corpus* and a trial by jury so important?

We have seen how the rights of Englishmen were developed over hundreds of years of British history. We also know that the Founders were familiar with these rights and their history. They believed several of these rights were so important they included them in the original Constitution. Others were added in the Bill of Rights.

The rights to *habeas corpus* and trial by jury are two of the oldest rights in British history. In fact, there is evidence that *habeas corpus* is found in English law before the Magna Carta, and there is evidence that an early form of the right to a trial by jury may have been brought to England from Europe. People have fought to establish and protect these rights for over a thousand years. Therefore, it is worth looking more closely to see why people have thought they were so important.

Critical Thinking Exercise

ANALYZING AND EVALUATING THE IMPORTANCE OF THE RIGHTS TO *HABEAS CORPUS* AND TRIAL BY JURY

The following exercise calls upon you to examine the rights of *habeas corpus* and trial by jury. Your class should be divided into groups, each assigned to read one of the selections and to develop answers to the questions that accompany it. Then discuss your answers with the entire class.

A. ***Habeas corpus.*** Your right to the protections of a writ of *habeas corpus*, the "Great Writ of Liberty," has sometimes been called an essential right in a free society. The term *habeas corpus* is from the Latin language. It means to "have the body," or person, of a prisoner present in a court of law. It was considered so important by the English Parliament that it was included in the Petition of Right and in two other acts passed shortly thereafter. Let's examine why this right was thought to be so fundamental.

Suppose you have been arrested and imprisoned by the English king. Although you have the right to be tried according to the law of the land, the king's jailers keep you in prison. They will not bring you before a court to be charged with a crime and tried.

How could the right to a writ of *habeas corpus* protect you from such arbitrary and unfair treatment? How could the king's jailers be forced to bring you to a court for a fair hearing?

Suppose you had a family member, a friend, or a lawyer who knew you were being kept in prison without being brought before a judge. That person could go to court and ask a judge to issue a writ of *habeas corpus*.

In this situation, a writ of *habeas corpus* would be an order by the judge to your jailer to bring you to court and present evidence that you have broken a law. If there is such evidence, you would be held for trial. If there is no evidence justifying a trial, you would be set free.

Examining the Right

1. What limits does the right to a writ of *habeas corpus* place upon the power of the king?

2. Why would the English Parliament want to place such limits on the power of the king?

3. What arguments can you make for this right today?

4. What examples of situations in the United States or other nations can you identify that uphold or violate this right?

5. **What do *you* think?** Under what conditions, if any, do you think this right should be limited?

B. **Trial by jury.** The right to a trial by a jury of your peers chosen from your community is another essential right in a free society. Let's examine why this might be so.

Suppose you had been arrested and imprisoned by the English king. A judge, appointed and paid by the king, has examined the evidence against you and decided you should be tried for breaking the law.

The English constitution guarantees you the right to be tried by a jury of your peers. This means that a jury of people chosen from your community will listen to the evidence the king's prosecutor has against you. They will also hear your side of the story.

The jury has the power to decide if you are guilty or innocent of breaking the law. The jury cannot be prejudiced against you and its verdict must be unanimous to find you guilty. Jurors may, if they think a law is unfair, declare you innocent even if you have broken the law.

Examining the Right

1. What limits does the right to a trial by jury place upon the power of the king?

2. Why would the English Parliament want to place such limits on the power of the king?

3. What relation does the right to a trial by jury have to the separation of powers and checks and balances?

4. What arguments can you make for this right?

5. **What do *you* think?** Under what conditions, if any, do you think this right should be limited?

How did the English experiences affect the Founders' beliefs?

By the end of the eighteenth century, many Americans had come to believe that government was created by citizens who consent to live under its laws in order to protect their rights. They also thought that a written constitution was necessary for such a government. The Founders had learned from their experience with British history that it was important to have written documents to protect people's rights.

The belief in the importance of a written constitution and bill of rights came as much from practical experiences in government as from the study of history and political philosophy. In the following lessons we will learn more about these experiences in self-government and how they influenced Americans' ideas about the best way to protect the rights of the people.

Using the Lesson

1. Why was the Magna Carta important to the people of England? What is its significance to you today?

2. Why would the nobles want their rights in written form? What disadvantages, if any, might result from having rights in written form?

3. What rights were established by the Petition of Right and the English Bill of Rights? What values and interests did those rights protect?

4. Many of the Founders had studied English history. How might their knowledge of this history have influenced whether they would want to have a written bill of rights?

LESSON 7

How Did the Differences Between American and European Society Influence the Founders' Beliefs About Rights?

Purpose of Lesson

You have learned about some events and ideas that influenced the Founders' thinking about rights and the purposes of government. We also need to understand the social and economic conditions of America at the time of the Revolution. As a result of these conditions, the Founders chose to borrow certain ideas from the past, adapt others, discard some as not being useful or desirable, and create some entirely new ones.

When you have completed this lesson, you should be able to explain how the differences between colonial America and Europe affected the Founders' political views. You should also be able to explain the relationship between property and political rights. Finally, you should understand what experiences led the Americans to declare their independence from Great Britain.

Terms to Know

suffrage
right to property
Massachusetts Body of Liberties
sovereignty

Critical Thinking Exercise
EXAMINING AN ORIGINAL DOCUMENT ABOUT COLONIAL LIFE

In the mid-eighteenth century, Philip Taylor wrote about his life on the border of what today is the state of Vermont. Read what he wrote and then be prepared to discuss your answers to the questions that follow.

We now have a comfortable dwelling and two acres of ground planted with potatoes, Indian corn, melon, etc. I have 2 hogs, 1 ewe and a lamb; cows in the spring were as high as 33 dollars, but no doubt I shall have 1 by fall.

I am living in God's noble and free soil, neither am I slave to others....I have now been on American soil for two and a half years and I have not been compelled to pay for the privilege of living. Neither is my cap worn out from lifting it in the presence of gentlemen.

1. What was it that Philip Taylor liked about life in America?

2. What rights did he enjoy? How are they related to the ideas of the natural rights philosophers? Do you enjoy these rights today?

3. **What do *you* think?** Given what you know of Philip Taylor's experiences, explain why he would be more or less likely to favor laws that

   a. guarantee each individual the right to own property

   b. limit an individual's right to buy and sell goods to anyone he or she chose

   c. give people certain rights because they were wealthy or from a certain family background or group

How did life in colonial America affect people's ideas about rights?

What was unique about the American experience?

American colonists had far greater opportunities to live well and gain wealth than most people in Europe. Land was cheap and available. Almost any white man with ambition could gain the fifty acres of land required to vote in most colonies.

Colonial society had its class and social distinctions. Yet, because of the economic opportunities that were available, such distinctions were less important than in the older societies of England and Europe. As Philip Taylor boasted, "Neither is my cap worn out from lifting it in the presence of gentlemen."

Americans had a greater sense of equality because feudalism and its inherited social distinctions never became established here. There was no nobility whose social and economic positions were protected by law. In Great Britain, the laws prohibited the land of the nobility from being sold and required that it be inherited by the oldest son. Since economic and political power was based on this land, it was passed down in the families of nobility for generations. Although such laws had existed in some areas in the colonies, all were eliminated soon after the Revolution.

It is true that those people who came from educated British families or those with great personal wealth had an advantage over those who arrived in the colonies almost penniless and unknown. But wealth and family name did not mean automatic success in a land without a rigid class system; and their lack rarely held back for long those with ambition.

Americans were far more equal than most Europeans in their economic, social, and political life. As one British gentlewoman commented on her visit to the colonies, "In America, there is a disgusting equality." While some upper-class Americans may not have liked the situation, a high degree of opportunity and equality was a central and permanent characteristic of American society.

In this land of almost unlimited opportunity, one of a candle-maker's seventeen children, Benjamin Franklin, could rise to become a great inventor, statesman, and diplomat. A corset-maker's son, Thomas Paine, could become an important and famous leader of public opinion. And Alexander Hamilton, an illegitimate son of poor parents, could become the first Secretary of the Treasury of the newly formed United States.

What property and political rights did most Americans enjoy?

The rights to life, liberty, and property were mentioned in many of the documents of the colonial period. Americans, like many of the English, thought there was a close relationship between property and liberty. If property was not secure, they argued, neither was liberty. Thus, property and liberty, as well as life itself, were thought to require special protection.

As a result, political rights such as **suffrage** (the right to vote) were seen as essential to protect the individual's property. If one of the major purposes of government was to protect property, it seemed reasonable to limit the right to vote to people who possessed at least a small amount of property. Fifty acres was the usual requirement. Since land was easily gained, this requirement did not exclude large numbers of white males.

Colonial voters used their political rights to protect their **right to property**. As early as 1641, for example, voters passed the **Massachusetts Body of Liberties**, one of many colonial documents that formed the basis for our Bill of Rights. It protected the right of free men to own property and made it illegal for the government to take that property away without fair compensation. Today, that same right is protected by the Fifth and Fourteenth Amendments.

In addition, the Body of Liberties forbade the government to tax property without the consent of citizens or their representatives. This limitation on government is also found in the Petition of Right and the English Bill of Rights of 1689. Other protections included the right to a trial by jury, free elections, and the prohibitions against self-incrimination (testifying against yourself in court) and cruel and unusual punishment, rights protected today by our Bill of Rights.

Although the Body of Liberties limited suffrage, it also granted non-voters certain political rights:

> *Every man whether Inhabitant or foreigner, free or not free, shall have the libertie to come to any publique Court, council or Towne meeting and either by speech or writing...present any necessary motion, complaint, petition, bill or information.*

Today, these same rights—our rights to assemble, to petition our government, and to speak and write freely—are protected by the First Amendment.

Did all Americans have political rights?

Not all Americans, however, enjoyed the right of property and the political rights that accompanied it, such as the right to vote. In some colonies, for example, only Protestants were allowed to vote and hold political office.

Laws also limited women's ability to own property and manage their own legal and personal affairs. Although laws varied in different colonies, women usually had the legal status of under-age children. The following are just two examples of such laws:

> *A man may lawfully own and retake his wife or child wherever he finds them.*

> *The husband may put an end to his wife's sole trade whenever he pleases, and at the end of it, the profits of it will be his sole property.*

The most glaring example of the violation of rights was seen in the slave system which treated human beings as property and denied them their basic rights. By 1760, one million people lived in the colonies; one-fifth of these were African Americans. Most blacks were slaves who clearly did not enjoy the natural rights of life, liberty, and property.

The contradiction between the colonists' demands for liberty and their continued tolerance of slavery was often noted by the British. As one observer asked, "How is it that we hear the loudest yelps for liberty among the drivers of negroes?" The Reverend Samuel Hopkins criticized his fellow Americans for "making a vain parade of being advocates for the liberties of mankind, while...you at the same time are continuing this lawless, cruel, inhuman, and abominable practice of enslaving your fellow creatures."

How did the practice of slavery contradict the principles of the natural rights philosophy?

In the years following the adoption of the Constitution and Bill of Rights, slave owners would claim that forcing them to free their slaves would be a violation of their right to property. Opponents would argue that every human being had a natural right to liberty. This argument over natural rights and to whom they applied eventually contributed to the Civil War.

In some places, slaves were allowed a limited amount of self-government during the colonial period. In addition, there were free blacks who owned property, ran businesses, and later participated in the Revolution. In many instances, they gave their lives in the cause of freedom.

Critical Thinking Exercise
EVALUATING THE IMPORTANCE OF THE RIGHT TO PROPERTY

Work either independently or in small groups to discuss the Founders' ideas about the importance of the right to property. Be prepared to explain your responses to the questions that follow.

A. The Founders believed that their right to own and control property gave them a sense of independence that made them better able to assume the responsibilities of citizenship and less likely to be controlled by others.

B. The Founders believed that their right to own property made them more concerned about all the other rights required to protect their property.

What do *you* think?

1. What arguments can you make for and against the Founders' ideas about property rights?

2. In your opinion, do the Founders' ideas about property rights apply to our society today? Why or why not?

3. What arguments can you make to justify the right to property?

What led to the American Revolution?

For much of the colonial period, Great Britain paid little attention to the American colonies. Britain had become a world power and was often at war with European nations. In addition, the colonies were a long way from Britain and communications were slow. As a result, for more than 150 years before the Revolution, the American colonists had been largely free to govern themselves. They had achieved considerable experience in self-government.

The colonists had also enjoyed even greater freedoms than were actually allowed by British law. For example, British law did not give the colonists the right to trade directly with foreign nations. For many years, however, the British did not enforce these laws. Therefore, the colonists had grown accustomed to trading with almost anyone they wished. Many colonists had become quite wealthy doing so.

All of this changed with Britain's victory over France in 1763. The Seven Years' War had been expensive and Britain saw the colonies as a source of much needed money from taxes and trade. Disputes soon developed between the colonists and the British government over both economic and political issues.

Parliament passed a series of laws intended to raise taxes to help pay the debts left by the Seven Years' War. These taxes would also pay the expenses of keeping British troops in America to protect the colonists. In 1765, for example, Parliament passed the Stamp Act which required the colonists to pay for stamps to be attached to legal documents, liquor licenses, playing cards, newspapers, pamphlets, and almanacs. (These taxes had already been used in Britain.) The Stamp Act set off a storm of protest, including riots and the destruction of the stamp distributor's house in Boston.

Why did the British government want to limit the colonists' freedom of expression?

As the conflict grew, the British government began to limit further the rights of the colonists. The British began to restrict the Americans' right to express their opposition to the acts of Parliament that affected them. When the colonists disobeyed laws they thought unfair, they found themselves denied the legal protections traditionally enjoyed by Englishmen. They were refused the protections of the writ of *habeas corpus* and trial by jury.

How did the colonists justify their armed rebellion?

Each time Parliament tried to regain some sort of control over the colonies, the Americans resisted. They complained that the British were plotting "designs for destroying our constitutional liberties." In April 1775, the governor of Massachusetts sent 700 British soldiers to Lexington and Concord to arrest the colonial leaders and seize their arms and ammunition. There they met the resistance of "Minutemen" who had been alerted and "fired the shot heard 'round the world." By the end of the day, 273 British and 95 American casualties had been inflicted.

Richard Henry Lee introduced a resolution in the Continental Congress on June 7, 1776, which called for a declaration of independence. By that time, the Americans were already at war with the British. "Nothing is left now but to fight it out," said a North Carolinian.

What was the conflict over sovereignty?

The Americans and the British were fighting over two conflicting principles: parliamentary sovereignty and natural rights. **Sovereignty** is the ultimate power in a state. The British and Americans had different views about where sovereignty lay. The British believed sovereignty rested with Parliament; Americans thought that the people were sovereign.

The British believed that the supremacy of Parliament, the great achievement of the Glorious Revolution, provided the best protection for their rights. The Americans believed strongly in the ideas of the natural rights philosophy, which said there were certain rights that no one, even Parliament, could violate. This belief directly contradicted the idea of parliamentary sovereignty. If Parliament's powers were limited in any way, then it did not have the supreme or sovereign power of government. While the British saw parliamentary sovereignty as the protector of rights, the Americans had come to view it as the violator of rights.

There was no compromise possible between these two principles. The Declaration of Independence states that "governments are instituted among men, deriving their just powers from the consent of the governed," that is, the ultimate power of government, or sovereignty, lies with the people, not in Parliament.

How can you protect your rights?

The situations you have just discussed illustrate the need the Founders saw for the protection of various rights. If you were to review the Declaration of Independence, you would see that several of the violations noted above are contained in the list of criticisms made of the British government. The experiences of the Revolution had a profound impact on how Americans viewed the problem of protecting rights. This impact is clearly seen in the various provisions of the Constitution and Bill of Rights.

In the next lesson, we will look at examples of other documents developed by the newly freed colonists to protect the basic rights of all Americans.

Using the Lesson

1. In what ways was life in colonial America an improvement over that in Europe?

2. Describe the relationship between property rights and political rights in colonial America.

3. What groups were excluded from enjoying full property and political rights?

4. How did the unique experience of the American colonists, their knowledge of history, and the ideas of the natural rights philosophers contribute to the Founders' views on individual rights and limited government?

5. Read the Bill of Rights and identify those provisions which clearly reflect the Americans' experiences during the Revolution.

LESSON 8

What Rights Were Protected by the New States?

Purpose of Lesson

In this lesson, we will look at some of the declarations of rights written by the newly independent states. These documents were designed to protect individual rights and limit the powers of the state governments. We will concentrate on the Virginia declaration which served as a model for the other states. These state declarations had a considerable influence on the development of our Bill of Rights.

When you have finished this lesson, you should be able to explain the importance of the state declarations of rights and how they protected individual rights. You should also be able to describe the similarities and differences between these state declarations and the Bill of Rights.

Terms to Know

declaration of rights
Virginia Declaration of Rights
inherent rights

What were the state declarations of rights?

The American colonists declared their independence from Great Britain in 1776. The Second Continental Congress was composed of representatives from the thirteen former colonies. Congress asked each of the new states to create its own government. All adopted written constitutions before the U.S. Constitution was written in 1787. Eleven of these states wrote new constitutions. Connecticut and Rhode Island merely modified their colonial charters.

Never before in history had people worked together to create so many new governments based on the ideas of classical republicanism, the natural rights philosophy, and their own experiences. In a world where most nations were ruled by kings, it was truly a revolutionary period in the history of government and the rights of the people.

Most state constitutions began with a **declaration of rights**. Although the rights listed differed from state to state, they were all based on the idea that people have certain rights which must be protected. It was only after safeguarding these rights at the very start, that the framers of these constitutions went on to form state governments.

Taken together, the rights protected in the state declarations included all the fundamental rights guaranteed today by our Bill of Rights. By looking at these declarations and how they were developed, we can learn a great deal about how we came to have the rights we enjoy today under both our state and federal constitutions.

By the time the Constitution was written, Americans had over 150 years experience of limited self-government in the colonies and ten years of experience with self-government under their state constitutions. As you will see in the next unit, this experience greatly influenced the way the Framers wrote the Constitution and the Bill of Rights.

Critical Thinking Exercise
EXAMINING SLAVES' CLAIMS FOR RIGHTS

Shortly after Americans declared their independence, New Hampshire townspeople chose representatives to draft a constitution for their new state. While the representatives were meeting in a popular tavern, twenty slaves owned by the revolutionaries rowed across Portsmouth harbor to deliver a petition to them. The petition asked that the new constitution guarantee liberty for all people,

so that the name of slavery may not be heard in a Land gloriously contending for the Sweets of Freedom.

The slaves wanted the new state constitution to ban slavery and give them the same rights others held.

What arguments might be made for and against the slaves' petition? Use the following questions to help you.

1. What rights did the slaves want to have?

2. What argument could the slaves have used to support their claim to these rights? What ideas from the natural rights philosophy might the slaves have used to support their position?

3. What argument do you suppose some of the Founders may have used to deny the slaves their rights? What ideas from the natural rights philosophy might the Founders have used to support their position?

What important ideas were expressed in the Virginia Declaration of Rights?

On June 12, 1776, Virginia was the first state to adopt a declaration of rights—almost a month before independence was formally declared. The Virginia Declaration of Rights helped convince other colonies to vote for independence and influenced Thomas Jefferson's writing of the Declaration of Independence.

The Virginia declaration was written primarily by George Mason (1725-1792), who later became a leading opponent of the federal Constitution because, among other things, it lacked a declaration of rights. In writing the Virginia Declaration of Rights, Mason relied heavily on the writings of John Locke. However, he also drew from the classical republican philosophers, and, of course, from the experiences of the colonists themselves.

The Virginia Declaration of Rights declared:

- "That all men are by nature equally free and independent, and have certain **inherent rights**, of which, when they enter into a state of society, they cannot, by any compact, deprive or divest their posterity; namely, the enjoyment of life and liberty, with the means of acquiring and possessing property, and pursuing and obtaining happiness and safety."

- That all power is derived from and kept by the people.

- "The government is, or ought to be, instituted for the common benefit, protection, and security of the people."

- If a government does not serve these purposes, the people have an unalienable right to alter or abolish it.

Other rights in the Virginia declaration are rights we enjoy today under both our state and federal bills of rights. Examples include the rights to trial by jury, the protection against cruel and unusual punishment, freedom of the press, and the free exercise of religious beliefs.

> "That religion, or the duty we owe to our Creator, and the manner of discharging it, can be directed only by reason and conviction, not by force or violence; and therefore, all men are equally entitled to the free exercise of religion, according to the dictates of conscience."

The Virginia Declaration began with a statement based on the ideas of natural rights, the social contract, and the purpose of

George Mason and Virginia House of Burgesses

What philosophical ideas and experiences influenced the Virginia Declaration of Rights?

government. It ended with a statement based on the ideas of classical republicanism about civic virtue and responsibility.

The framers of this document believed that listing rights and establishing a government were not enough to guarantee people their freedom. They argued that each individual must accept the responsibility to live according to certain moral principles and ideals. The last section of the Virginia declaration stressed the importance of civic virtue and religious values:

> "No free government, or the blessings of liberty, can be preserved to any people but by a firm adherence to justice, moderation, temperance, frugality, and virtue....it is the mutual duty of all to practice Christian forbearance, love, and charity, towards each other."

Thus, the Virginia Declaration of Rights combined many of the ideas Americans had learned from studying the past and from their own personal experiences with government.

It is important to note, however, that the Virginia Declaration of Rights omitted some important rights. It did not include freedom of speech or assembly. Nor did it provide for the writ of *habeas corpus*. The right to counsel, freedom from double jeopardy, and the prohibition against bills of attainder and *ex post facto* laws (all of which will be discussed in later units) were left out. These omissions were later used by some Framers as an argument against adding a bill of rights to the new federal Constitution. They claimed that if some rights were included and others omitted, it could be said that the rights omitted were not protected against violation by the federal government.

What rights were protected by the other states?

Most states adopted declarations or bills of rights that resembled Virginia's. Each began with a statement expressing the views of the natural rights philosophers about government. In addition, each included the idea that civic virtue and a commitment to certain moral and religious principles were essential to preserving freedom. Some of them included rights that had been omitted from the Virginia declaration.

Several states, including Virginia, provided for the free exercise of religion, while at the same time permitting state religious establishments. They allowed tax money to be spent for the support of the Protestant religion generally or, in some cases, for a particular denomination. For example, taxes could be used to pay for the salaries of ministers and teachers of religious education or even for a new church roof. In most states there were religious requirements for holding public office that were designed to exclude Roman Catholics and Jews.

Property qualifications for voting were established in most states. The right to vote and hold public office was essentially limited to adult white males who owned certain amounts of property.

In what way were the state declarations different from the Bill of Rights?

In many ways, the state declarations resemble the Declaration of Independence more than they resemble the Bill of Rights. The state documents were meant to establish the moral and philosophical foundations of the state governments. They were written as preambles to the state constitutions, describing the purpose of government and setting forth the principles of the natural rights philosophy and classical republicanism.

The Bill of Rights, on the other hand, was written after the Constitution had created the federal government. The principles of government had been established. The Framers believed there was no need to list these principles again. What was needed was a list of specific rights that should be protected from government interference. The Bill of Rights is such a list.

The state declarations were written while Americans were in the midst of a violent revolution. The framers of these documents thought of themselves as principled, law-abiding citizens who were forced into armed rebellion to protect their rights. It was important to them to explain why they had taken the drastic steps they had.

The framers of the state constitutions and state declarations of rights were shrewd politicians. They knew that they needed to gain support for their cause in the colonies where many people still remained loyal to the king, or were "fair weather patriots," sitting on the political fence. They also needed to influence opinion in Europe where they hoped to find not only moral, but also political and financial support.

Finally, the Founders were individuals who were inspired by the justice of their cause. They wanted to share their ideas for a new nation and to tell the world that people could band together to create a society based on principles of freedom, justice, and equality. They knew that they themselves did not always live up to these ideals. But they sincerely believed that it was possible to do so if people had the courage and conviction to make their dreams a reality.

People today, not only in our own country but around the world, have been inspired by the vision of society expressed in the Declaration of Independence and our state declarations of rights. In the 1990s, people in South Africa, China, and Eastern Europe marched, fought, and died under placards with the words FREEDOM and DEMOCRACY written on them. And at a rally in Prague, Czechoslovakia, a brewery worker

Why do you suppose the ideas in the Declaration of Independence have inspired people throughout the world?

climbed up on a platform to recite these words to the crowd gathering below:

> *We hold these truths to be self-evident, that all men are created equal.*

The Founders of our nation had inspired not only their own generation, but generations to come. Today we inherit not only their dreams of liberty and justice for all, but the responsibility to make those dreams a reality.

Critical Thinking Exercise
CREATING A BILL OF RIGHTS

Work in small groups to use what you have learned to develop a list of rights you would include in a bill of rights designed to prohibit the federal government from violating the rights of individuals. Be prepared to explain the reasons for the rights you have included and not included.

Save your lists to discuss again after completing the next unit about the creation of our Bill of Rights. Then you will be able to compare your ideas with those of the Founders.

Using the Lesson

1. What basic ideas of the natural rights philosophers and classical republicanism were found in the state declarations of rights?

2. What groups were not given full rights under the state declarations? Do these groups have such rights today?

3. What important rights have you studied that were not included in the Virginia Declaration of Rights? What problems might be caused by having an incomplete list of rights?

4. In what ways did the state declarations of rights resemble the Declaration of Independence more than the Bill of Rights? Why?

Unit Two: How Was the Bill of Rights Created?

What did the Framers think was the greatest threat to their rights?

Purpose of Unit

Americans in the eighteenth century thought that the greatest threat to their rights was from the powers of a national government. This belief was partially due to their experiences with the British government which they thought had continually violated their rights. As soon as they were free from Great Britain, the Founders had to create their own national government. They then faced the problem of how much power to give to the government without enabling it to threaten their rights.

The Founders thought that the best way to protect individual rights was to give their government as little power as possible. In addition, that power should be limited by a complicated system of separated powers and checks and balances. This would help insure that the limited powers of the government would only be used to provide security for the people.

Some of the Founders thought that the Constitution adopted in Philadelphia in 1787 did not provide adequate protection for individual rights. George Mason of Virginia was one of the convention delegates who refused to sign the Constitution. He, and others, insisted that a bill of rights be added to the Constitution to make it absolutely clear that individual rights were not to be violated by the new federal government. A large part of the argument over the ratification of the Constitution was whether a bill of rights should be added to it. The issue of rights, which had been important during the Revolution, took center stage during the ratification debates.

In this unit you will learn how the experiences and ideas of the Founders affected the development of our two constitutions, the Articles of Confederation and our present Constitution. You will learn of the conflict over adding a bill of rights to the Constitution and why one was eventually added. Finally, you will learn about the relatively insignificant impact of the Bill of Rights in 1791 compared to its great importance today.

New state governments 1776-1780   Treaty of Paris 1781   Northwest Ordinance 1787   Constitution ratified 1788   Bill of Rights proposed 1789

1776 - 1791

Articles of Confederation 1781   Shays's Rebellion 1786-87   Philadelphia Convention 1787   Washington elected first president 1789   Bill of Rights ratified 1791

Lesson 9

How Were Rights Protected Under Our National Constitutions?

Purpose of Lesson

Once the Founders declared their independence, they needed a national government to coordinate the relationships between the states and conduct the war against the British. Between 1776 and 1787 the Founders created two national constitutions. The first was called the Articles of Confederation. It was under this constitution that the United States won independence from Great Britain. However, as you will learn, several problems with this government led to the development of a second constitution.

Neither of the constitutions developed by the Founders contained a bill of rights. Considering Americans' strong beliefs about protecting rights, this might seem surprising. In this lesson, you will learn about some of the most important reasons bills of rights were not included in these constitutions.

When you have finished this lesson, you should be able to explain why neither of the constitutions developed by the Founders contained a bill of rights. You should also be able to explain why they thought that the Constitution did not need one.

Terms to Know

Articles of Confederation
Northwest Ordinance of 1787
legislative supremacy
Shays's Rebellion
Philadelphia Convention
federal system/federalism
separation of powers
checks and balances

How did the Founders try to protect rights under the Articles of Confederation?

In the last lesson you learned that in 1776 the Second Continental Congress asked each of the newly independent states to create its own government. In addition to creating these state governments, Americans also needed to create a national government. The Continental Congress appointed a committee headed by John Dickinson of Pennsylvania to draft a constitution for the first national government. The Founders soon realized it would not be easy to agree on what type of national government to establish. Members of the Continental Congress argued on and off for more than a year. Finally, they agreed on a constitution to present to the states for approval. It was called the **Articles of Confederation**. The states argued about the Articles for four more years before all of them approved it. Two major fears made it difficult for the Founders to agree:

- They were afraid of creating a national government so strong that it would be a threat to the rights of citizens.

- They were afraid that the powers they were giving to the national government would enable it to dominate the state governments.

Americans had experienced how unresponsive a powerful and distant national government could be. They believed government should be close to their homes to allow citizens to make sure their rights were protected. Many of the Founders believed that republican governments were successful only in small communities where people shared common ideas and beliefs.

A republican government had never been tried in a nation as large and diverse as the United States. The Founders believed republican governments could function within their states and local communities. They did not think it possible to create one for the entire nation. Because of these fears, the Founders created a national government that had little power over the states and their citizens.

The Articles of Confederation did not include a list of the rights of citizens. The Founders believed that their rights were already protected by their state declarations of rights and state constitutions. More important, the Articles did not give the national government any direct power over the citizens of the states. The Founders thought that denying this power to the national government was the best way to protect their rights. For example, the national government could not force citizens to obey its laws or collect taxes from them. The power to make and enforce laws directly affecting citizens was left with the various state governments.

What were some of the national government's achievements under the Articles of Confederation?

What were the achievements of the first national government?

The national government under the Articles of Confederation was responsible for several important achievements:

- It successfully waged the war for independence against Great Britain.

- It negotiated a peace treaty, the Treaty of Paris in 1781, to end the American Revolution.

- It required each state to recognize the laws of the other states.

- It passed the **Northwest Ordinance of 1787**. This was the most important law passed by Congress under the Articles. It gave people in the north-western lands the right to organize their own govern-ments and eventually become states. It provided for public education and forbade slavery. It provided protections to settlers in the territory not given to other citizens under the Articles of Confederation, including the rights to freedom of religion, trial by jury, and due process of law.

Despite these major accomplishments, some people argued that the national government did not have enough power to deal with important problems facing the newly independent states.

What problems arose under the Articles of Confederation?

Problems arose under the Articles of Confederation that threatened the new nation. Some of these were economic difficulties brought about by the cost of fighting the war with Great Britain. Others were caused by the way the new state governments had been organized.

Most states created governments which gave most of the power to the legislature. This is known as **legislative supremacy**. Americans believed that because the legislature was elected by the people, it was the most democratic branch of government. They were afraid of giving too much power to the executive. They remembered how the king and the royal governors had abused their power. So most of the state gover-nors were given limited power.

Legislative supremacy led to serious problems in most states:

1. **High taxes.** The state legislatures passed laws that taxed their citizens far more than the British had. The level of taxes during the 1780s was ten to twenty times more than before the Revolution.

2. **Violation of personal rights.** Many new state laws were passed which interfered with the private lives of the citizens. Laws were passed telling people what they should eat, drink, wear, and believe.

3. **Violation of property rights.** A number of Founders argued that the state legislatures were controlled by majorities that passed laws violating the property rights of creditors and land owners.

The economic problems of the nation had made it necessary for many Americans, especially farmers, to borrow money to support their families. Many of these people had debts they were unable to pay. They demanded that their state legislatures help them by passing laws that forced their creditors to postpone collecting these debts.

Such laws were seen by many as violations of the property rights of creditors. Because of these laws, creditors were either not able to collect the money owed them or were forced to accept payment in paper money that was of little value.

According to James Madison, these attacks on property rights were among the most important reasons people demanded that the Articles of Confederation be improved or replaced. Moreover, they demonstrated the potential tyranny of majority rule in a democratic system. The states all had declarations of rights, but this did not stop majorities in the state legislatures from violating the rights of property owners. It was clear that bills of rights alone were not enough to protect individual rights.

The Confederation Congress was powerless to collect taxes to pay for the expenses of the Revolution, including wages for the soldiers who had fought for independence. Congress had no power to prevent unfair competition among the states or to enforce trade agreements with foreign nations. States taxed goods from other states and trading often became impossible.

Finally, **Shays's Rebellion** in Massachusetts convinced many leaders that a stronger national government was necessary to protect property rights. Daniel Shays led a group of armed farmers in an attempt to close down the county courts. They wanted to stop the courts from ordering foreclosures on their

What problems led to Shays's Rebellion?

farms. The rebellion was finally defeated by the Massachusetts militia.

Shays's Rebellion had a great impact on public opinion. Massachusetts had requested the help of the national government to put down the rebellion, but Congress had been powerless to do anything. Many Americans concluded that a stronger national government had to be established.

Shortly afterward, Congress invited the states to send delegates to a convention in Philadelphia. Congress directed the delegates to limit their work to improving the Articles of Confederation.

What were the major concerns of the Framers?

Our present Constitution was written at the **Philadelphia Convention** in the summer of 1787 and sent to the states for ratification that September. Delegates from most of the states arrived in Philadelphia by May 25. George Washington was unanimously elected to be the presiding officer. Almost immediately the Framers agreed to ignore the instructions they had been given to limit their work to improving the Articles of Confederation. Instead, they began to draft a new constitution.

The Framers believed that the purpose of government should be to protect individual rights and promote the common welfare. They also believed strongly that the power of government should be limited to prevent an abuse of people's rights.

However, the Framers often disagreed about how these ideas should be put into practice. For example, they argued over what powers should be given to the national and state governments. Many people did not want any important powers to be given to the new national government. They did not want their state governments to be dominated by a strong central authority. And they were afraid some states might have more power than others.

How did the Framers organize the government to protect rights?

After much debate and several important compromises, the Framers agreed on a new constitution. They believed they had created a government that was organized in a way that made it almost impossible for anyone to gain enough power to dominate the government and violate the rights of others.

The most important ideas the Framers used to organize the new government and limit its powers are explained below.

1. **Federalism.** The Framers created a new system of government called a **federal system** or **federalism**. Under a federal system, the people delegate certain powers to their federal government. For example, the federal government is given the power to declare war and

regulate commerce among various states. Other powers, such as creating and enforcing most civil and criminal laws, are left to the states. The remaining powers are kept by the people.

The Founders divided the powers between the federal government and the state governments for two reasons:

- They believed it was the best practical solution to the problem of governing a territory as large and diverse as the United States.

- They believed this division of power between the federal and state governments would reduce the chances that the federal government could use its powers to violate the rights of the people.

2. **Separation of powers and checks and balances.** The Constitution also includes several other ways to limit the power of the federal government. It divides the powers of the federal government among three branches. This **separation of powers** makes it less likely that any one branch of the government will gain so much power that it can ignore the limitations placed on it by the Constitution.

Why did the Framers think the separation of powers would protect the rights of the people?

Thus, the Constitution creates the

- **legislative branch**, or Congress, which is given the power to create laws

- **executive branch**, or presidency, which is given the power to carry out and enforce the laws

- **judicial branch**, headed by the Supreme Court, which is given the power to decide cases and interpret how the laws apply in those cases and how they should be enforced

The Constitution also contains a complicated system of **checks and balances**. Each branch is given powers that enable it to check the use of power by the other branches. For example, the president can check the powers of Congress by vetoing its bills. Congress can check the powers of the president by refusing to approve members of the executive branch or Supreme Court who are nominated by the president. The Supreme Court can check the powers of the other branches of the federal government by declaring their actions unconstitutional.

How did the Framers defend the way they had organized the government?

The Framers believed that the complicated federal system they had created, with its separation of powers and checks and balances, was essential for the protection of the rights of the people. In addition, James Madison argued that the great advantage of a country as large as the United States was that it had many different sections, interests, and classes of citizens.

Madison believed that the complicated system of government and the variety of competing interests in such a large and diverse nation would make it impossible for any group—or even a majority—to completely control the government. Thus, no group could promote its selfish interests at the expense of individual rights or the common welfare.

Critical Thinking Exercise
EVALUATING POSITIONS ON A CONSTITUTIONAL ISSUE

Some people have made the following argument to support the position that a bill of rights is not necessary:

Your rights are adequately protected from government violation by federalism, the separation of powers, and checks and balances.

If possible, before discussing this issue, interview adults familiar with local, state, or federal government to get their opinions on the statement. Then work in small groups to discuss and take positions on the statement and present them to the class.

Roger Sherman, Connecticut (1721-1793) George Mason, Virginia (1725-1792) Elbridge Gerry, Massachusetts (1744-1814)

Why didn't the Framers include a bill of rights in the Constitution?

By September 1787 the delegates had been working on the Constitution for more than four months. They had argued and compromised and had settled many strong disagreements. Some delegates had walked out of the convention. Those remaining knew they had not created a perfect government.

During the convention a bill of rights had not been a serious matter of debate. The only formal discussion of the topic was begun by George Mason. On September 12, 1787, the weary delegates prepared to vote on the final version of the Constitution. Mason said that he "wished the plan had been prefaced by a bill of rights."

Only Elbridge Gerry of Massachusetts spoke in favor of Mason's proposal. Roger Sherman of Connecticut disagreed. He argued that since the Constitution did not replace the state declarations of rights, they alone were adequate protections of individual rights.

Sherman's reasoning and the delegates' weariness and eagerness to go home persuaded them that a bill of rights was unnecessary. The motion to appoint a committee to draft a bill of rights was voted down 10-0. Every state delegation then present voted no.

You should understand that the Framers were not opposed to a bill of rights. They just believed that one was not necessary for reasons we will examine in a later lesson. However, as you will see, the Framers did include protections of some specific rights in the Constitution itself. Later events caused them to add the Bill of Rights as the first ten amendments to the Constitution.

Using the Lesson

1. In what ways did the Founders try to protect the rights of citizens under the Articles of Confederation? What problems arose about rights under the Articles?

2. In what ways did the Framers try to protect the rights of citizens and the powers of their state governments under the Constitution?

3. Why didn't the Framers include a bill of rights in the Constitution?

4. If you had been a member of the Philadelphia Convention, what rights, if any, would you have tried to include in the Constitution? Explain your position.

5. What evidence of federalism, the separation of powers, and checks and balances can you identify in your daily life?

6. What arguments can you make for and against the position that your state government should have more power than the federal government?

Lesson 10

What Rights Were Included in the New Constitution?

Purpose of Lesson

The Framers believed that the way they had organized the new government was the best way to protect the rights of individuals. The Framers also included provisions in the new Constitution that prohibited both the federal and state governments from violating several important rights. In this lesson you will examine the rights the Framers did include in the Constitution and discuss their importance.

After completing the lesson, you should be able to describe the rights the Framers included in the Constitution, explain why they might have chosen to include these particular rights, and explain their importance.

Why is it important to protect freedom of speech in congressional debates?

Terms to Know

provision
impeachment
ex post facto law
bill of attainder

What specific rights were protected in the Constitution?

The Framers believed that the way they had organized the government was the best way to protect rights. Nevertheless, they included a number of **provisions**, or clauses, in the Constitution to protect specific rights. These provisions protected rights of individual citizens and persons holding public office in the federal government. Each provision was designed to prevent abuses the Framers had seen in British history, their colonial and state governments, and the national government under the Articles.

It is worth examining the rights the Framers included in the Constitution to see why they thought they were necessary. We have divided these rights into three groups to make it easier to understand their functions and importance.

1. **Protections of the political independence and other rights of public officials.** Several provisions are designed to protect the political independence and other rights of members of the government. One of these protects freedom of speech for members of Congress.

Members of Congress cannot be arrested for anything they say on the floor of Congress. Neither can they be arrested for minor crimes they commit while Congress is in session.

The **impeachment** clauses protect the right of members of the executive and judicial branches to a fair hearing if they are accused of misconduct in office.

2. **Protections of individual rights against violation by the state governments.** The Constitution includes provisions limiting the powers of state governments in order to protect the rights of their citizens. One of these provisions protects the property rights of citizens who have loaned money. It says that no state can pass any law "impairing the obligation of contracts." This means, among other things, that a state legislature cannot pass a law releasing people from the responsibility to pay their debts.

The protection of property rights was a result of problems that had arisen under the Articles of Confederation. As you know, the country was in a financial crisis after the Revolution and many people were in debt. Some state legislatures passed laws to provide relief for persons who owed money to others. The Framers believed these laws violated the property rights of citizens. They included in the Constitution a provision that prohibited the states from passing such laws.

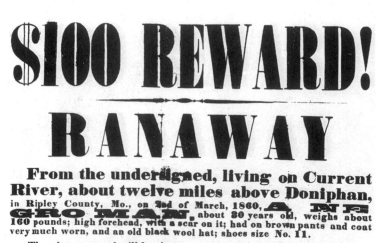

$100 REWARD!

RANAWAY

From the undersigned, living on Current River, about twelve miles above Doniphan, in Ripley County, Mo., on 3rd of March, 1860, A NE GRO MAN, about 30 years old, weighs about 160 pounds; high forehead, with a scar on it; had on brown pants and coat very much worn, and an old black wool hat; shoes size No. 11.

The above reward will be given to any person who may apprehend this said negro out of the State; and fifty dollars if apprehended in this State outside of Ripley county, or $25 if taken in Ripley county.

APOS TUCKER.

Another provision of the Constitution protected the property rights of citizens who owned slaves. Slaves were considered the personal property of their owners. This provision required state governments to return to their owners any slaves who might have escaped from another state.

The Constitution also prohibits both the federal and state governments from passing *ex post facto* laws and **bills of attainder**. These protections will be examined in the exercise following the next section.

3. **Protections of individual rights against violation by the federal government**. It is this group of rights that we are most concerned with in this lesson. Two of these rights, *habeas corpus* and trial by jury in criminal cases, you have already examined in the last unit. Four more of these protections will be examined in the exercise that follows this section.

The Framers included these protections of individual rights in the Constitution because of their experiences as British subjects. Each provision is related to a traditional right of Englishmen that was denied by the British to control religious dissenters, political opponents, and critics of the government. The Framers wanted to make sure that in their new nation they would be free to criticize the government without fear of having their property taken from them, being imprisoned, or being executed. They were also concerned about abuses of these rights that had occurred under the state governments.

Critical Thinking Exercise
EXAMINING THE IMPORTANCE OF RIGHTS GUARANTEED IN THE CONSTITUTION

Work in small groups to complete this activity. Each group should be assigned one of the following readings concerning rights guaranteed in the Constitution. Discuss your answers to the questions. Then select a spokesperson to present your group's opinions to the rest of the class.

A. **"No bill of attainder...shall be passed"** (Article I, Section 9, Clause 3 and Section 10, Clause 1). It is 1778 and the United States is fighting against British rule. Your name is Josiah Phillips. You live in Virginia and you are against the war. You are a Loyalist—an outspoken supporter of the king of Great Britain and the Church of England. Thomas Jefferson has introduced a bill of attainder in the state legislature against you.

A bill of attainder is a law passed by a legislature that calls for the arrest and punishment of a named person or group without a trial in a court of law. Bills of attainder were first used in England in 1459. They give the government the power to imprison persons, take their property, and even order their execution without a trial. Because bills of attainder allow the government to ignore the court system and due process of law, they are a dangerous instrument of tyranny.

If the bill of attainder passes the Virginia legislature, you will be ordered to surrender to the government or you will be arrested. The bill passes, but you refuse to surrender. You and all your property are seized.

What do *you* think?

1. Would you give your government the right to pass bills of attainder? Why or why not?

2. Why might a legislature want the power to pass bills of attainder? Against whom might they be used?

3. What limitations on government would be gained by prohibiting bills of attainder?

4. What relationship, if any, does prohibiting bills of attainder have to the separation of powers and checks and balances?

5. What other rights, if any, would you want included to protect yourself further against this type of government activity?

B. **"No...*ex post facto* law shall be passed"** (Article I, Section 9, Clause 3 and Section 10, Clause 1). You are James Iredell. You write and publish pamphlets on political topics. It is late at night and you are working to finish a manuscript for the printer. You want the Constitution to prohibit the federal and state governments from passing *ex post facto* laws.

An *ex post facto* law declares an act a crime after the act has already taken place. It punishes people for acts that, when they did them, were not against the law. This prohibition would forbid the government from passing laws that

- make something a crime that was not a crime when it was done

- make a crime greater or more serious after the act was committed

- make the punishment for a crime more severe after the crime was committed

- change the rules of a trial after an act was done in order to make it easier to convict a person

You agree with Alexander Hamilton's criticisms that *ex post facto* laws have been "in all ages" one of "the favorite and most formidable instruments of tyranny." You know they have been used by political leaders to prevent people from opposing them, or to imprison their opponents. You publish your opinions in a pamphlet:

> *This very clause I think is worth 10,000 declarations of rights....A man must feel some pride in his security when he knows that what he does innocently and safely today, in accordance with the laws of his country, cannot be tortured into guilt and danger tomorrow.*

What do *you* think?

1. What arguments can you make for prohibiting *ex post facto* laws?

2. Why might a legislature want the power to pass *ex post facto* laws? Against whom might they be used?

3. What limitations on government would be achieved by prohibiting *ex post facto* laws?

4. What relationship, if any, does prohibiting *ex post facto* laws have to the separation of powers and checks and balances?

5. What other rights, if any, would you want included to protect yourself further against this type of government activity?

C. **"Treason against the United States, shall consist only in levying war against them, or in adhering to their enemies, giving them aid and comfort. No person shall be convicted of treason unless on the testimony of two**

witnesses to the same overt act, or on confession in open court" (Article III, Section 3, Clause 1). Your name is Flora Mc-Donald. You were arrested in Scotland for rebellion against the king. You were pardoned and sent to the American colonies after swearing an oath that you would remain loyal to the king.

Flora McDonald (1720-1790)

You have stood by this oath. As a result you and your family have been branded traitors by the American revolutionaries. You know of many others who have been called traitors. Some have fled. Others have been imprisoned. Even some patriot women have been persecuted and evicted from their homes, not because they had been traitors, but because their husbands were!

You have been accused of treason by both the British government and the new government of the United States. You want to see that people with different political views are not persecuted under the new Constitution. You want treason to be defined very narrowly in the new Constitution in order to protect people who may be merely disagreeing with the government. You think treason should refer only to citizens who are fighting against the United States or giving aid and comfort to its enemies. Finally, you want the Constitution to set very strict standards for proving that a person has committed treason.

What do *you* think?

1. In what way could a loose definition of treason lead to a denial of your rights?

2. How would the power of government be limited by defining treason very narrowly and requiring you to be tried in a court?

3. What arguments can you make for including the protections you have discussed in the Constitution?

4. What other rights, if any, would you want included to protect yourself further against unfair accusations of treason?

D. **"no religious test shall ever be required as a qualification to any office or public trust under the United States"** (Article VI, Section 3). Your name is

Haym Solomon. You are a descendent of Jews who fled Europe in the seventeenth century to seek religious freedom in America. You are one of about 2,000 Jews living in the American colonies at the time of the Revolution.

You have been a strong and active supporter of the revolution against British rule. You abandoned your home and successful business in British-occupied New York to escape to Philadelphia.

Throughout the war, you used your skills and business connections to help finance the fight against the British. Now you are bankrupt because of your generous personal loans to Congress. You still believe that freedom was worth the price. However, you think it is unfair that several of the new state constitutions prohibit Jews from holding public office.

You hope that a provision will be included in the Constitution to enable men like you to run for office in the new nation you helped create. You believe there should be no religious qualifications or test to hold political office.

What do *you* think?

1. Would you give your government the right to require you to belong to a particular religion or to take a religious test before you could hold a public office? Why or why not?

2. Why might a government wish to require a religious test for public office?

3. How might requiring a religious test for public office be related to the ideas of classical republicanism? To the natural rights philosophy?

4. What other rights, if any, would you want included to protect yourself further from discrimination because of your religion?

What task did the Framers have after drafting the Constitution?

As you have seen, many of the Framers believed they had adequately protected the rights of citizens in the Constitution. However, they faced a difficult task convincing all the states to accept the Constitution as the basis for the new federal government. The Framers knew that many members of Congress and the state governments were against the new Constitution. They were afraid it reduced the powers of the state governments. Opponents of the Constitution also believed a bill of rights was necessary to protect people from the power of the federal government. As you will see in the next lesson, the demand for a bill of rights became so strong that the Framers agreed to add one to the Constitution.

Using the Lesson

1. What important values and interests underlie the rights the Framers included in the new Constitution? For example, how do they promote fairness, security, freedom, and respect for human life?

2. Why do you suppose the Framers included these particular rights in the new Constitution?

3. What additional protections, if any, of your rights do you think should have been included in the Constitution? Why?

4. Why do you think the Framers protected some rights just from the federal government and others from the state governments?

5. Which of the rights included in the Constitution before the Bill of Rights was added appear most important to you today?

Lesson 11

Why Was the Bill of Rights Added to the Constitution?

Purpose of Lesson

Once the Framers had completed the Constitution, they faced the task of getting it accepted by the states. In this lesson you will learn how the issue of a bill of rights was raised in the struggle to get the Constitution ratified. You will examine the plan developed by the supporters of the Constitution, called the Federalists, to get it ratified and the opposition to its ratification by the Anti-Federalists. Finally, you will examine the arguments of both the Federalists and Anti-Federalists over adding a bill of rights.

When you have completed this lesson, you should be able to describe the major differences between the Federalists and the Anti-Federalists over the issue of a bill of rights. You should also be able to explain how and why the decision was made to add the Bill of Rights to the Constitution.

Terms to Know

ratifying conventions
Federalists
Anti-Federalists
The Federalist
amendment

What happened after the Philadelphia Convention?

Imagine that you are one of the Framers of the Constitution. You know that many leaders in Congress and the state governments will be against it. They fear the new Constitution will reduce the power of the state legislatures. Consequently, members of these legislatures oppose ratification. In addition, many of them oppose it on philosophical grounds: they believe the state governments are the best protector of individual rights. However, you have developed the Constitution in secret. Your opponents do not know everything that is included in the final version. They have not yet had time to prepare all their arguments against the Constitution.

What plan can you develop for getting the Constitution ratified? Who do you think should have the right to vote for ratification? How soon should the ratification process take place? These are some of the questions raised by the Framers as the convention drew to a close.

How did Madison suggest the Constitution be ratified?

Why did the Framers ask the voters to approve the Constitution?

James Madison developed the plan for ratifying the Constitution. He was sure that the Constitution would be rejected if either Congress or the state legislatures were asked to ratify it. To avoid this, he thought the best plan would be to get the voters to approve the Constitution at special **ratifying conventions** to be held in each state. The delegates to these conventions would be elected by popular vote of the people, for the sole purpose of approving the Constitution.

Madison's plan was based on the idea contained in the Preamble to the Constitution, which says, "We the People...do ordain and establish this Constitution...." The people were asked to consent to their new government. Thus, the Constitution can be considered a social contract—an agreement among the people to create a government.

The Framers approved this plan. Article VII said the Constitution would go into effect after it had been ratified by nine of the thirteen states. The Framers only required approval by the voters of nine states because they were afraid they might not be able to get the support of all thirteen.

Once they had agreed upon their plan, the **Federalists**, those who supported the Constitution, went to work. They encouraged the states to organize and elect delegates to the state ratifying conventions as quickly as possible. They knew their opponents, the **Anti-Federalists**, had not had much time to prepare their arguments. By contrast, the Federalists had worked on the Constitution for almost four months. They knew the arguments for and against it. They thought if the state conventions acted quickly, the Constitution would be ratified before the Anti-Federalists could organize their opposition.

The struggle for ratification

Despite the advantages of the Federalists' position, the Anti-Federalists put up a strong fight. The debates in the states over ratification lasted ten months. It was an intense and sometimes bitter political struggle.

One of the most difficult fights was in New York. To help the Federalist cause, Alexander Hamilton, James Madison, and John Jay wrote a series of articles supporting ratification. These articles, now called *The Federalist*, appeared in three New York newspapers. They were also used in the Virginia ratification debates and are an important source of information about the conflict over the Bill of Rights.

Anti-Federalist leaders included George Mason and Elbridge Gerry. Both had attended the Philadelphia Convention but had refused to sign the Constitution. Richard Henry Lee was a leading revolutionary and signer of the Declaration of Independence but fought against the ratification of the Constitution. Patrick Henry had always opposed the idea of a strong national government; he became a leading Anti-Federalist. Mercy Otis Warren, a playwright, also opposed ratification. She, like the others, wrote pamphlets explaining why she did not support the Constitution.

Many arguments were made both for and against the Constitution. Most of them had to do with three basic questions:

- Would the new Constitution maintain a republican form of government?

- Would the federal government have too much power?

- Was a bill of rights needed in the Constitution?

We are focusing upon the story of the Bill of Rights in this text, not on the history of the entire Constitution. Therefore, we will limit our discussion of the ratification struggle to the conflict between the Federalists and Anti-Federalists over the issue of a bill of rights.

Patrick Henry (1736-1799)

Richard Henry Lee (1732-1794)

Mercy Otis Warren (1728-1814)

Why did the Anti-Federalists demand a bill of rights?

Critical Thinking Exercise
TAKING, DEFENDING, AND EVALUATING POSITIONS ON THE NEED FOR A BILL OF RIGHTS

Your class should be divided into an even number of small groups for this exercise. Each group should read and discuss the following arguments of the Federalists and Anti-Federalists. Half the groups should be assigned to present and defend the Federalists' position. The other half should defend the Anti-Federalists' position. Finally, the entire class should evaluate the different positions.

What arguments were used by the Federalists against adding a bill of rights?

The following are the major arguments the Federalists used in opposing the addition of a bill of rights to the Constitution.

1. **The complexity of the government and diversity of the nation protect rights.** You have discussed Madison's argument that the way the Constitution organizes the government, and the size and diversity of the nation, provide citizens with enough protection from the federal and state governments. This was a principal argument the Federalists used against their opponents.

2. **The Constitution contains protections of specific rights.** The Constitution contains provisions protecting some of the rights included in various state constitutions and declarations of rights. These include the right to *habeas corpus*, prohibition of *ex post facto* laws and bills of attainder, protection against violations of contracts, the guarantee in criminal cases of a trial by jury in the state where the crime was committed, and the protection of persons accused of treason. These rights, in addition to those contained in the state declarations, are adequate.

3. **A bill of rights is unnecessary in a nation with popular sovereignty.** Most bills of rights, such as the English Bill of Rights, protect the people from a king who has the ultimate power of government and over whom they may have little or no control. In the United States, the situation is entirely different. The people are the ultimate source of power and the members of government are their servants, selected by them, and not their masters. The people can remove anyone from office who is violating their rights. Therefore, there is no need to protect the people from government officials over whom they have the ultimate power.

4. **The Constitution does not give the federal government the power to deprive people of their rights.** The Constitution only gives limited and specific powers to the government. It does not give the government the power

to limit such rights as freedom of belief or expression, or freedom of the press. Therefore, there is no need to list such rights since the Constitution does not give the government any power to violate them.

5. **Declarations of rights are ineffective and dangerous.** Most states listed rights in their state declarations or constitutions. Yet, these lists had not stopped the state governments from violating such rights. In addition, no state had a comprehensive list of rights. As a result, some state governments apparently felt free to violate important basic rights because they were not listed in their state documents.

It would be almost impossible to list all the rights of the people. Therefore, it would be better not to list any. This would avoid giving government officials the impression they could violate any right that was not specifically protected.

What arguments were used by the Anti-Federalists for adding a bill of rights?

The lack of a bill of rights proved to be the strongest and most powerful weapon of the Anti-Federalists in their fight to defeat the Constitution. Their most frequent arguments are as follows:

1. **The organization and complexity of the government do not adequately protect rights.** The way the government is organized is not an adequate protection of individual rights. Only the House of Representatives is chosen directly by the people. The federal government is too far away from the average citizen to share his concerns. Because of its great power, the federal government could still violate individual rights.

2. **The unlimited power given the federal government to act directly on citizens will allow it to violate rights.** The Constitution allows the federal government to act directly on citizens. The argument that the Constitution only gives the federal government specific powers is not true. Some provisions are so general and vague that they can be used to give the government almost unlimited power. For example, the Constitution gives Congress the power to make any laws that it thinks are "necessary and proper" and to promote the "general welfare."

3. **The federal government would feel free to violate rights it is not specifically prohibited from violating.** The Federalists' argument is inconsistent. They claim that listing rights is unnecessary and possibly even dangerous. Yet they have included provisions in the Constitution protecting some rights but not others. And several important rights are not included. For example,

the Constitution does not protect freedom of religion, speech, the press, assembly, or petition. These are rights essential to a free society. By omitting such important rights, the Constitution leaves the federal government free to violate them.

4. **A bill of rights is necessary to quiet the fears of the people.** The people have just fought a war to secure their rights. Not including a bill of rights is a major objection many people have to the Constitution. To add a bill of rights would reassure the people that the Framers do not intend to establish a federal government with the power to violate their rights.

5. **A bill of rights is necessary to remind the people of the principles of our political system.** As one Anti-Federalist expressed it, there is a necessity of "constantly keeping in view...the particular principles on which our freedom must always depend."

How did the demand for a bill of rights unite the Anti-Federalists?

The Anti-Federalists often disagreed with each other about why they opposed the Constitution, and they were not a well organized group. However, they were united in their opposition to the new federal government called for in the Constitution. They soon realized that the best way to defeat the Constitution was to use the issue of a bill of rights.

There was a widespread fear of a strong and powerful federal government, combined with the belief that a bill of rights was necessary to protect people from government. If people needed to be protected from their relatively weak state governments, they certainly needed protection from the vastly more powerful federal government. In addition, it was easier for the Anti-Federalists to dramatize the lack of a bill of rights than the issues of taxes or the powers of the state governments.

The lack of a bill of rights became the focus of the Anti-Federalist campaign. It was a highly emotional issue for the men and women who had just fought a revolution to secure their rights. In several states, the question of a bill of rights was used effectively to organize opposition to the ratification of the Constitution.

Many Anti-Federalist leaders, like George Mason, hoped to defeat the Constitution so that a second constitutional convention would be held. There, the Anti-Federalists hoped, they would have more influence in creating a new government.

Why did the Federalists give in to the demand for a bill of rights?

The Federalists used a number of strategies to get the different states to ratify the Constitution. One of these was to give in to the Anti-Federalists' demand for a bill of rights. This decision deprived the Anti-Federalists of their most powerful weapon. In some states, Massachusetts for example, the agreement to add a bill of rights was enough to win ratification by the close vote of 187 to 168.

The Federalists worked hard to overcome the objections of the Anti-Federalists. New Hampshire was the ninth and last state needed to make the Constitution the highest law of the land. It voted for ratification, but included a list of twelve **amendments** suggested as a bill of rights for the new nation. Many other states had also recommended amendments.

The Anti-Federalists had lost their battle to reject or revise the Constitution. However, they had won an agreement to add a bill of rights. The next lesson will explain how that agreement was fulfilled.

Using the Lesson

1. Explain the plan the Framers used to get the Constitution ratified and why they used it.

2. How were the Federalists, who were against adding a bill of rights to the Constitution, able to use the issue to get the Constitution ratified?

3. If you were afraid of giving too much power to the federal government, why would you be especially concerned with the "necessary and proper" and "general welfare" clauses of the Constitution?

4. If you had lived in the United States during this period, would you have agreed with the Federalists or Anti-Federalists? Why?

Lesson 12

How Was the Bill of Rights Added to the Constitution?

Purpose of Lesson

In this last lesson of Unit Two, you will learn of the struggle to add a bill of rights to the Constitution. You also will learn of the reactions of Americans in 1791 to the Bill of Rights, and the reasons it was of limited usefulness in protecting the people's rights.

When you have finished this lesson, you should be able to explain the conflict over adding a bill of rights to the Constitution, the result of the conflict, and why the Bill of Rights had such a limited effect on the lives of Americans at that time.

Terms to Know

Ninth Amendment
enumeration

The beginning of the new government

On April 30, 1789, George Washington was sworn into office as the first president of the United States. For the first time in history, the people of a nation held the ultimate power of government and had selected the person to lead their government. Most important, the powers of that person were limited by the written Constitution he was sworn to uphold.

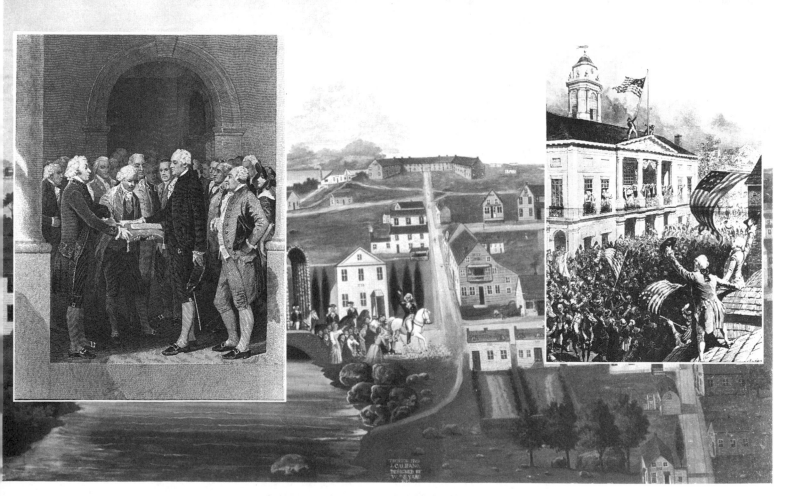

In our system of government, who holds the ultimate power?

Washington was not dressed like a king. He saw himself as a man of the people. He wore a brown suit made of American-woven cloth bought through a newspaper advertisement. President Washington spoke of freedom in his first inaugural address, and about what should be done to secure it. He urged Congress to fulfill the promise to add a bill of rights to the Constitution.

Who was responsible for adding a bill of rights to the Constitution?

The Constitution had been ratified. Nevertheless, the Anti-Federalists had not given up their fight to place more limitations on the powers of the new federal government.

James Madison had been elected to Congress as a representative from Virginia. Although he had been opposed to a bill of rights and often referred to it as a "parchment [paper] barrier," during the ratifying debates he had made a promise to add one. His fulfillment of that pledge entitles him to be known as the "father of the Bill of Rights" as much as his better-known title, "father of the Constitution."

Madison knew he needed to get a bill of rights approved quickly. He did not want to give the Anti-Federalists time to gain enough support to call for a second constitutional convention. He also felt strongly that he should fulfill his promise to protect individual rights.

Madison began his task by sorting through the more than two hundred amendments recommended by the states during the ratification debates. Most fell into one of two groups. They either (1) placed additional limitations on the powers of the federal government or (2) protected individual rights.

What amendments did Madison propose?

Madison ignored all the amendments that were designed to limit severely the power of the federal government. His draft of the Bill of Rights did include many of the suggestions from the states that protected individual rights such as freedom of conscience, speech, press, religion, assembly, petition, and trial by jury. He also relied on the colonial bills of rights and

charters of liberty. For example, the Massachusetts Body of Liberties was adopted in 1641, forty-eight years before the English Bill of Rights and almost one and a half centuries before our Bill of Rights. It contained twenty-three of the twenty-seven rights listed in our Bill of Rights.

Madison's proposals included all the amendments that became the Bill of Rights. However, several of his ideas were not accepted by Congress.

On June 8, 1789, Madison introduced his amendments on the floor of the House of Representatives. In his speech, he tried to assure the Federalists that his amendments would not radically change the Constitution they had supported. He also tried to convince the Anti-Federalists that his amendments would protect individual liberties.

Madison suggested that an introductory statement be added to the Constitution containing some of the basic ideas about government included in the Declaration of Independence. This statement would contain the ideas that the purpose of government is to protect the rights of the people and that the people are the ultimate source of its authority.

As you have learned from previous lessons, some Americans had become increasingly concerned about what they saw as the violations of minority rights by powerful majorities in the state legislatures. By this time, Madison had become convinced that the greatest danger to individual rights came not from the federal government, but from groups who could use their state governments to serve their selfish interests at the expense of others.

Madison believed that state governments were a greater threat to individual rights than the federal government. So he included what he considered "the most valuable amendment in the whole list." This amendment stated that:

No State shall violate the equal rights of conscience, or the freedom of the press, or the trial by jury in criminal cases.

Madison also included an amendment to deal with the criticism that an incomplete list of rights would endanger those rights not listed. This is the **Ninth Amendment** which clearly states that the Bill of Rights is only a partial list of the people's rights. It says:

*The **enumeration** [listing] in the Constitution of certain rights shall not be construed [interpreted] to deny or disparage [make less important] others retained by the people.*

Finally, Madison argued that the amendments he had drafted should be included in the Constitution itself. He did not think they should be added as a list at the end of the Constitution.

How did Congress respond to Madison's proposals?

Although Madison's speech was eloquent, members of the House of Representatives appeared completely uninterested in his suggestions. Every speaker who followed him either opposed a bill of rights or believed the House had far more important business. Six weeks later Madison again asked the House to vote on his amendments, but the House sent them to a committee instead of debating them.

Finally, in August, the House agreed to consider Madison's amendments. Only one significant change was made. At the insistence of Roger Sherman, the amendments were added at the end of the Constitution instead of placed in the body of the document as Madison had suggested. Also, of the forty-two rights proposed by Madison, only twenty-seven were in the final Bill of Rights.

The amendments were then sent to the Senate. Since Senate debate was not open to the public, little is known about what happened there. However, Anti-Federalist senators eliminated the amendment that would have prohibited state governments from violating freedom of conscience, speech, press, and trial by jury in criminal cases. As a result, it was not until almost 150 years later (by use of the Fourteenth Amendment) that citizens would be protected by the Constitution from violations of these rights by their state governments.

A joint committee of the House and Senate made a few other changes in Madison's proposed amendments. Then, in September of 1789, Congress approved the Bill of Rights and sent it to the states for ratification. The Bill of Rights passed by Congress contained twelve amendments. Of these, two were not ratified by the states. These dealt with reapportionment of the House of Representatives and the effective dates of pay raises for members of Congress. On December 15, 1791, the Bill of Rights became a part of the Constitution when it was ratified by Virginia, the last state required for its approval.

What did people think of the Bill of Rights in 1791?

The reaction of most Americans to the Bill of Rights was lukewarm at best. Its passage had little effect on the average man and woman on the street. The Bill of Rights only prohibited the federal government from violating rights. State governments could and did pass laws that limited the rights of citizens in their states.

Why was the Bill of Rights of such limited importance in the eighteenth century?

The Anti-Federalists, who had based much of their opposition to the Constitution on the lack of a bill of rights, were unhappy with its passage. They thought it spoiled their chances to rewrite the Constitution. They said the amendments were "good for nothing." "I believe," said Senator William Grayson of Virginia, "as many others do, that they will do more harm than good."

At the same time, many Federalists were angry with Madison for pushing the Bill of Rights through Congress. At best, they considered it of little importance. Even Madison, tired of all the disagreement and dissent, had come to think of the whole experience as a "nauseous project."

Thomas Jefferson was serving as the first secretary of state. He was responsible for notifying the state governors of the actions of Congress. In 1792 Jefferson informed the governors that Congress had taken action concerning fisheries, the post office, and postal roads. At the end of his letter, almost as a postscript, he informed them of the ratification of the Bill of Rights: "the ratification by three fourths of the...States, of certain articles in addition and amendment of the Constitution."

Critical Thinking Exercise
TAKING AND DEFENDING A POSITION ON A CONSTITUTIONAL AMENDMENT

A well regulated Militia, being necessary to the security of a free State, the right of the people to keep and bear Arms, shall not be infringed.
Second Amendment

One of the basic beliefs of classical republicanism was that a standing army was the enemy of freedom. Only a citizen militia, in which each member of the community had the duty to serve, provided security without threatening the liberties of the people.

This fear of standing armies and the belief in a citizen militia was supported by political philosophers as well as by historical experience. For example, when the American colonists began to oppose British policies, Parliament passed a law banning the shipment of arms to the colonies. Indeed, the first armed rebellion was not the famous battle at Lexington and Concord in April 1775, but a patriot raid on the British fort of William and Mary on the New Hampshire coast six months earlier. It was there that arms and ammunition were seized and secretly distributed throughout the colonies—arms that were later used to fire the "shot heard 'round the world."

James Madison argued during the ratification debates that one reason Americans need not fear the power of the new federal government was because the citizens had "the advantage of being armed, which you possess over the people of almost every other nation....In the several Kingdoms of Europe...the governments are afraid to trust the people with arms."

The Anti-Federalists also strongly supported the right of citizens to bear arms. Patrick Henry declared, "The great principle is that every man be armed. Everyone who is able may have a gun." Richard Henry Lee argued that "to preserve liberty, it is essential that the whole body of the people always possess arms, and be taught alike, especially when young, how to use them."

Why do you suppose the Bill of Rights is so important today?

It was with this understanding that the Second Amendment was written. It was passed on a voice vote, without objection, and was approved by the Senate. It was ratified by the people with little debate.

What do *you* think?

1. Do you think the Second Amendment is as important today as it was in the eighteenth century? Explain your answer.

2. What argument would you make for the right of the citizens to bear arms today? How might that argument differ from the arguments Americans made in the 1790s?

3. What limitations, if any, do you think should be placed on the right to bear arms? How would you justify those limits?

Were the Framers aware of other threats to rights?

Some people have argued that the Framers were not sufficiently aware of important threats to rights from sources other than government. They did not appear to pay adequate attention to threats arising, for example, from economic power and religious and racial prejudice. Therefore, some people would argue, the Framers did not appreciate that the power of government can be used to protect the rights of some individuals against threats from other individuals, groups, or organizations.

In the twentieth century, the Bill of Rights has become what it never was in the eighteenth century. It is, perhaps, the most important single document protecting individual rights. However, the struggle to extend its protections to all Americans has taken more than two hundred years, and the struggle continues. The rest of this book will be devoted to examining these rights and how they have been protected and extended to Americans deprived of them in the past.

Using the Lesson

1. Why did the Anti-Federalists change their minds and oppose the Bill of Rights?

2. What types of rights did Madison include and exclude in the Bill of Rights?

3. Where did Madison think the greatest danger to individual rights came from? Why did he think this?

4. What were the reactions of Congress and the American people to the Bill of Rights in 1791? How can you explain this reaction?

5. Why did the Bill of Rights only limit the powers of the federal government and not the state governments?

6. In 1791, what protections, if any, did the Bill of Rights appear to provide for the rights of individuals from violation by other individuals or groups?

Unit Three: How Were the Protections of the Bill of Rights Expanded?

What responsibility should the federal government take to protect individual rights?

Purpose of Unit

Today the Bill of Rights has become something it never was in the eighteenth and most of the nineteenth centuries. It is perhaps the most important document protecting your rights from the abuse of power by the federal, state, and local governments. The struggle to extend the protections of the Bill of Rights to all Americans has taken more than two hundred years, and the struggle continues not only to protect individuals and groups from government actions, but also from actions by private agencies.

In this unit you will learn how the protections of the Bill of Rights have been extended to Americans deprived of them in the past as a result of the Supreme Court's interpretation of the equal protection and due process clauses of the Fourteenth Amendment. The result of this use of the Fourteenth Amendment has greatly increased the power of the federal government over the states. You will also examine alternative means of remedying the effects of past discrimination and the importance of the Supreme Court's power of judicial review over state governments.

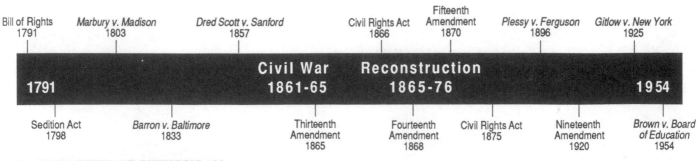

Bill of Rights 1791 · Marbury v. Madison 1803 · Dred Scott v. Sanford 1857 · Civil Rights Act 1866 · Fifteenth Amendment 1870 · Plessy v. Ferguson 1896 · Gitlow v. New York 1925

1791 · Civil War 1861-65 · Reconstruction 1865-76 · 1954

Sedition Act 1798 · Barron v. Baltimore 1833 · Thirteenth Amendment 1865 · Fourteenth Amendment 1868 · Civil Rights Act 1875 · Nineteenth Amendment 1920 · Brown v. Board of Education 1954

LESSON 13

How Well Did the Bill of Rights Protect Individual Rights Before the Civil War?

Purpose of Lesson

This lesson examines the role played by the Bill of Rights from the time it was adopted in 1791 to the outbreak of the Civil War in 1861. You will learn that during this period, the Bill of Rights had very little effect on the lives of most Americans. This was because it only limited the powers of the federal government and the federal government had very little to do with the average citizen.

When you have completed this lesson, you should be able to explain why the Bill of Rights did not protect individuals from their state governments or private individuals. You should also be able to explain the major sources of threats to rights during this time.

Terms to Know

Sedition Act
Marbury v. Madison
judicial review
null and void
Dred Scott v. Sanford
Barron v. Baltimore
Emancipation Proclamation

Why did the Bill of Rights provide so little protection for individuals during the early years of the nation?

As you have learned, the Bill of Rights only prohibited the federal government from violating individual rights. During the early period of our history, the federal government had very little to do with the daily lives of Americans. In fact, often the only contact most people had with the federal government was with their postmaster. Therefore, the Bill of Rights was of little importance to them.

The Bill of Rights did not place any limits upon the powers of the state and local governments or upon private persons and groups, and they had the greatest influence on the day-to-day lives of most people. Until the beginning of the Civil War in 1861, the state governments had almost unlimited authority over the rights of individuals. If a state government violated a right listed in the Bill of Rights, you could not ask the federal

government for help since the Bill of Rights did not limit the powers of the states.

The primary protections of individual rights were provided by the state constitutions, state bills of rights, and state civil and criminal laws. If an individual or group violated the rights of other individuals protected by a state's laws, they could sue in a state court. Under this system rights were sometimes violated. Although various groups were treated unfairly, the most notable were African Americans, Native Americans, and women. Religious tests and property requirements for voting also violated the rights of white men.

Neither the federal or state bills of rights protected many of the same rights for women that they did for men. Finally, the Constitution itself permitted slavery to continue. The federal government even made money on the slave trade by placing import taxes on slaves brought into the country. Since the Constitution protected an individual's right to own property, it protected the right to own slaves who were considered at the time to be a form of property.

How well did the Bill of Rights protect individuals from the federal government?

James Madison had warned that written guarantees of rights might be merely "parchment barriers." Just because rights are listed on a piece of paper does not mean that rulers will not violate them. Madison's warning soon proved to be true. In 1798, Congress passed the **Sedition Act** which violated the right to freedom of expression. The circumstances which led to this act were as follows.

During the 1790s, soon after the new government was established, rival political parties developed:

- The **Federalists**, led by Alexander Hamilton, favored a strong federal government. They also wanted to renew ties with Great Britain which was at war with France.

- The **Republicans**, led by Thomas Jefferson, wanted less power in the federal government and more power in the state governments. They supported France in its war with Great Britain.

The Republicans criticized the Federalists for being in favor of the British instead of the French who had helped the United

Alexander Hamilton (1757-1804)

Thomas Jefferson (1743-1826)

John Adams (1735-1826)

States gain their independence from British rule. They also favored France because its people were overthrowing their king and establishing a republican form of government.

In 1796, John Adams, a Federalist, was elected president. The nation prepared for war with France. Republicans severely criticized the government's actions in speech and in the press. The Federalists were furious at such criticism. They claimed that Jefferson's and the other Republicans' favoring of France during a national emergency was dangerous to the unity of the nation. Congress, dominated by the Federalists, passed the Sedition Act of 1798. This act made it a crime for anyone to engage in "false, scandalous and malicious" criticism of the government or its leaders. Persons found guilty could be fined and imprisoned. However, criticism that could be proven to be true could not be punished.

Federalist government officials used this act against their Republican critics. Twenty-five Republican printers and writers were arrested. Fifteen were indicted and ten were convicted, fined, and imprisoned for as long as nine months.

The Republicans claimed that the Sedition Act violated the First Amendment, but the act was never ruled upon by the Supreme Court. While the Republicans accused the Federalists of instituting a "reign of terror," this was probably an overstatement. The success of the Republicans in the election of 1800 suggests that the Sedition Act was not as effective as the Federalists had hoped in silencing their critics. In the so-called "revolution of 1800," Thomas Jefferson was elected president of the United States and the Republicans gained control of the Congress. It is worth noting that the attacks under the Sedition Act on the rights of the citizens to criticize the government were not eliminated by the courts, but through the election of a new government that did not support the act.

Marbury v. Madison (1803)

In 1803, during Jefferson's first term as president, the Supreme Court made a decision in the case of *Marbury v. Madison* that is of great importance in the history of individual rights in America. This decision clearly established the Supreme Court's power of **judicial review** over the other branches of the federal government. Judicial review is the power of the court to decide whether laws and actions of the government are allowed under the Constitution. When the Court decides they are not allowed, it orders that the law or action be considered **null and void**. A law that is null and void cannot be enforced.

It is clear that the Constitution gives the Supreme Court the power of judicial review over the state governments. Whether it gives the Court this power over the federal government is less clear. The Supreme Court claimed this power in its opinion in the case of *Marbury v. Madison*. As you will learn in later lessons, the consequences of this opinion for American constitutional law and American politics have been enormous.

From the time of the adoption of the Constitution to the Civil War, the Supreme Court only used its power of judicial review over the federal government two times. The first was in the case of *Marbury v. Madison*. The second was in the case of *Dred Scott v. Sanford* (1857) which helped bring about the Civil War. We will discuss this case later in the lesson.

The Supreme Court did review numerous state and local laws during this period. One of the most important of these was in the following case which dealt with the question of whether the Bill of Rights applied to the states.

Barron v. Baltimore (1833)

Barron v. Baltimore (1833) was one of the first important cases in which the Supreme Court used its power of judicial review over the actions of a state government. In this case the Supreme Court decided that the Bill of Rights did not extend to actions by state governments.

The case involved a man who claimed that people working for the city government of Baltimore had left his wharf useless by diverting the stream that flowed under it from its natural course. When the city refused to compensate him, the man went to court and claimed that his rights under the Fifth Amendment of the Bill of Rights had been violated. This amendment says that the government cannot take a person's property for public use without paying a fair price for it. The man argued that by making his wharf useless and refusing to pay for it, the city had violated his rights under the Fifth Amendment.

The Supreme Court ruled that the Fifth Amendment was written only to protect individuals from violation of their rights by the federal government, not the state governments. State constitutions were meant to protect individuals from actions by state governments.

The decision in *Barron v. Baltimore* was of major importance because of Chief Justice Marshall's statement that the Framers of the Bill of Rights did not intend it to apply to actions of state governments. The Bill of Rights had been added to the Constitution because of the widespread fear that the powerful new federal government would be such a threat to individual rights. Its only purpose was to limit the actions of the federal government, not those of the states.

Protections of rights by state governments

The decision in *Barron v. Baltimore* did not mean people had no protection when state governments violated their rights. It meant, however, that citizens must look to their state constitutions to protect those rights.

During the nineteenth century, state courts frequently declared state laws unconstitutional when they violated individual rights. However, as you learned previously, not all rights were protected under each state constitution. For example, one state constitution might prohibit *ex post facto* laws, while another would not. One state might specifically protect freedom of speech, while another had no such guarantee.

In addition, on many occasions, state governments violated rights. Sometimes this was the result of the wishes of the majority of citizens. At other times, it was because a small but powerful minority was influencing the state government.

Interest groups often pressured state legislators to pass laws that helped them at the expense of the rights of others. For example, the constitution of each state in New England included provisions similar to the Fifth Amendment to protect property from being taken by the government without fair compensation. Nevertheless, when railroad companies became powerful in New England, state legislatures often violated the property rights of their citizens.

The state governments took land "for the public good," giving the farmers who owned it only a fraction of what it was worth. The states then turned the land over to railroad companies in exchange for stock and free rail passes for all legislators and governors.

When citizens took the cases to the state courts, judges often sided with the state at the individual's expense. When courts did not rule the way the powerful railroad companies wanted, they influenced legislators to change the laws to add more judges to the courts. Then the companies pressured governors to appoint judges favorable to their wishes.

In one state, the railroad companies went so far as to hire all the attorneys in the state. This made it a conflict of interest for the attorneys to accept any cases against the companies. As a result, citizens could not find an attorney to represent them in court. Yet the state constitution supposedly protected citizens' rights to counsel and to have a fair trial.

In the southern states, most blacks were slaves and were not protected by their state or federal constitutions. They were merely regarded as property and had no rights. Slaves and their children could be sold at any time. They could not move about freely, had no freedom of speech or right to testify in court, and had no protection against unreasonable searches and seizures.

Although slavery was abolished in the northern states by 1805, free blacks living in both the North and South did not enjoy full rights. As an 1826 editorial in an African American newspaper in Baltimore charged:

> We reside among you...surrounded by the freest people and most republican institutions in the world, but we enjoy none of the immunities of freedom....Though we are not slaves, we are not free.

Dred Scott v. Sanford (1857)

The U.S. Supreme Court refused to protect freedom for African Americans in 1857 in the *Dred Scott* case. In this case, the Court formally declared that neither free blacks nor slaves were citizens of the United States. It denied Congress the power to prevent slavery from entering the western territories. This decision prevented Congress from stopping the further spread of slavery by limiting it to the states where it already existed. Some believe that the *Dred Scott* decision was one of the principal causes of the Civil War.

How was the ideal of equality used in the fight against slavery?

The ideal of equality is contained in the familiar phrase from the Declaration of Independence, "We hold these Truths to be self-evident, that all Men are created equal." In the years before the Civil War, many Americans, most notably free blacks and abolitionists, argued that this ideal of equality was the foundation of American government. They used this ideal to support their argument that racial discrimination and slavery were not permissible in the United States.

Despite this argument, the Supreme Court and many state courts upheld racial discrimination. However, some state legislatures did not. In Massachusetts, free blacks and abolitionists tried to get their state supreme court to declare segregated schools unconstitutional. When the court ruled in favor of segregation, the blacks and their supporters among the abolitionists went to their state legislature for help. They claimed that the court had violated their state constitution's guarantee of equality. The state legislature was persuaded by their arguments and passed a law prohibiting segregation in the public schools of Massachusetts.

The Civil War

The Civil War between the northern and southern states began in April of 1861. It was a result of years of conflict between the states over political power, economic interests, and social issues such as labor and slavery. As a result of this conflict,

What conflict between the right to liberty and property was raised by the <u>Dred Scott</u> case?

Inauguration of Jefferson Davis
as president of the Confederacy
February 1861

What arguments could the southern states have made to justify secession?

the South claimed it had the right to secede from the Union and form a new government. The southern states created their own government, the Confederate States of America. Jefferson Davis was elected president. In his inaugural address he said, "All we ask is to be let alone."

The federal government refused to recognize the South's right to secede. For President Abraham Lincoln, and for most northerners, the primary purpose of the Civil War was to preserve the Union. Lincoln had said that he believed all African Americans should have the natural rights described in the Declaration of Independence. However, in 1862 he also said:

My paramount object...is to save the Union....If I could save the Union without freeing any slave, I would do it; and if I could save it by freeing all the slaves, I would do it; and if I could do it by freeing some and leaving others alone, I would also do that.

The Emancipation Proclamation

Lincoln was true to his word. In order to preserve the Union, he issued the **Emancipation Proclamation** to take effect in January 1863. This act freed the slaves in the southern states

which were still fighting the North and were not under federal control. It did not free the slaves in any state controlled by the federal government.

There had always been some sentiment in the United States for freeing the slaves. The American Colonization Society, founded in 1816, had advocated the gradual emancipation of slaves coupled with their return to Africa. The American Anti-Slavery Society was founded on January 1, 1831. As the war progressed, the movement to end slavery in the United States gained support. The Society of Friends (Quakers) and various other religious groups were active in attempting to abolish slavery. Many people saw the war as an opportunity to achieve this goal. The result was that after the defeat of the South, amendments were added to the Constitution to eliminate slavery throughout the United States.

In the next lesson, you will learn about these amendments which narrowed the gap between the ideals of our government stated in the Declaration of Independence and the Preamble to the Constitution, and the reality of American life. However, as you will also learn, it has taken more than a hundred years since the Civil War to come close to realizing the goal of equality for all Americans.

Critical Thinking Exercise
TAKING AND DEFENDING POSITIONS ON THE PROTECTION OF RIGHTS

Work in small groups to develop positions agreeing or disagreeing with the following statements. Be prepared to present and defend your positions before the class.

1. James Madison argued that a bill of rights was no more than a "parchment barrier" protecting rights that could easily be violated by government. He claimed that the separation of powers, checks and balances, and the federal system were a better protection of rights. Taking into account what you have learned, do you agree? Explain your position.

2. Judge Learned Hand said that if liberty does not lie in the hearts of men, no constitution or law can save it. How, if at all, are his ideas relevant to the period of history you have just studied?

Using the Lesson

1. Why was the Bill of Rights of such little importance before the Civil War?

2. During the period you have studied, where were the greatest threats to individual rights found? Which, if any, of the Framers had foreseen such threats?

3. Why do you suppose some of the Framers were more concerned with threats to individual rights from the federal government than from their state governments?

4. What is the power of judicial review? Why do you suppose it is more important now than it was in the early 1800s?

5. Why do you suppose Lincoln's Emancipation Proclamation did not free slaves in states under federal control?

6. What violations of rights in our country or other countries have you observed that have been due to racial or ethnic prejudice or to religious intolerance? What do you think might be the best way to protect people from such violations of their rights?

COME AND JOIN US BROTHERS.
PUBLISHED BY THE SUPERVISORY COMMITTEE FOR RECRUITING COLORED REGIMENTS

LESSON 14

What Amendments to the Constitution Were Added to Protect the Rights of African Americans?

Purpose of Lesson

You have learned how limited the protections of rights were under the Bill of Rights before the Civil War. You also learned of some of the common violations of rights during this period.

In this lesson we will examine the amendments added to the Constitution after the Civil War. These were intended to free the slaves and give them the same rights other Americans had. However, you will see that these amendments were not enough to guarantee the newly freed slaves their rights.

When you have completed this lesson, you should be able to explain how the federal government attempted to use amendments to the Constitution and civil rights legislation to protect the rights of African Americans. You should also be able to explain why these attempts failed to protect these rights.

Terms to Know

Civil War Amendments
black codes
Civil Rights Act of 1866
privileges and immunities clause
due process clause
equal protection clause
poll taxes, literacy tests, and grandfather clauses
Slaughterhouse Cases
Civil Rights Act of 1875
Nineteenth Amendment

Political parties of the times

In order to understand some of the conflicts surrounding this period of history, it is necessary to know something about the two most prominent political parties. These were the Democratic and Republican parties. The Democratic party was the former Republican party begun by Thomas Jefferson. The Federalist party was defeated in the election of 1800 and it ceased to exist a few years later.

The new Republican party was an anti-slavery party formed in 1854. It nominated its first presidential candidate, John C. Fremont, in 1856. He ran against James Buchanan, the Democratic candidate. In this election, Fremont ran on a platform that would have prohibited slavery in the territories.

Fremont was supported by the North and Buchanan by the South. Buchanan won.

Four years later, Abraham Lincoln ran as a Republican on a platform which allowed slavery in the states in which it already existed, but prohibited slavery in the western territories. He defeated Stephen O. Douglas, the Democratic candidate, and became president. With the admission of Minnesota and Oregon to the Union in 1858-59, there were eighteen free states and fifteen slave states. From this time through the period following the Civil War, the Republican party controlled both the executive and legislative branches of the federal government.

Why did Lincoln and the Republicans want to prohibit slavery in the territories?

The Reconstruction period

The period after the Civil War, during which states that had seceded were being brought back into the Union, is called Reconstruction. During this time, the Republican party dominated the federal government as it had done during the war. The Republican party gained most of its strength from the northern states. The Democratic party was strongest in the South. Many of the leaders of the Confederacy had been members of the Democratic party.

CONVENTION OF FREEDMEN DISCUSSING THEIR POLITICAL RIGHTS.

Why was the right to vote so important to the newly freed male slaves?

Since most of their former masters had been members of the Democratic party, it was expected that most of the newly freed slaves would vote for the Republican party. As you shall see, this expectation strongly influenced some of the political battles fought over the rights of African Americans during Reconstruction.

The Civil War Amendments

The Civil War ended slavery in America after it had existed for more than two hundred years. Shortly after the war, three amendments, commonly called the **Civil War Amendments**, were added to the Constitution. As you will see, they were added for both moral and political reasons.

- The **Thirteenth Amendment** abolished slavery "within the United States, or in any place subject to their jurisdiction."

- The **Fourteenth Amendment**, among other things, made all persons born or naturalized within the United States citizens. It also prohibited any state from making or enforcing any law that limited the rights of citizens.

- The **Fifteenth Amendment** prohibited the national and state governments from denying citizens the right to vote because of their race, color, or status as former slaves.

The first postwar session of Congress was held in December 1865. Congress and many state governments immediately passed laws designed to protect the rights of blacks. When Congress tried to implement these laws vigorously, its efforts were strongly resisted by whites, especially in the South, who opposed racial equality. Eventually public support for protecting the rights of the newly freed blacks grew weaker and, by the late 1870s, the Civil War Amendments became useless as a tool for protecting their rights.

What was the effect of the Thirteenth Amendment?

The Thirteenth Amendment, ratified in 1865, was intended to end slavery and the unfair treatment of African Americans throughout the nation. In reality, it did very little.

Several northern states did pass laws to expand blacks' rights. In 1865, both Illinois and California passed laws allowing blacks to testify against whites in trials. Massachusetts passed a law prohibiting racial discrimination in public accommodations. In 1868, both Minnesota and Iowa passed laws giving blacks the right to vote. However, not one southern state passed a law protecting the right of African Americans to vote or enjoy any of the other political, economic, and social rights held by most other citizens.

Some states had refused to ratify the Thirteenth Amendment. Others demanded that the federal government pay their citizens for the loss of their slaves.

Although some Southerners were in favor of freeing the slaves, many were not. Slavery had accustomed Southerners to seeing blacks as inferior. Plantation and farm owners had grown used to slaves as a cheap form of labor.

Many northern businesses were also interested in cheap labor. White workers had been organizing into labor unions and were demanding better pay and working conditions. Owners of factories and other businesses saw the newly freed slaves as a source of cheap labor.

Some workers in the North were afraid that blacks might compete with them for jobs. They wanted the blacks to stay in the South and West where they would not threaten their jobs.

The black codes

After the Civil War, the federal government had kept Union troops in the South to protect the newly freed slaves. Southern legislatures passed laws called the **black codes** in an attempt to convince the federal government that they would treat African Americans fairly. Supposedly, these laws protected the rights of blacks. For example, they protected the rights of blacks to marry, own property, travel, work for pay, and sue in court.

In fact, the black codes severely limited these rights. African Americans could only marry other African Americans. They could own property, but few white people would sell it to them. They could travel, but only after dark in the baggage cars of trains. They could work for pay, but few people would pay them fair wages. They could sue for damages in court, but their right to sue white people was meaningless because cases were tried by white judges and juries who were hostile to blacks.

In the southern states, the educational opportunities of blacks were far less than those of whites. Schools for black students were usually inferior to those for white children. Blacks could only go to school with other blacks. People were discouraged

Why were equal educational opportunities denied to blacks?

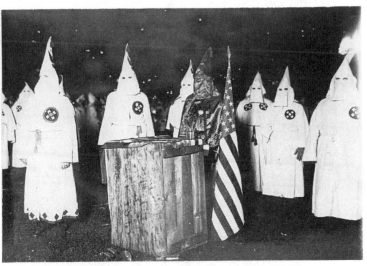

Why did vigilante groups threaten all people who supported equal rights for African Americans?

from starting black schools and sometimes such schools were burned. Blacks found with books were sometimes whipped. White supremacists did not want blacks to gain an education.

Vigilante groups of whites such as the Ku Klux Klan intimidated, terrorized, and sometimes killed black people and whites who helped them claim their rights. African Americans could rarely look to their local or state governments for protection from such treatment. Law enforcement agencies and the courts were biased against blacks and the whites who sympathized with them. Blacks were tried by all-white juries who rarely decided a case in their favor no matter what the facts were.

When the Union troops withdrew, a reign of terror began in the South. Blacks trying to gain their rights were assaulted and lynched. A white state senator who was sympathetic to the cause of the blacks was found with his throat slit. Others were lynched with signs hung around their necks saying such things as "Beware, ye guilty, both white and black."

The black codes were intended to prevent the former slaves from developing the political power they might have gained with education and the right to vote. Black codes clearly placed the political power of the southern states in the hands of white men.

Why did Congress pass the Civil Rights Act of 1866?

It became clear to members of Congress that the Thirteenth Amendment was not enough to protect the rights of African Americans. In an attempt to provide help to blacks, Congress passed the **Civil Rights Act of 1866** over the veto of President Andrew Johnson.

Despite the passing of this legislation, it had little effect. This was because the president refused to enforce the laws and the Supreme Court refused to listen to people who complained that their rights, supposedly protected by the Civil Rights Act, had been violated.

Frederick Douglass (1817-1895)

Many political leaders in the North and elsewhere were outraged by the treatment of African Americans in the South. Republicans were also concerned that their power in the federal government might soon be endangered by the new Democratic representatives elected to Congress by the southern states.

As a result of these concerns, Republicans in Congress drafted the Fourteenth and Fifteenth Amendments to be added to the Constitution. These amendments were written for both moral and political reasons. Many Republican leaders strongly believed in protecting the rights of blacks. For this reason, they argued that only if southern blacks had the right to vote would the officials of their state and local governments be responsive to them and protect their rights. In addition to protecting the rights of African Americans, Republicans were also interested in increasing the political power of blacks in the southern states. This was intended to keep the Republican party in power in the federal government and to limit the growing power of the Democratic party.

The Fourteenth Amendment

Seeing the failure of the Thirteenth Amendment and the Civil Rights Act of 1866 to protect the rights of blacks, Congress drafted the Fourteenth Amendment. This amendment, ratified in 1868, contained several provisions designed to reduce the problems of African Americans. These provisions are set forth below.

- **Defining citizenship.** "All persons born or naturalized in the United States are citizens of the United States and of the State wherein they reside." This clause made it clear that African Americans who met its requirements were citizens.

- **Rights of citizens.** "No state shall make or enforce any law which shall abridge the **privileges or immunities** of citizens of the United States." This clause was intended to forbid states from violating the rights of all citizens, regardless of their race.

- **Due process of law.** "nor shall any state deprive any person of life, liberty, or property, without **due process** of law." While the concept of due process is not easy to define, it has been described as meaning

that the government must govern fairly and according to the law and not in an arbitrary way.

- **Equal protection of the law.** "...nor shall any state...deny to any person within its jurisdiction the **equal protection** of the laws." This clause was intended to prevent state governments from unfairly discriminating against their citizens.

As you can see, this amendment was intended to prevent discrimination against blacks and to guarantee them the rights of equal citizenship. But as we shall see, it did not serve this purpose until almost one hundred years later.

Two clauses of the Fourteenth Amendment have been considered by many scholars to be among the most important in the entire Constitution. These are the due process and the equal protection clauses. These clauses have been used by attorneys and the courts to protect individual rights from being violated by state and local governments. In Lessons 15 and 17 you will learn how this was done.

The ratification debate over the Fourteenth Amendment was filled with conflict. President Johnson and others who did not wish to "punish the South" worked to defeat the amendment. People who did not want blacks to gain equal rights promoted racial fear and hatred to develop opposition to the amendment. Nevertheless, the Fourteenth Amendment was passed in 1868 over the objections of ten states which refused to ratify it.

The Republicans had gained their objective and they dominated Congress. Strong laws were passed by Congress to enforce the Fourteenth Amendment. During the late 1860s and 1870s, state legislatures and courts in both the North and the South expanded the rights of blacks and enforced laws against discrimination.

The Fifteenth Amendment

The failure of the Fourteenth Amendment to adequately protect the rights of black citizens led to the adoption of the Fifteenth Amendment in 1870. This amendment contains the following two sections:

Section 1. The right of citizens of the United States to vote shall not be denied or abridged by the United States or by any state on account of race, color, or previous condition of servitude.

Section 2. The Congress shall have the power to enforce this article by appropriate legislation.

This amendment was clearly intended to protect the right of African Americans to vote. Like the other Civil War Amendments, it was passed for both moral and political reasons. People believed that black citizens should have the same rights as all other citizens. The immediate effect of this amendment and the legislation passed to support it was that, during the late

1860s through the 1880s, large numbers of blacks voted. They gained considerable political power and they used it to protect their rights.

Eventually, however, after the Reconstruction period, southern states passed laws that destroyed the political power of blacks in the South. The following are the major types of laws that were used to eliminate blacks from participating in politics in the southern states.

- **Poll taxes.** Some states passed laws that required citizens to pay a tax before voting. Since most blacks were desperately poor, these taxes greatly reduced the number who could vote.

- **Literacy tests.** Some states required men to take tests proving they could read or write before they were allowed to vote. Since most southern blacks had been prevented from learning how to read or write, these tests denied them the right to vote. Furthermore, these tests were administered by whites who prevented even literate blacks from passing.

- **Grandfather clauses.** Laws were passed that allowed people in the South to vote, even if they could not read or write, if their grandfathers had voted. Since no blacks had grandfathers who had voted, these laws denied blacks the right to vote.

How well did the Civil War Amendments protect the rights of African Americans?

In the years following the Civil War, there was less and less talk about the rights and living conditions of African Americans. Unfortunately, the federal Bill of Rights offered little relief against injustice.

You may remember that the Fourteenth Amendment contains the clause, "No state shall make or enforce any law which shall abridge the privileges or immunities of citizens of the United States." The Supreme Court was asked in the **Slaughterhouse Cases** of 1873 to rule that this clause protected the rights listed in the Bill of Rights from violation by state governments. The Court refused to do so. The states were left with the power to continue to pass laws that violated the rights contained in the Bill of Rights. As a result of the Court's opinion in these cases, the privileges and immunities clause of the Fourteenth Amendment has been of no use in protecting individual rights to this day.

Congress passed the **Civil Rights Act of 1875** to give the federal government the power to enforce the protections of citizens' rights under the Fourteenth Amendment. However, this act was not enforced by the executive branch. Later, the Supreme Court declared the Civil Rights Act unconstitutional.

In what ways did the laws illustrated deny blacks the right to vote?

Rutherford B. Hayes of Ohio was the Republican candidate for president in 1876. He ran against the Democratic candidate, Samuel Tilden of New York. Hayes won the election with a minority of the popular vote, but a majority of the electoral vote.

Hayes had campaigned under the promise that he would remove the remaining federal troops from the South. In 1877, soon after he was elected, he appointed a former Confederate leader to his cabinet. It was a symbolic gesture, but a clear signal. The president and the majority of Americans believed it was time to get on with expanding the economy and territory of the United States. Reconstruction was over.

Hayes and his supporters did not want to spend more time and money on the former slaves. They wanted to let southern leaders handle their own problems. As the president told African Americans on a supposed "good will tour" of the South, "Your rights and interests would be safer if this great mass of intelligent white men were left alone by the federal government."

Hayes refused to enforce the Fourteenth and Fifteenth Amendments. From this time forward, government officials and the majority of Americans whom they represented failed to protect the rights and promote the welfare of black citizens. One result of this failure was that African Americans learned to look to themselves and their own community institutions for self-help.

Ministers, teachers, and community leaders became the backbone of the continuing struggle for the rights of African Americans. They formed the leadership of the black community for the next one hundred years.

Nevertheless, despite their limited effectiveness, the Civil War Amendments had created a constitutional basis for expanding the rights of individuals and minorities. In the next lessons, you will look at the special role the Fourteenth Amendment came to play in protecting the individual rights of all Americans.

The continued discrimination against women

During the time Congress was considering the Civil War Amendments, leaders of the women's movement asked that the right to vote be expanded to include women. These leaders, including Susan B. Anthony, hoped their long support of the anti-slavery cause would be rewarded. Their appeal was denied. Male anti-

Susan B. Anthony (1820-1906)

slavery leaders refused to extend the vote to women. Instead, they specifically included the term "male citizen" for the first time in the Constitution. The Fourteenth Amendment prohibits any state from denying the right to vote to males.

The omission of women in the Fourteenth Amendment did not deny states the right to grant women the right to vote. In 1869 the Wyoming Territories gave women this right.

In 1875 the Supreme Court ruled that being a citizen did not automatically give a person the right to vote. States could deny this right to women if they chose. It was not until 1920, fifty years after black men won the right to vote, that women were guaranteed that same right under the **Nineteenth Amendment**.

Critical Thinking Exercise
EXAMINING ALTERNATIVE MEANS OF PREVENTING UNFAIR DISCRIMINATION

You have seen that neither the Civil War Amendments nor the civil rights acts passed during the Reconstruction period achieved their goals. Work with a study partner or in small groups to discuss and answer the following questions.

1. What were some of the main reasons why these amendments and laws had so little effect?

2. Suppose that Congress passed civil rights legislation today that was intended to protect racial and ethnic minorities from unfair discrimination. Suppose this legislation met resistance similar to what happened during Reconstruction. Suppose you were a member of a group that wanted to see the goals of the legislation achieved. What are some actions your group could undertake to insure that the legislation is properly enforced?

Using the Lesson

1. What were the reasons some groups did not want African Americans to gain their rights? What were some of the means they used to deny blacks their rights?

2. Why do you suppose that women were not given the right to vote in the Civil War Amendments?

3. What current events are you aware of that raise the same issues found in this lesson?

4. What remedies, besides passing laws, might reduce or prevent unfair discrimination? What might be the advantages and disadvantages of each of these remedies?

5. What remedies, if any, for unfair discrimination besides laws are presently being used in your community or state? Explain them.

LESSON 15

How Does the Fourteenth Amendment Promote Equal Protection of the Laws?

Purpose of Lesson

The guarantee of the right to equal protection of the laws in the Fourteenth Amendment made an especially important change in the Constitution. For many years, this guarantee meant very little because of the continuing prejudice against blacks, women, Native Americans, and other minorities. However, since 1954 the equal protection clause has had a significant effect on reducing unfair discrimination.

This lesson will introduce you to two different uses of the term equality and explain the type of equality protected by the Fourteenth Amendment. It will also explain some of the obstacles that have stood in the way of providing people equal opportunity under the law.

When you have finished this lesson, you should be able to explain the difference between the two uses of the term equality contained in the lesson. You should also be able to explain how the use of the equal protection clause of the Fourteenth Amendment has changed from its adoption to the present day. Finally, you should be able to take and defend a position on a contemporary issue involving the equal protection clause.

Terms to Know

equality of condition
segregation
Plessy v. Ferguson
separate but equal doctrine
Brown v. Board of Education

The idea of equality

The natural rights philosophers argued that all people have an equal right to life, liberty, and property. Thomas Jefferson included the idea of equality in the Declaration of Independence which states that all people are created equal, they have certain inalienable rights, and it is the purpose of government to protect these rights. Despite this long-standing belief in equality, however, the original Constitution made no mention of equality.

The idea of equality strongly influenced the American Revolution. Americans rejected monarchy with its unequal classes of royalty, nobles, and commoners, and established a government by the people. The government they created was meant to promote individual rights and the common welfare, not the interests of special privileged groups. The Constitution even forbids the use of titles of nobility.

The fact that Americans often contradicted the ideal of equality is well known. Slavery and the status of women were among the most notable examples of the unequal and unfair treatment of persons during this period. However, compared with other nations of the time, there was a high degree of social equality in America.

As you have learned, public sentiment against slavery eventually grew so strong it contributed to the outbreak of the Civil War and the writing of the Civil War Amendments. Most of the authors of these amendments had fought against slavery and racial discrimination. They believed such practices violated the principle of equal rights. Racial discrimination denied equal opportunities for blacks and others, created special privileges for certain people, and prevented others from achieving what they were capable of doing.

What is the importance of the right to equal opportunity under the law?

What type of equality is protected by the Fourteenth Amendment?

The Fourteenth Amendment placed the idea of equality in the Constitution for the first time. It is contained in the clause that provides people the equal protection of the laws. This addition made an important change in our constitutional system. The extent of that change, however, depended on how equality was defined.

The authors of the Fourteenth Amendment did not intend to protect a right to **equality of condition**. This would mean that the government would be responsible for guaranteeing, for example, that all people were equal in the amount of property they possessed, their living standards, the medical care they received, their education, and their working conditions.

Few Americans at this time thought it was desirable for the government to try to establish equality of condition. They believed that individuals have different abilities and talents. Some are more resourceful, motivated, strong, or intelligent than others. Most Americans favored a competitive society in which individuals had the freedom to use their talents to advance as far as they could. They knew that differences among people would eventually lead to some enjoying greater success than others. The wealth of society would not be distributed equally; some people would become rich and some would be poor. However, everyone would have the opportunity to succeed, unlike most other countries of the time where rigid class systems denied most people the opportunity to better themselves.

The authors of the Fourteenth Amendment were interested in creating a society in which all people were treated equally by the law. This is why the Fourteenth Amendment contains the phrase "equal protection of the laws." This meant that no individual or group was to receive special privileges nor be deprived of certain rights under the law.

However, the Fourteenth Amendment does not prevent legislatures from passing laws that treat some people differently when it is reasonable and fair to do so. For example, it does not prevent a legislature from passing a law granting the privilege of a driver's license to those over sixteen, and thus denying the privilege to twelve-year-olds.

The equal protection clause is intended to prevent legislatures from passing laws that unreasonably and unfairly favor some groups over others. For example, as it is currently interpreted, it prevents legislatures from establishing certain schools for white students and other schools for non-white students.

What is the difference between equality of opportunity and equality of condition?

What was the effect of the equal protection clause?

As you learned in the last lesson, the promised protection of rights under the Fourteenth Amendment did not last long. During the Reconstruction period, former slaves used their new right to vote to achieve a considerable amount of political power. They were able to gain fairer treatment by their state governments. However, by the late 1870s, federal troops protecting blacks and their supporters were withdrawn from the South. Southern whites soon regained control of their state governments and reduced blacks to second-class citizenship.

Southerners quickly passed laws to establish racial **segregation**. These laws required blacks to use separate schools and other public facilities. The states claimed that these laws did not violate the equal protection clause because the separate facilities were supposedly equal. Many people disagreed, claiming that such laws were meant to mark African Americans as an inferior group, not fit to associate with whites.

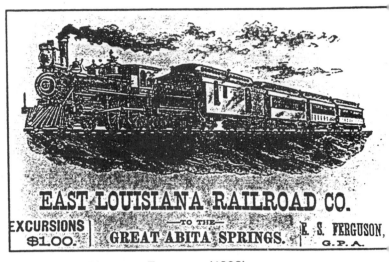

Plessy v. Ferguson (1896)

In the case of *Plessy v. Ferguson,* the Supreme Court established the **separate but equal doctrine** that was to deny blacks equal rights for almost sixty years. Louisiana had passed a law requiring railroad companies to provide separate but equal cars for white and black passengers.

Black leaders claimed this law violated their rights under the equal protection clause of the Fourteenth Amendment. They decided to challenge the constitutionality of this law in court. They chose Homer Plessy to make their test case. He bought a ticket but insisted on riding in the "whites only" car. Plessy was arrested and convicted. He appealed his case to the Supreme Court.

The question before the Supreme Court was whether the Louisiana law violated the equal protection clause. The Court said that to separate the races did not in itself suggest one race was inferior to the other. Since the law required that blacks and whites be provided equal facilities, the Court concluded no unfair discrimination had occurred. The Louisiana law was constitutional.

What rights and values were endangered by the separate but equal policy?

The rights of women also were not protected. While some western states extended full citizen rights to women, most states prohibited them from voting, holding political office, and serving on juries. In 1873, the Supreme Court said a state law denying women the right to be lawyers did not violate their right to equal protection of the laws.

Both the state courts and the Supreme Court upheld the right of states to pass such laws which treated women and minorities differently despite the equal protection clause.

Not all members of the Court agreed with the majority. Justice John Marshall Harlan wrote a strong dissenting opinion. He argued that the segregation law, passed by whites who controlled the state government, clearly was unfair to blacks. The law implied that African Americans were inferior. Therefore, it was a violation of the Fourteenth Amendment. He wrote, "Our Constitution is color-blind and neither knows nor tolerates classes among citizens. In respect of civil rights, all citizens are equal before the law."

As a result of the majority decision in *Plessy,* segregation became even more widespread in the South. In most states, there was no attempt to provide educational equality. Black schools were inferior to those provided for whites and black teachers were paid far less than whites with comparable training and experience. As a result, generations of black children received an inferior education.

The struggle for equality

Despite the way the Fourteenth Amendment had been interpreted and applied, the principle of equality under the law remained alive. Year after year, many Americans fought to make reality live up to the ideal. For years, they received little help from the federal government. The Court continued to uphold racial segregation. Other branches of the federal government failed to support legislation or constitutional amendments to prohibit the unequal treatment of blacks, women, and other groups suffering from unfair discrimination.

Why do you suppose it took so long for women to gain the right to vote?

At last, in 1920 the Nineteenth Amendment was ratified, giving women the right to vote throughout the United States. In 1924, Congress passed the Citizenship Act granting Native Americans full citizenship rights for the first time. And finally, in 1954, a historic case set the stage for extending the equal protection of the law to all people denied this right in the past.

Brown v. Board of Education (1954)

It was not until 1954 that the Supreme Court overturned its decision in the *Plessy* case. This landmark decision came in *Brown v. Board of Education*.

Linda Brown lived five blocks from a neighborhood elementary school. Because of her race, she was forced to attend the school for black children which was twenty-one blocks from her home. Her parents sued the school board of Topeka, Kansas, for denying their daughter admission to the neighborhood school for whites.

What was the significance of Thurgood Marshall's victory in the case of *Brown v. Board of Education*?

The Browns were represented by an attorney for the National Association for the Advancement of Colored People, an interracial group founded in 1909. Thurgood Marshall, who later became the first black justice of the Supreme Court, argued the case. He said that segregated public schools violated the equal protection clause because they placed black children at a severe disadvantage.

Chief Justice Earl Warren delivered the unanimous decision of the Supreme Court:

> *To separate* [children] *from others of similar age and qualifications solely because of their race generates a feeling of inferiority as to their status in the community that may affect their hearts and minds in a way unlikely ever to be undone....*[Therefore] *separate educational facilities are inherently unequal...*[and deny] *the equal protection of the laws guaranteed by the Fourteenth Amendment.*

Although it met with sharp resistance, the Court's decision in the *Brown* case marked a major turning point in American history. During the next decades, the Supreme Court struck down cases of segregation in other areas. The Court's assumption was that laws that distinguished between people on the basis of race violated the equal protection clause.

The expanded protections under the Fourteenth Amendment

In recent years, the equal protection clause has been expanded to prevent unfair discrimination on the basis of age, sex, or ethnic background as well as race. Decisions of the Court which have expanded the protections of the Fourteenth

Amendment have been reinforced by laws passed by Congress and policies instituted and enforced by the executive branch. For example, President Dwight D. Eisenhower ordered federal troops into the South to protect black students attempting to integrate schools.

Meanwhile, Congress passed a series of civil rights bills including the Civil Rights Acts of 1957 and 1964 and the Voting Rights Act of 1965. In 1968, the Equal Employment Opportunities Act became law. It has been used to prevent job discrimination on the basis of sex or age. The Education Act of 1972 has banned discrimination on the basis of sex in any educational program that receives federal aid.

The tension between equality of condition and equal protection of the laws

There has been remarkable progress in recent years in providing equal protection of the laws to people deprived of this right in the past. However, some people argue that the American emphasis upon protecting equality of rights instead of equality of condition results in an unacceptable inequality in our society.

They argue that an emphasis on equal rights not only allows, but encourages, wide differences in wealth, power, and education. These differences in condition make equality of rights meaningless. Consider three examples:

1. **Political influence.** All persons have an equal right to participate in the political process by voting, expressing their views, and petitioning and lobbying government officials.

   Despite this equal right, however, not all Americans have the same ability to influence the government to promote their interests. Many poor people are not well educated and do not understand how their system of government works well enough to influence its decisions. On the other hand, people who are wealthy, well-educated, and well-connected often know more about politics and government. They are more able to contact people in power, from the president to leaders of their state and local governments. As a result, despite equality of political rights, wealthy and more educated people have greater influence than do the poor.

2. **Rights of the accused.** All persons accused of a crime have the right to a lawyer to defend them. If they are too poor to hire a lawyer, the court will provide one. However, a wealthy person can afford to hire the best criminal lawyer available. In such a situation, the poor person is likely to have a less skilled lawyer in his or her defense than the wealthy person.

3. **Right to an education.** Although the Constitution does not guarantee the right to education, every state offers all children a free public education. However, the quality of education varies widely. Public education is largely supported by property taxes. Therefore, children who live in poor communities usually attend schools that have larger classes, fewer educational materials, fewer special classes, lower teachers' salaries, and poorer buildings and equipment than children who live in wealthy areas.

Even within a school district, there may be great differences between schools in rich and poor neighborhoods. Parents in rich neighborhoods often raise money to provide books, computers, and special classes not available in poor areas.

Critical Thinking Exercise
PROPOSING REMEDIES TO PROBLEMS ARISING FROM INEQUALITY OF CONDITION

The above situations raise some difficult questions resulting from inequality of condition. Does inequality of condition give some people a greater opportunity to enjoy their rights than others? Does this undermine the ideal of equality of rights? If so, does the Fourteenth Amendment's equal protection of the laws clause provide any remedy?

Review each example. Then work in small groups to develop proposed remedies for the problems they involve. Be prepared to present and discuss your proposals with the class.

Using the Lesson

1. What are the differences between the ideas of equality of condition and equal protection of the laws?

2. What consequences were the authors of the Fourteenth Amendment prepared to accept as a result of their belief in the importance of equal protection of the law? What arguments can you give for their position?

3. How did the separate but equal doctrine affect the rights of blacks? What do you suppose were the consequences of this doctrine for the educational opportunities of blacks? Employment opportunities? Opportunities to gain political power?

4. What was the significance of the decision in *Brown v. Board of Education* for the extension of equal protection of the laws?

LESSON 16

How Should the Effects of Past Discrimination Be Remedied?

Purpose of Lesson

One of the most difficult problems faced by the United States is to make the goal of equality of opportunity a reality for all people. It is particularly difficult to find fair and reasonable ways to remedy the effects of discrimination suffered by various groups in our society. One attempt to do so has been through affirmative action programs. This lesson addresses the policy of affirmative action and its relationship to equality of opportunity.

When you have finished this lesson, you should be able to explain the purpose of affirmative action programs, their relationship to the Fourteenth Amendment, and some of the issues they raise. You also should be able to propose your own remedies to some of the problems addressed by affirmative action programs. Finally, you should be able to take and defend positions on the guidelines used to determine which kinds of affirmative action programs are constitutional.

Terms to Know

affirmative action
aggressive recruitment programs
remedial programs
preferential treatment programs
reverse discrimination

Why do some people claim equality of opportunity is not enough to remedy past injustice?

Conflicts continue over the meaning and application of the right to equal protection of the laws provided by the Fourteenth Amendment. Some people argue that the government is not going far enough to protect the rights of individuals deprived of them in the past. Others say the government is going too far and is applying the equal protection clause in ways never intended by those who wrote and ratified it.

The decision of the Supreme Court in *Brown v. Board of Education* tried to make the ideal of equal opportunity under the law a reality by prohibiting racial segregation in public schools. Later rulings by the Court and civil rights legislation passed by Congress attempted to further this ideal for members of all groups who were treated unfairly in the past.

Why were affirmative action programs started?

Many people argue that just eliminating the official, legal barriers to equal opportunity is not enough. The effects of past discrimination and continued prejudice against women, racial and ethnic minorities, and others still exist. This history of prejudice and established patterns of discrimination handicap the ability of people to take advantage of their new-found opportunities provided by the law.

Many people have argued that it is not enough to sit back and passively wait for the effects of past legal discrimination to disappear. They believe that something positive, or affirmative, must be done to further the goal of equality of opportunity.

Why did President Johnson believe affirmative action programs were necessary?

As a result of such concerns, in the 1960s President Lyndon Johnson and others urged Congress to create programs that would go beyond merely removing legal barriers to equal opportunity. Such programs would open up opportunities in education and employment, provide remedial help and, in some cases, preferential treatment for members of groups discriminated against in the past. These programs were called **affirmative action**. People justify them by claiming that they are designed to make equality of opportunity a reality. They say affirmative action helps remedy the wrongs and reduce the handicaps caused by the unjust way women and minorities have been treated in the past. Affirmative action programs include the following:

- **Aggressive recruitment programs** that are conducted by business, industry, and government to make sure that when opportunities in education and employment occur, women and members of minority groups are encouraged to apply for them. For example, it is common for many people to learn of jobs from friends. Such practices may perpetuate existing patterns which deny equal employment opportunities to members of other groups. In this type of situation, providing equal opportunity would mean widely advertising the availability of jobs to members of all groups that might be interested.

- **Remedial programs** include special education programs in elementary and secondary schools and in pre-schools. They are designed to help students with particular educational and economic needs gain the basic skills to succeed in school and in the job market. Some are designed to help students learn useful occupations. Others give remedial tutoring and assistance to students in college as well as adults who want to improve their knowledge and skills. These include adult literacy programs and English as a second language programs.

What are some of the purposes of affirmative action programs?

There has been little controversy over providing remedial programs except for the complaint that, even though many have proven effective, the federal government does not provide enough money to make the programs available for all children and adults who need them.

- **Preferential treatment programs** are also designed to compensate for the effects of past discrimination against women and minorities. These programs are designed to give members of these groups preferred treatment in gaining jobs and entrance to colleges and universities. People argue that preferential treatment for such groups is required to

  - make up for the advantages of white men who have benefitted from preferential treatment for hundreds of years

  - promote diversity in colleges and universities to produce a less race conscious and more racially fair society

  - include people of different racial, religious, and ethnic groups whose perspectives help to improve educational programs for all

What issues have been raised by affirmative action programs?

Critics of some affirmative action programs, particularly those calling for preferential treatment, have claimed that these programs violate the right of individuals to equal protection of the law guaranteed by the Fourteenth Amendment. For example, some of the earliest preferential treatment programs called for setting aside a certain number of positions in colleges or businesses for qualified members of minority groups. Sometimes these programs had goals and timetables which called for filling enough positions with women and minorities to reflect their proportion in the community. Thus, if 25% of a community were Hispanic or Native American, a college might have set a goal of recruiting enough students from those groups to make the student body reflect that number or quota.

The use of quotas in education and employment has led to claims of unfairness from members of other groups. These people feel that quotas result in qualified individuals being denied equality of opportunity because of their race, sex, religion, or ethnic background. Opponents of quotas claim that such programs lead to **reverse discrimination**. They argue, for example, that admission to college should be color blind. Just as it was wrong in the past to discriminate *against* people because of their sex, race, religion, or ethnic background, it is wrong now to discriminate *in favor* of people on the same basis.

Critics of affirmative action programs point to the long struggle to establish individual rights as opposed to group rights. They point to past practices in which certain groups received special rights and favors regardless of how deserving they might have been. Some argue that today special programs or treatment should only be provided to individuals based on their educational or economic need, their capacity to benefit from such programs, and how deserving they may be of such treatment.

Today few people disagree with the general goals of affirmative action programs. Most agree that something should be done to help groups unfairly treated in the past. Most agree to support remedial programs. Conflicts continue to arise, however, over preferential treatment programs and the use of quotas. Such programs raise the charge that they violate the right of individuals to equal protection of the law.

The following exercise provides you an opportunity to discuss a Supreme Court case which illustrates the difficulty of designing reasonable and fair programs to promote the goals of affirmative action while not violating the right of the individual to equal protection of the law.

Critical Thinking Exercise
EXAMINING A SUPREME COURT OPINION ON AFFIRMATIVE ACTION

Read the summary of the facts and opinions in this case and then be prepared to take and defend positions on the questions that follow.

Regents of the University of California v. Bakke (1978)

As a part of its affirmative action program, the Medical School of the University of California at Davis had set aside sixteen places for minorities out of its entering class of one hundred. Alan Bakke, a non-minority applicant, had been denied admission even though his test scores were higher than most of the minority applicants that were accepted.

Bakke sued in the state courts claiming that the admissions policy of the university denied him the right to equal protection of the laws guaranteed by the Fourteenth Amendment. The California Supreme Court agreed with Bakke's claim. The case was appealed to the U.S. Supreme Court which also ruled in Bakke's favor in a 5-4 decision. Bakke entered the medical school.

The five-member majority of the Court was not in agreement on why they voted in Bakke's favor. Four of the justices said the university quota system violated the Civil Rights Act of 1964 which prohibited excluding anyone on the basis of race from any program receiving federal funds. (The university received federal funds.)

The fifth justice, Lewis F. Powell, concluded that the racial quota was a violation of the equal protection clause of the Fourteenth Amendment. Powell's opinion contained several points:

- He stated that it was a violation of the Constitution to place the burden of remedying the effects of past discrimination on individuals who had nothing to do with such discrimination.

- He rejected quotas.

- He approved the consideration of race as one factor to take into account in an admissions policy meant to promote diversity in the student body. Such diversity is an acceptable goal for universities.

The four dissenting members of the Supreme Court claimed that the university quota system was a reasonable way to help remedy the effects of past discrimination against racial and ethnic minorities.

What is the importance of diversity on university campuses?

What do *you* think?

1. What arguments could you make to support the majority opinion in this case? The minority opinion?

2. What values and interests underlie each position?

3. Does Justice Powell's opinion eliminate the use of quotas based on race? Explain your position.

4. Should a university be allowed to have an admissions policy designed to promote racial, ethnic, and religious diversity on campus? Explain your position.

5. How, if at all, is it possible to have an admissions policy based on sex, race, ethnicity, or religious beliefs that does not violate the right to equal protection of the laws guaranteed by the Fourteenth Amendment? Explain your position.

What considerations are presently used to deal with affirmative action programs?

Since the *Bakke* decision in 1978, a number of legal and constitutional guidelines have been developed to determine what affirmative action programs are acceptable under the equal protection clause of the Fourteenth Amendment. Below are brief descriptions of these guidelines. After reviewing them, be prepared to take and defend positions on the questions that follow.

1. **Remedial programs.** Government and private activities do not violate the Constitution if they are

   - designed to help students that are not adequately prepared for school by providing them special pre-school, elementary, and secondary school programs or occupational skill programs, regardless of cost.

   - special classes or supplementary training programs on any level of education from pre-school to the highest levels of education, regardless of cost.

   Eligibility for these programs must be based on educational or economic need, not upon a person's race or any other group characteristic. Thus, all people who meet the criteria for educational or economic need must be eligible for these programs, regardless of their sex, race, or ethnic background.

2. **Strict enforcement of non-discrimination.** All affirmative action programs must strictly enforce the prohibition against discrimination on the basis of race, sex, religion, nationality, and age.

3. **Recruitment programs.** Programs that clearly attempt to recruit members of groups formerly treated unfairly for employment and educational opportunities are constitutional.

4. **Preferential treatment.** Programs in employment and education that give applicants special consideration upon the basis of their sex, race, or religion are acceptable in deciding between applicants who are equal in all relevant respects. For example, a college can choose to admit a woman or Mexican-American applicant over a white male applicant if all three have equal scores on all entrance requirements.

5. **Quotas.** No quotas or set-aside programs may be used that are based on race, religion, sex, age, or nationality. Such programs establish, for example, a percentage or number of jobs or places in a college for women or minorities. "Goals" and "guidelines" that are really the same things as quotas or set-asides are not allowed. The only criteria for receiving such benefits must be individual merit and ability.

6. **Double standards.** No programs may use double standards for admitting applicants. This means a program cannot ask members of one group to meet certain requirements and others to meet different requirements. The requirements for all must be the same.

Critical Thinking Exercise
EVALUATING PRESENT GUIDELINES

Your class should be divided into an even number of groups. Half the groups should review the above guidelines and present arguments in their favor. The other half should present criticisms of the guidelines. In conclusion, the entire class should address the following questions:

1. What appear to be the strengths and weaknesses of the guidelines?

2. What values and interests do the guidelines appear to be promoting? Endangering?

3. What modifications, if any, would you suggest be made in the guidelines? Explain your position.

Using the Lesson

1. Suppose a university sets aside a number of positions in its first-year class for outstanding athletes who, though qualified for admission, have lower scores on entrance exams than others who were not admitted. Should this practice be considered a violation of equal protection of the law? Explain your position.

2. What current situations are you aware of in which affirmative action is an issue? Be prepared to explain what position you would take on the issues involved in such situations.

LESSON 17

How Does the Fourteenth Amendment Protect Substantive Due Process?

Purpose of Lesson

In addition to the equal protection clause, the Fourteenth Amendment contains a clause that prohibits state governments from depriving "any person of life, liberty, or property, without due process of law." This short clause has had a profound effect on how the Constitution has been interpreted to protect individual rights.

In this lesson, you will learn that there are two types of protections provided under the due process clause. These are the protections of substantive due process and procedural due process.

After completing this lesson, you should be able to explain the difference between substantive and procedural due process. You should also be able to explain the development of the idea of substantive due process and what rights it has been used to protect. Finally, you should be able to take and defend positions on what rights, not listed in the Bill of Rights, you think should be protected by substantive due process.

Terms to Know

due process of law
procedural due process
substantive due process
laissez-faire

What is the history of the right to due process of law?

The following are the due process clauses contained in the Fifth and the Fourteenth Amendments:

No person shall...be deprived of life, liberty, or property, without due process of law.
Fifth Amendment, 1791

nor shall any State deprive any person of life, liberty, or property, without due process of law.
Fourteenth Amendment, 1868

You can see the language is similar in both amendments. However, as you have already learned in Lesson 13, there is an important difference between the two amendments. The Fifth Amendment only applies to the federal government. The Fourteenth Amendment applies to state governments.

The phrase **due process of law** is one of the oldest in English constitutional history. The clause appears for the first time in 1354, but the concept was found even earlier in the Magna Carta (1215). "Due process" refers to the requirement that the actions of government must be conducted according to the law of the land. As you remember from Unit Two, no one, not even the king, was supposed to be above the law. The natural rights philosophers of the eighteenth century also argued that government must be limited by law.

The idea of a social compact in the natural rights philosophy did involve individuals giving up some of their freedom to the government in exchange for security and welfare. However, these philosophers argued, there were certain natural rights, such as freedom of conscience, that were so much a part of human nature, they could not be given away. There were some rights, as Jefferson phrased it in the Declaration of Independence, that are unalienable. Many of the "abuses and usurpations" Jefferson listed in the Declaration were examples of the king and Parliament putting themselves above the law and violating these rights.

Numerous state declarations also described certain rights with which the government could not interfere. Examples of such natural rights included the right to

- "defend life and liberty"

- "worship God according to the dictates of his own conscience and reason"

- be free of being compelled to bear arms if a "person... is conscientiously scrupulous about the lawfulness of bearing arms"

You can see that the idea underlying these rights is that there are some areas of life in which the government is not to interfere. This basic idea underlying our system of government has been developed further as we will see shortly.

What is meant by due process of law?

Neither the Declaration of Independence nor the Constitution of 1787 uses the term "due process of law." However, both documents include the idea of due process. The Constitution prohibits the government from passing bills of attainder and *ex post facto* laws. It requires the government to respect the right to *habeas corpus*. These parts of the Constitution were included to prevent the government from unfairly depriving persons of their rights to life, liberty, and property. This is the goal of the due process clauses of the Fifth and Fourteenth Amendments.

What is procedural due process?

Due process originally meant that government cannot use unfair procedures in fulfilling its responsibilities. This is known as **procedural due process**. It requires that the procedures used by government in making, applying, interpreting, and enforcing the law be fair and reasonable.

Procedural due process limits the powers of government in order to protect individual rights. Some of the most prominent examples of these protections limit the powers of law enforcement officers and the courts. For example, police must use fair procedures in investigating crimes, arresting, and questioning suspects. They cannot arrest or search people or their property without having a very good reason for doing so. They cannot force people to give evidence against themselves. Courts must use fair procedures in trying people suspected of crimes. They must provide accused persons the right to counsel and to cross examine witnesses against them.

Law enforcement agencies and the courts are not the only branches of government whose powers are limited by due process. Congress must use fair procedures in holding hearings. The executive branch of government must use fair procedures, for example, in deciding whether to ban the use of pesticides. You will learn more about this important topic in Unit Five.

What is substantive due process?

Over the years the Supreme Court has made a number of decisions which have interpreted the due process clause to place another type of limitation on the powers of government. This is the requirement that government cannot make laws that apply to situations in which the government has no business interfering. This is known as **substantive due process**. It requires that the substance, or purpose, of laws be constitutional. It does not refer to the procedures used to attain those purposes.

The right to substantive due process prohibits government from making laws or taking actions that interfere with certain areas of your life. These are areas, such as personal privacy, that the government has no right to regulate. In these areas, people claim the right to be left alone by their government. For example, it is not the business of government to interfere with what you believe, what friends you wish to associate with, what kind of work you want to do, or whom you want to marry. Such rights, although not specifically listed in the Constitution or Bill of Rights, are clearly outside of the proper scope of government under our constitutional system. Consequently, it can be argued that they are protected by the right to substantive due process.

How has the right to substantive due process been interpreted and applied?

There is no definition of due process in the Constitution. As with other rights, due process has been continually redefined by the judicial and legislative branches of government in an attempt to live up to the fundamental values and principles upon which our nation is based.

The idea of substantive due process appeared as early as 1798 when Justice Samuel Chase wrote that any law that "takes property from A and gives it to B" is unconstitutional. He claimed this was true even if the Constitution does not specifically forbid the federal government from making such a law (*Calder v. Bull*).

Before the Civil War, there were several other times when the Supreme Court used the idea of substantive due process in its decisions regarding laws made by Congress. However, it was after the adoption of the Fourteenth Amendment that the idea of substantive due process became more widely used and developed. This was because the due process clause of the Fourteenth Amendment applied to the states. State legislatures were more active than the Congress in passing laws that affected various economic activities.

In the years following the ratification of the Fourteenth Amendment, the Court heard many cases involving laws passed by state governments that attempted to regulate working conditions, establish maximum hours, and otherwise involve the government in the economic activities of individual citizens.

Substantive due process and property rights

nor shall any State deprive any person of life, liberty, or property without due process of law.
Fourteenth Amendment

What arguments were used by the Supreme Court in declaring laws governing child labor and working hours unconstitutional?

From 1897 to 1937 the Supreme Court declared over two hundred laws passed by state legislatures to be unconstitutional violations of the property rights of business and industry. These were laws passed by the states to limit child labor and establish maximum hours and minimum wages for workers. They also imposed safety and health regulations on employers and protected the rights of workers to organize into labor unions.

Most of these laws were declared unconstitutional because the Supreme Court claimed that state legislatures could not pass laws that interfered with the property rights of employers. The Court also claimed the laws violated an individual's freedom or liberty to enter into a contract and use property as he or she wished. It was the substance or the purpose of these laws, not the procedures used to attain that purpose, that made the laws unconstitutional. The Court saw these laws as violations of the due process clause of the Fourteenth Amendment. In effect, the Court was saying that such laws take property from A and give it to B and agreed with Justice Samuel Chase's opinion that such laws are an unconstitutional violation of the right to liberty and property.

For forty years, the Supreme Court declared laws passed by state legislatures that controlled business and industry to be unconstitutional violations of the rights to liberty and property. These decisions were not without their critics. Some argued that the Court was more influenced by the doctrines of **laissez-faire** than any requirements of the due process clause of the Fourteenth Amendment. People believing in the doctrine of laissez-faire argued that government should not interfere with business, industry, or commercial activity. The economy would function best if the government left it alone. Moreover, they claimed, the Constitution did not give the government the authority to regulate economic affairs.

As a result of changes on the Court as well as various political and economic changes, the Court gradually began to stop declaring laws regulating business and industry unconstitutional. The current view of the Court is expressed in the opinion of Justice William O. Douglas in a 1955 case. He wrote, "The day is gone when this Court uses the Due Process Clause of the Fourteenth Amendment to strike down state laws, regulatory of business and industrial conditions, because they may be thought unwise, improvident, or out of harmony with a particular school of thought."

Substantive due process and liberty

As early as 1923, the Supreme Court had used substantive due process to protect individual freedom or liberty. For example, in *Meyer v. Nebraska* (1923) it ruled unconstitutional a Nebraska law which prohibited the teaching of foreign languages before the eighth grade. The Court said that teachers should be free to teach and parents to raise their children as they saw fit. It was not the business of government to interfere in such matters. Justice James McReynolds wrote in his majority opinion:

> *Without doubt,* [the liberty protected by the due process clause] *denotes not merely freedom from bodily restraint but also the rights of the individual to contract, to engage in any of the common occupations of life, to acquire useful knowledge, to marry, establish a home and bring up children, to worship God according to the dictates of his own conscience, and generally to enjoy those privileges long recognized at common law as essential to the orderly pursuit of happiness by free men.*

Today the Supreme Court is more likely to use the idea of substantive due process to protect the individual's right to privacy and to be left alone and free from government interference. For example, the right to privacy is the basis for the Court's opinions limiting government interference with birth control and abortion.

Over the past fifty years, the Supreme Court has interpreted due process to include most of the Bill of Rights in the Fourteenth Amendment. As a result of these interpretations, the Bill of Rights now protects you from your state and local governments as well as the federal government. The means by which this has been accomplished is the subject of the next lesson.

Critical Thinking Exercise
PROPOSING AND DEFENDING RIGHTS

The idea of substantive due process has been used to protect rights not listed in the Constitution or Bill of Rights that people argue are related to the right of privacy and to be left alone by government. These are rights with which the government has no business interfering.

Work in small groups to develop a list of from five to ten rights, not listed in the Constitution or Bill of Rights, that you think should be protected by substantive due process. Be prepared to explain the rights you have listed and why you think the government has no business interfering with them.

Using the Lesson

1. How is due process of law related to the idea of a rule of law?

2. What is the difference between substantive and procedural due process of law?

3. How was the due process clause used to protect property rights?

4. How has the due process clause been used to protect liberty and other rights?

LESSON 18

How Does the Fourteenth Amendment Prohibit States from Violating the Bill of Rights?

Purpose of Lesson

Ratification of the Fourteenth Amendment radically changed our system of government. For the first time, the Constitution specifically prohibited the states from violating a person's right to life, liberty, and property. In effect, this completely changed the intent of the Anti-Federalists who had wanted the Bill of Rights added to the Constitution to limit the federal government's power over the states. The Fourteenth Amendment instead has given the federal government immense power over the states.

The Fourteenth Amendment opened the way for the judicial branch of the federal government to declare acts of state governments that violated provisions of the Bill of Rights to be unconstitutional. As you will see in this lesson, over the past hundred years, this has greatly increased the power of the federal government over state governments.

After completing the lesson, you should be able to explain how the Bill of Rights was made applicable to the states. You should also be able to explain the concerns this process has raised about our federal system. Finally, you should be able to take and defend a position on the importance of the Supreme Court's power of judicial review over state governments.

Terms to Know

incorporation
Gitlow v. New York
capital offense
double jeopardy
fundamental rights
Adamson v. California
dissent
unenumerated rights

What is meant by the incorporation of the Bill of Rights?

During the 1930s, the Supreme Court began to interpret the due process clause of the Fourteenth Amendment in a new way. This change focused on the meaning of the words "nor shall any state deprive any person of...liberty...without due process of law." Attention had shifted from protecting property rights to protecting the civil liberties of the people.

Since the 1930s, the word "liberty" in the due process clause has been interpreted to include almost all the rights guaranteed in the first eight amendments of the Bill of Rights. The process of including these rights is called **incorporation**. By incorporating these rights into the Fourteenth Amendment, the federal government has protected them from violations by state and local governments. This has resulted in the federal government gaining far more power over state governments than in the past. As you will see, this process has caused considerable controversy which continues today.

Did the authors of the Fourteenth Amendment intend to incorporate the Bill of Rights?

As you have seen, before the adoption of the Fourteenth Amendment the Bill of Rights only applied to the federal government. State constitutions and laws were expected to protect individuals from violations of their rights by state and local governments. Whether the authors of the Fourteenth Amendment deliberately meant to change this is unclear.

Several influential congressmen who had drafted the Fourteenth Amendment said they thought it protected all the rights listed in the Bill of Rights from being violated by state and local governments. Although historical records are sketchy, it is unlikely that these representatives spoke for the majority of Congress. There is even less evidence to suggest that most of the state legislators who ratified the Fourteenth Amendment thought that it prohibited the states from violating the rights listed in the federal Bill of Rights.

The result was that the meaning of the Fourteenth Amendment was left for the Supreme Court to decide. The justices were faced with the difficult task of giving concrete meaning to the vague, general language of the Fourteenth Amendment. For example, what meaning should be given to the rights to be protected by such general terms as "equal protection" and "due process"?

Why were people concerned over the incorporation of the Bill of Rights?

Whatever the intentions of those who wrote the Fourteenth Amendment, the justices of the Supreme Court were initially very hesitant to interpret it to mean that all of the protections of the Bill of Rights should be applied to the states. Primarily, they were concerned with preserving federalism. The Framers of the Constitution had carefully created a complicated federal system to protect the rights of the people by limiting the power of the federal government. This system left considerable power in the state and local governments and the ultimate power of the government in the hands of the people.

Before the 1930s, the federal government had very limited responsibilities. Basically, it was limited to such duties as conducting defense and foreign policy, regulating commerce among the states, creating national currency, and managing the postal system. Most other duties of government were performed by state and local governments. They were responsible, for example, for preserving law and order, public education, and public health programs.

Members of the Supreme Court, like most other Americans, believed that the federal system allowed the states to adopt policies that citizens thought best suited their needs. It was the backbone of self-government. It was also a system well-suited to a nation as large and diverse as the United States.

How was the Bill of Rights incorporated?

Most justices were very reluctant to change the balance of power in the federal system by interpreting the Fourteenth Amendment's due process clause to incorporate the Bill of Rights. To do so would dramatically expand federal control over the criminal justice systems of the state governments, as well as other areas that had been under local control since colonial times.

At first, the Supreme Court incorporated only those rights it felt were essential to protect liberty or justice. In the case of *Gitlow v. New York* (1925), for example, the Court incorporated the rights of freedom of speech and of the press. The justices

Why might freedom of expression be considered a fundamental right?

reasoned that these rights were fundamental to liberty. By 1947, the Fourteenth Amendment had been interpreted to prohibit the states from violating all of the individual liberties protected by the First Amendment, just as the Bill of Rights prohibited the federal government from doing.

The Supreme Court, however, hesitated to apply the Bill of Rights to state criminal trials. The justices on the Court believed that very few protections in the original Bill of Rights were essential to guarantee justice. As a result, they only applied certain rights to the states.

In the Scottsboro cases (1932), for example, the Court ruled that persons charged with **capital offenses** (crimes for which the punishment is death) have a right to an attorney. This ruling extended the Sixth Amendment to cover both state and federal crimes. However, in *Palko v. Connecticut* (1937), the Court ruled that the prohibition against **double jeopardy** (being tried more than once for the same crime) did not apply to the states. The justices on the Court at that time did not think this right was essential to guarantee justice.

Justice Benjamin N. Cardozo (1870-1938)

Justice Benjamin N. Cardozo was concerned by this "berry picking" approach which incorporated one right but not another. He wanted to set up criteria for deciding which rights should be incorporated. He suggested that only **fundamental rights** of life, liberty, and property should be guaranteed to all Americans, regardless of the state in which they lived. Other rights should be protected, as in the original federal scheme, by state constitutions.

The majority of the justices agreed with him. They said that the due process clause of the Fourteenth Amendment prohibits the states from violating only those rights which are essential to a "scheme of ordered liberty." These protections must be "so rooted in the traditions and conscience of our people as to be ranked as fundamental."

What should be the criteria for incorporation?

Justice Cardozo and others argued that the criteria for incorporating a right should be whether or not it is fundamental. But other justices, like Hugo Black, disagreed. They thought that the way the majority was interpreting the Fourteenth Amendment was very subjective, unfair, and illogical.

Justice Black feared that the justices were writing their personal preferences into law. The only way to avoid this, in his opinion, was to incorporate all the specific protections of the Bill of Rights into the due process clause of the Fourteenth Amendment.

The question of incorporation came to a head in the case of *Adamson v. California* (1947). The defendant, Dewey Adamson, had been convicted of murder and sentenced to die. He appealed his conviction because he claimed his right to remain silent had been violated by the California court. Adamson argued that the protection against self-incrimination (the Fifth Amendment) was an essential part of a fair trial. Therefore, the state of California should be prohibited by the due process clause of the Fourteenth Amendment from violating this right.

Why might the right to remain silent be considered a fundamental right?

The Supreme Court rejected Adamson's argument. The majority of justices said that not all the protections of the Bill of Rights were part of due process—only those necessary to guarantee justice and fairness. The right to remain silent, in their opinion, was not essential to justice.

Justice Black wrote a stinging **dissent**. He claimed that in order to "follow...the original purpose of the Fourteenth Amendment [it was necessary] to extend to all the people of the nation the complete protection of the Bill of Rights." He believed that total incorporation would accomplish the following:

- It would provide a fixed definition of due process and prevent the justices from relying on their own personal preferences.

- It would offer a reasonable way to define fundamental rights. Fundamental rights were any rights considered so important that they had been included in the Bill of Rights.

Justice Felix Frankfurter argued against total incorporation. He said that only those protections of the Bill of Rights which are fundamental to our system of government should be incorporated. His position included the following points:

- Not all rights are fundamental. The justices should look to the historical and philosophical traditions of the American people to decide which rights are fundamental and should be incorporated.

- The protections included in the Bill of Rights reflect the ideas and practices of eighteenth-century America. Some of these rights were truly fundamental; others were practices inherited from Britain that were not essential to ensure fairness and justice.

- Total incorporation would force all the provisions of the Bill of Rights on the states whether or not each one was important. The result would be that the states would no longer experiment and reform their legal systems so as to better protect the basic rights of their citizens.

These arguments for and against total incorporation still form the basic positions of those debating this issue today.

Which rights are incorporated today?

From the 1930s to the 1950s, the Court decided on a case-by-case basis which rights should be incorporated. Then, during the 1960s, the Supreme Court dramatically expanded the meaning of the Fourteenth Amendment's due process clause.

Chief Justice Earl Warren and the majority of justices at that time were personally committed to the ideal of equality. They believed it was their duty to use the Court to actively extend equal protection to disadvantaged and minority groups in order to combat injustice.

Under the Warren Court, the Constitution was interpreted very broadly. For example, the justices ruled that the states were prohibited from denying all trial rights listed in the federal Bill of Rights. The Court thought that it had to hold state law enforcement officials to strict standards to insure that minority defendants would be treated justly. As Justice William Brennan explained in a 1964 decision, "The Court has rejected the notion that the Fourteenth Amendment applies to the States a 'watered-down...version' of the individual guarantees of the Bill of Rights."

The Warren Court incorporated most, but not all, the protections of the Bill of Rights. For example, the right to bear arms which the Founders described as "essential to preserve liberty" and the people's final check on the government's arbitrary use of power, was not incorporated by the Warren Court. Other rights also not incorporated include the

- protection against quartering troops in private homes (Third Amendment)

- right to indictment by a grand jury (Fifth Amendment)

- right to a jury trial in civil cases where the amount involved was more than $20 (Seventh Amendment)

- prohibition against excessive bail (Eighth Amendment)

- **unenumerated rights** of the Ninth Amendment

In addition, the Warren Court prohibited states from violating additional rights which do not specifically appear in the Bill of Rights. For example, in 1965 the Court ruled that the due process clause contains a right to marital privacy that forbids states from making laws which prohibit married couples from using contraceptives (*Griswold v. Connecticut*). In 1970 the Court decided that the due process clause contains a right of persons accused of crimes that requires states to prove them guilty beyond a reasonable doubt (*In re Winship*).

What are the results of incorporation?

One of the most important results of the due process clause of the Fourteenth Amendment has been to prevent state and local governments from violating most of the provisions of the Bill of Rights. It is also worth noting that many of the people who insisted upon a Bill of Rights wanted it to limit the federal government to protect the powers of the state governments. And that was indeed how the Bill of Rights was understood throughout most of our history.

For reasons we have examined, when the Bill of Rights only limited the powers of the federal government, it was of almost no importance in protecting individual rights. The great change occurred when the Supreme Court decided that state governments could not violate the individual rights contained in the Bill of Rights. It is interesting to see that using the Bill of Rights to limit the powers of the state governments is the opposite of what the Framers intended.

Using the Lesson

1. What is meant by the incorporation of the Bill of Rights?

2. Why were people concerned about using the Bill of Rights to limit the powers of state governments?

3. What were the differences between Justices Cardozo, Frankfurter, and Black regarding incorporation? With whom do you agree? Why?

4. What current issues are you aware of that involve the Supreme Court's use of its power of judicial review over state governments? Be prepared to explain the issues and what positions you would take on them.

Unit Four: What Rights Are Protected by the First Amendment?

Purpose of Unit

The First Amendment today protects the rights to freedom of religion and expression from both the federal and state governments. When it was first adopted, the First Amendment only protected individuals from the federal government. Through the process of incorporation, which you examined in Unit Three, it now applies to the states as well.

Many people have argued that the rights protected by the First Amendment are among the most important rights in the Constitution and Bill of Rights. After you have studied this unit, you will have a better idea of why these rights are thought to be so important.

This unit will look at the history of the rights contained in the First Amendment and examine their purpose and importance. The words of the First Amendment may seem, at first glance, brief and to the point. However, the interpretation and application of these protections have been a source of continued controversy. These controversies focus upon the proper scope and limits of First Amendment rights, and the need to balance them against conflicting rights, values, and interests.

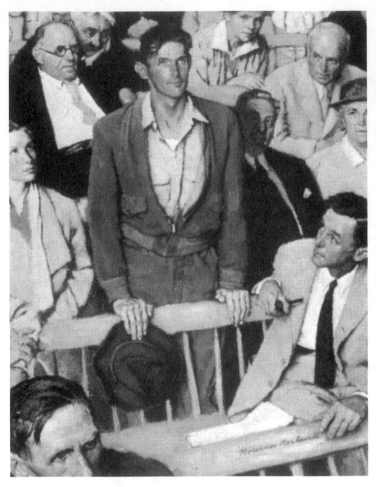

Why are First Amendment rights fundamental to a free society?

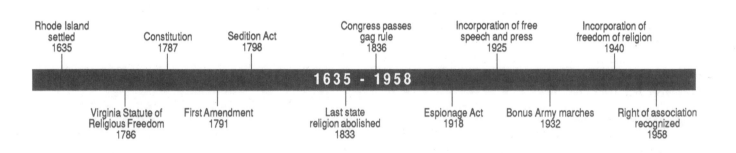

Rhode Island settled 1635 — Constitution 1787 — Sedition Act 1798 — Congress passes gag rule 1836 — Incorporation of free speech and press 1925 — Incorporation of freedom of religion 1940

1635 - 1958

Virginia Statute of Religious Freedom 1786 — First Amendment 1791 — Last state religion abolished 1833 — Espionage Act 1918 — Bonus Army marches 1932 — Right of association recognized 1958

LESSON 19

Why Does the First Amendment Prohibit the Establishment of Religion?

Purpose of Lesson

Two clauses in the First Amendment protect freedom of religion. These are the establishment and the free exercise clauses. This lesson will focus upon the first of these clauses. It will examine the sources of the Founders' beliefs about the need to separate religion and government. It will give you an opportunity to consider some of the conflicts that have arisen over the interpretation of the establishment clause. The next lesson will deal with the free exercise clause.

When you finish this lesson you should be able to explain the purposes of the establishment clause and explain the differences between the establishment clause and the free exercise clause. You also should be able to take and defend positions on issues involving the establishment clause.

Terms to Know

establishment clause
free exercise clause
established church
Great Awakening
separation of church and state
religious tests

What are the establishment and free exercise clauses?

The First Amendment opens with the words "Congress shall make no law respecting an establishment of religion, or prohibiting the free exercise thereof." The Supreme Court has interpreted the Fourteenth Amendment to make these protections from the federal government applicable to state and local governments. Let's examine these two clauses protecting your right to religious freedom.

- **The establishment clause.** At a minimum, this clause prohibits the federal government from establishing one or more official religions or churches for the nation.

- **The free exercise clause.** This clause prevents the federal government from interfering with your right, in most cases, to practice your beliefs.

As we have noted, this lesson will deal with the establishment clause. The next will examine the free exercise clause.

Religious conflict in Europe

At the time of the first settlements in America, Europe was still suffering from the religious wars and bloodshed that had torn apart much of the continent since the Reformation.

The religious revolt known as the Reformation ended the domination of Europe by the Roman Catholic Church that had existed for more than a thousand years. It led to more than a century of religious wars as Catholics and Protestants struggled for power. Each group, once in power, attempted to eliminate its opponents—through torture, banishment, jail, or death. In one country after another, men and women were burnt at the stake for refusing to convert to the official faith.

Mary I of England (1516-1558), for example, was known as "Bloody Mary" because she was determined to reassert the Catholic faith if she had to burn every Protestant in England to do so. In France, the religious wars led to the massacre of over three thousand Huguenots (Protestants) on St. Bartholomew's Day, 1572. This type of bloodshed, repeated throughout Europe, was justified by many people because they believed their religion was the only true faith.

Almost every nation in Europe had an official religion, known as the **established church**, supported by the government. Sometimes, everyone had to attend its services, obey its requirements, and pay taxes to support it. There was only one established church. Whether it was the Church of England in Great Britain, the Roman Catholic Church in Spain, or the Lutheran Church in Sweden, each nation had its official religion.

Where different churches were allowed to exist, people who did not belong to the established church were denied the rights of people who did. They were often excluded from universities and disqualified from civil and military offices. Sometimes they were severely persecuted or killed for their beliefs.

How much religious freedom was there in the colonies?

The colonists brought to the New World their experiences with an established church. In many cases, those who left Europe

How might an established religion threaten freedom of belief?

did so because they disagreed with the church in power—not because they believed in religious freedom. Most Europeans in the seventeenth century accepted the idea of an established religion. The idea that several different religions could coexist was not yet widely accepted.

It should not be surprising, therefore, that in most of the early colonies, there was little tolerance for religious differences. Not only did most colonies have an established religion, but in many cases there was intolerance for those who did not follow this church. The Puritans who settled Massachusetts, for example, did not come to the New World in search of religious liberty. They came to save pure religion from what they believed to be the corruption of religion in Europe. They thought they were called by God to establish a Holy Commonwealth based on a covenant between themselves and Him. They were unwilling to accept those who did not conform. Indeed, they thought that toleration of religious error was a sin. Consequently, they drove many dissenters out of their colony, punished others, and in 1659 hanged two Quakers and banished a third, Mary Dyer, who was hanged the following year when she returned to the colony.

There are many stories of religious dissenters who were persecuted in these early years. Anne Hutchinson, a brilliant and talented woman, arrived in Massachusetts in 1634 with her husband and seven children. She gained great respect as a midwife, healer, and spiritual counselor. Before long she began preaching a theory of salvation that went against the official Puritan beliefs. Not only was she a dissenter, as a woman she was particularly offensive to the male leaders of the community. Brought to trial, she was cast out of the colony as "a heathen and a leper."

Hutchinson fled Massachusetts to Rhode Island where religious dissenters were tolerated. It was the first colony to grant freedom of conscience to everyone. The charter of 1663 provided that "noe person...shall bee any wise molested, punished, disquieted, or called in question, for

any differences of opinione in matters of religion." Jews, Quakers, Catholics, and others not welcome elsewhere found a haven in Rhode Island.

Rhode Island was established by a dissenter, a Puritan minister who had fled Massachusetts because of his beliefs. Roger Williams opposed any established religion because he believed government involvement would corrupt religion. People should be free to worship according to their own conscience, Williams argued, and not be forced to attend any particular church. Requiring people to attend a particular church "stinks in God's nostrils," he proclaimed. Religion was only meaningful when freely chosen—"forced worship is false worship."

What led to increased religious toleration in the colonies?

By the time of the American Revolution, people had become more tolerant of others. Diverse religious groups existed in the same community and people became used to living and working with others who had different beliefs. The large number of religious groups also made it highly unlikely that one particular church could dominate all others. As James Madison noted, the diversity "which pervades America is the best and only security for religion."

At the same time, the religious revivals of the eighteenth century, known as the **Great Awakening**, drew many away from the established religions and into new religious groups. The Awakening promoted the idea that all Christian religious groups were equal. As a leading preacher proclaimed, "Father Abraham, whom have you in heaven? Any Episcopalians? And the answer came back, No! Any Presbyterians? No! Any Independents or Methodists? No, no, no! Whom have you there? And the final answer came down from heaven, We don't know the names here. All who are here are Christians."

Why is it important to protect the right to dissent?

With this attitude, it became increasingly difficult for one church to claim special privileges.

As a result, even those states that had some sort of established religion did not support only one church as was common in Europe. Government support was given to a number of churches—it was support for religion rather than for a particular state church. However, preference was given to the Protestant form of the Christian religion. Catholics, Jews, or any other non-Protestant groups were not supported and were sometimes discriminated against.

By the time the Constitution was written, most Americans supported the idea that freedom of belief was an essential right that needed to be protected. They also believed in the importance of religion in developing the kind of character needed to maintain a free society. At the same time, they had become convinced that each person has a natural right to his or her own beliefs.

Why did the Founders believe in the separation of church and state?

In Virginia in the 1770s and 1780s, there were bitter debates over the aid the state government gave to the established church. Members of the state legislature were sharply divided over this issue and their angry disputes threatened the stability of the government. Thomas Jefferson believed that the only way to deal with such problems was to completely separate religion from politics. This, he argued, would eliminate the formal influence of religion on government and promote a free choice of political positions. He therefore urged the **separation of church and state**.

Jefferson wanted to protect debates over public policy from the influence of religious disputes. He and others were affected by the horrible example of the religious wars that had raged in Europe. Jefferson believed such wars were the results of religion and government becoming too closely connected. He was also influenced by the example of the religious disputes which had taken place in Virginia. Consequently, Jefferson argued, among other things, that members of the clergy should not be allowed to hold public office.

Madison also believed that individuals in a free society should have freedom of conscience—the right to decide for themselves what to believe. He worried that freedom of conscience would be threatened if government supported some religions and not others. He argued that throughout history there has been a great tendency for (1) government to dominate religion, (2) religion to dominate government, or (3) there to be a corrupt partnership between government and religion. Madison concluded that the best way to deal with this problem is to keep government from interfering in any way with religion. Government should only do what is necessary to keep the peace and protect each religious group from violating the rights of others.

There are two fundamental reasons why Americans have argued for the separation of church and state, that is, that religion and government should be separate. People such as Roger Williams believed it was essential in order to protect religion from being corrupted by the state. He insisted that there should be a "wall of separation between the garden of the Church and the wilderness of the world." Thomas Jefferson thought it was important in order to prevent religious conflict from corrupting good government. James Madison combined these two views in his opposition to a religious establishment. He, of course, was the one who wrote the First Amendment.

How was religious freedom protected in the Constitution?

Before the Bill of Rights, the only mention of religion in the Constitution was the ban placed on **religious tests** for public office in the federal government (Article VI). In 1787, most of the states still had established religions or religious tests for office. Many Americans did not believe that non-Protestants—Catholics, Jews, atheists, and others—could be trusted with public office.

At the Philadelphia Convention, Charles Pinckney of South Carolina proposed that "no religious test shall ever be required as a qualification to any office or public trust under the United States." His proposal passed with little dissent. For the first time in history, a nation had formally abolished one of the most powerful tools of the government for oppressing religious minorities.

Most states followed the example of the federal government and abolished tests for state office. But it was not until 1868 in North Carolina, 1946 in New Hampshire, and 1961 in Maryland that religious tests were abolished entirely.

At the same time, a number of states still supported Protestant Christianity as an established religion. The Virginia Declaration of Rights of 1776 had guaranteed the "free exercise of religion" but it did not end the establishment of the Episcopal Church. It took another ten years, and much effort by both Jefferson and Madison, to separate church and state in Virginia. It was not until 1833, when Massachusetts changed its constitution to separate church and state, that the last established religion in America was eliminated.

How have the courts interpreted the establishment clause?

The First Amendment says "Congress shall make no law respecting an establishment of religion." It is clear that the authors of the First Amendment wanted to put an end to the practice of having the government declare an official national religion. It is also fair to say that most of the Framers wanted to prevent the government from giving special benefits to some religions and not others.

Beyond this general agreement, however, there is considerable disagreement. These disagreements about the meaning of the establishment clause of the First Amendment can be summarized as follows:

1. **The broad interpretation**. People who hold this position argue that the government cannot

   ■ set up (or establish) a church

   ■ use tax money to support any religious activity, practice, or institution

   ■ give aid to all religions on an impartial basis

   People holding the broad interpretation argue that the Bill of Rights prevents the federal government from providing any support for religion whatsoever. The government may, however, provide the same support that everyone in the society receives, such as police and fire protection. It may also provide assistance that makes it easier for people to freely exercise their religion, such as by excusing students from school during religious holidays.

   However, supporters of this interpretation would argue that it is a violation of the First Amendment to place "In God We Trust" on money, to add "under God" to the Pledge of Allegiance, and to set up public displays on government property recognizing any kinds of religious holidays.

2. **The narrow interpretation**. People who hold this position argue that the government is only prohibited from giving one religious group preferred treatment over others. They believe the First Amendment does not prohibit government from supporting religion so long as it does so impartially.

   This group supports the placement of "In God We Trust" on money or other such actions that are opposed by people using a broad interpretation of the First Amendment.

   However, both people who hold the broad and narrow interpretations would say the First Amendment prohibits government recognition of Christmas, if the holidays of other religious groups are not also recognized. They would also prohibit the government from displaying a national Christmas tree if it does not display the symbols of other religions.

3. **The literal interpretation**. People who hold this view suggest that the First Amendment should only prohibit the establishment of an official government religion. This position would not prohibit the participation of government in, and approval of, the religious practices of particular religions. Thus, they would allow the government to participate in Christmas celebrations so long as the government did not declare Christianity to be an official established religion.

Debate continues throughout the nation on how the establishment clause should be interpreted to protect freedom of belief.

In 1940 the Supreme Court made the establishment clause and the free exercise clause applicable to the states through incorporation into the Fourteenth Amendment. Since that time, the court has heard numerous cases involving freedom of religion. These have involved a number of issues such as prayer in schools, Christmas displays of Nativity scenes, and various kinds of support for religious education. These are matters about which people have very strong feelings. While most people agree that church and state should be separated, we are no closer now than we were in 1791 to reaching a general consensus on exactly what this means.

Critical Thinking Exercise
TAKING AND DEFENDING POSITIONS ON ISSUES REGARDING THE ESTABLISHMENT OF RELIGION

Each of the four situations below is based on a case that reached the Supreme Court. Your class should be divided into small groups for the following activity. Each group should read one of the situations and answer the questions that follow as they relate to the situation you have read. Be prepared to explain your answers to the class.

1. A New Jersey law allowed local school districts to pay parents for the cost of student transportation to both public schools and private religious schools. Opponents claimed that the law made it easier for parents to send their children to religious schools and therefore violated the establishment clause of the First Amendment. Supporters argued that the law was designed as a safety measure for children, many of whom had to walk to school.

2. New York City arranged a voluntary program permitting its public schools to release students during school hours to go to off-campus centers to receive religious instruction. Several citizens complained that this violated the establishment clause.

3. The New York State Board of Regents required teachers to begin each school day leading their class in a "non-denominational" prayer written by state officials. Students who did not wish to participate were permitted to remain silent or be excused from the classroom. The parents of ten students claimed the prayer was against their religious beliefs and violated the establishment clause.

4. The city of Pawtucket, Rhode Island, put up a Christmas display that included a Santa Claus house, reindeer pulling Santa's sleigh, a Christmas tree, and a large banner saying "Season's Greetings." It also contained a creche with the figures of the Infant Jesus, Mary, Joseph, angels, shepherds, kings, and animals. Several citizens complained that this act violated the establishment clause.

What issues are raised by government-sponsored celebration of religious holidays?

Examining the Issues

1. What position would people who take the broad interpretation of the establishment clause take on this issue? The narrow interpretation? The literal interpretation? Explain your answers.

2. What arguments can you make for permitting the government to do what it did? What values and interests are involved?

3. What arguments can you make for prohibiting the government from doing what it did? What values and interests would be promoted?

4. What values and interests are in conflict in this situation?

5. **What do *you* think?** What position would you take on the situation you have examined? What arguments can you give to support your position? Be prepared to defend your position and evaluate others presented.

Using the Lesson

1. Why do you think most states at the time of the American Revolution had established churches and religious tests for public office?

2. Why was religious freedom so important to the Founders?

3. What do you believe was the Framers' intent in writing the establishment clause?

4. What was Roger Williams's position on the relationship between church and state?

5. Why caused the increase in religious tolerance in the American colonies?

6. What is the difference between teaching religion and teaching about religion? Do you think the establishment clause should be interpreted to prohibit teaching about the history of religion or about comparative religion? How would you decide which religions should be included in a public school course about religion?

7. What are the implications of the following statement written by Justice William O. Douglas in 1952? "We are a religious people whose institutions presuppose a Supreme Being....We cannot read into the Bill of Rights...a philosophy of hostility to religion."

8. What are the implications of the following position of Supreme Court Justice Hugo Black? He said the establishment clause means not only that the government cannot set up a church but also that the government cannot aid all religions impartially or levy a tax for the support of any religious activities, institutions, or practices. "In the words of Jefferson, the clause against establishment of religion by law was intended to erect 'a wall of separation between Church and State.'"

LESSON 20

How Does the Free Exercise Clause Protect Your Freedom of Religion?

Purpose of Lesson

The free exercise clause of the First Amendment prohibits the government from interfering with your right to practice your religious beliefs. However, religious practices may be limited if they endanger other important rights, values, and interests of society. This lesson will examine the importance of the free exercise clause and what considerations might be used in deciding when the right to practice one's religious beliefs should be limited.

When you have finished this lesson, you should be able to explain the importance of freedom of religion. You should also be able to take and defend positions on issues regarding the free exercise of religious beliefs.

Critical Thinking Exercise
EXAMINING THE IMPORTANCE OF FREEDOM OF RELIGION

Work in small groups to read the following hypothetical situation and answer the questions that follow it. Be prepared to explain your answers to the class.

> Suppose you lived in a country where there was one official religion, supported by government. Suppose the religion was a very admirable one which promoted peace, kindness towards others, and the common welfare.
>
> All people in the country were taught from an early age to believe in this religion. However, anyone who criticized the religion or refused to behave in ways required by the religion was denied certain rights and sometimes punished in other ways by the government.

Examining the Issues

1. What rights, if any, do you think would be violated in such a situation? Explain your position.

2. Why might a community or government want to promote such a situation? Explain your answer with references to what you have learned about the history of religious intolerance.

3. What position would Roger Williams have taken on this situation? Thomas Jefferson? Explain your answer.

4. In what way, if any, is the freedom to choose your beliefs and religious practices related to the idea of moral responsibility?

5. **What do *you* think?** If you had been drafting the Bill of Rights, what amendment, if any, would you have included to cover the rights involved in the above situation? Draft an amendment and be prepared to present, explain, and defend it before the class.

What rights are protected by the free exercise clause?

The establishment and the free exercise clauses of the First Amendment deal with two different parts of the idea of religious liberty. The establishment clause prevents the government from requiring citizens to support or believe in a particular religious faith. It is clearly intended to protect the rights of each individual to believe whatever he or she wishes. We have already examined the various ways in which different people interpret this clause. On the other hand, the free exercise clause is mostly concerned with making sure that people who want to practice their religion will have an opportunity to do so.

There are two parts to the idea of freedom of religion: the freedom to believe and the freedom to practice your religious beliefs. The Supreme Court has said that individuals have an absolute right to freedom of conscience or belief. The government may not interfere with this right. However, the right to practice one's beliefs may be limited under certain conditions to protect other important values and interests. The problem is deciding what religious practices should be protected by the First Amendment and what practices may be limited by government without violating the amendment.

Critical Thinking Exercise
TAKING AND DEFENDING POSITIONS ON ISSUES REGARDING THE FREE EXERCISE OF RELIGION

Each of the following situations involves an issue of whether the government should be allowed to interfere with an individual's right to freedom of religion. Work in small groups to examine each issue and develop answers to the questions that follow.

A. Should the government be able to require students to salute the flag if it is against their religious beliefs?

B. Should the government be able to require children to be vaccinated before they begin school if it is against their religious beliefs?

C. Should the government be able to require parents to permit blood transfusions for their children if it is against their religious beliefs?

D. Should the government be able to prevent people from having more than one wife or husband if their religious beliefs support their doing so?

E. Should the government be able to force people to serve in the armed forces during a national emergency if it is against their religious beliefs to do so?

Examining the Issues

Answer the following questions for each of the above situations:

1. If the government had this power, what rights of the individuals would be limited?

2. If the government did not have this power, what rights of individuals and interests of society might be promoted? Which would be endangered?

3. What values and interests should be considered when deciding whether or not to limit free exercise?

4. **What do *you* think?** Taking into account the conflicting rights and interests, what position would you take on each issue? Be prepared to explain and defend your position.

When should the practice of religious beliefs be limited?

There are no simple tests or criteria that can be used to give ready-made answers when difficult decisions must be made about whether the government should be allowed to limit the right to practice one's religious beliefs. Such decisions usually require balancing the right to practice one's beliefs against the rights of other individuals and other important values and interests of society. For example, the Supreme Court has held that although an adult can refuse a blood transfusion on religious grounds, the same adult cannot refuse to have a life-saving transfusion given to his or her child.

A number of different positions and considerations have been developed by judges and students of the Constitution to help decide when religious practices can be limited. Two approaches to deciding issues involving the free exercise clause are the following:

1. **Religious practices should be limited if they violate important and fair laws.** The free exercise clause protects freedom of belief. Government cannot make laws that punish people because of their beliefs. However, the clause does not necessarily protect the freedom to act on one's beliefs. Therefore, some would argue, government can make laws that limit people's religious practices if such practices would endanger an important interest the government is trying to protect.

   For example, the Native American Church has the tradition of smoking the drug peyote in their religious ceremonies. To do so violates laws against the use of illegal drugs. These laws are reasonable and fair methods of dealing with an important problem in our society. People who hold this position argue that the Native Americans have the right to believe in the use of drugs. However, the free exercise clause should not be interpreted to protect the right to use drugs in religious ceremonies.

2. **Religious practices that violate important and fair laws may be tolerated under certain circumstances.** The free exercise clause protects both belief and action. If a law interferes with the practice of one's beliefs, intentionally or unintentionally, courts must balance the importance of the government's interest against how great a burden the law places on religious freedom. If the government can serve its interest in some way other than limiting the free exercise of religion, it should do so.

   For example, people holding this position would say that smoking peyote is a very important part of the Native Americans' centuries-old, traditional religious ceremonies. It does little or no harm to the government's interest in fighting drugs. Therefore, the practice should not be prohibited.

What considerations are useful in deciding when the free exercise of religion should be limited?

Critical Thinking Exercise

TAKING AND DEFENDING POSITIONS ON ISSUES REGARDING THE FREE EXERCISE OF RELIGION

The following are the facts from a case heard by the Supreme Court regarding the right to the free exercise of religious beliefs (*Wisconsin v. Yoder*, 1972). Work in small groups to read the case and develop positions on the issue it involves. Be prepared to present and defend your positions before the class.

> The State of Wisconsin required parents to send their children to school until the age of sixteen. The purpose of the law was to provide all children with educational opportunities. Any parent convicted of violating this law could be fined or imprisoned.
>
> Jonas Yoder was a member of an Old Order Amish community in Wisconsin. Children in this community are expected to leave school after completion of the eighth grade and continue their education by working with their parents. The Amish believe that their children cannot be prepared for an adult Amish life by attending high school. They feel that students will be drawn away from traditional religious beliefs and occupations by exposure in high school to science, machines, and modern life-styles.
>
> Jonas Yoder refused to allow his fifteen-year-old son to attend high school. Mr. Yoder and several other Amish parents who had refused to send their children to school were arrested, tried, and convicted of breaking the state law.

Examining the Issues

1. What position would a person take on this issue who believed that religious practices should be limited if they violate important and fair laws promoting government interests? What arguments can you give for and against this position in the *Yoder* case?

2. What position would a person take who believed that a decision in this case should be made by balancing the right to religious freedom against other values and interests that government is responsible for promoting. What arguments can you give for and against this position in the *Yoder* case?

3. **What do *you* think?** Work in your group to develop a position on this case taking into account what you have learned and your own experiences and opinions. Be prepared to present and defend your position and to evaluate others presented.

The struggle to balance the rights of the individual against the interests of society

In deciding the issues you have been discussing, the Supreme Court justices have often been divided in their decisions. Sometimes they have overruled earlier decisions. In making their decisions, the justices have continually attempted to refine the tests or considerations used. We can expect this process to continue. The Court may well overrule some of its present decisions in its continued attempt to strike a fair and reasonable balance between the rights of the individual and those of society.

Some of the issues you have discussed and others the Court has considered have been dealt with in several decisions. For example, when the health of the community must be balanced against the religious beliefs of an individual or group, public health is considered to be more important. For this reason the Court has upheld the right of the government to require vaccinations before children attend school, even if this interferes with their religious beliefs. On similar grounds, the Court has upheld the right of the government to require blood tests before issuing marriage licenses.

By contrast, when the life, health, or safety of individuals, rather than the community, is involved, the Court has upheld the right of mentally-competent adults to make their own decisions. For example, an adult may refuse to receive a blood transfusion even if his or her life is at risk. Parents, however, may not refuse a transfusion for their children, and the courts may step in to protect the rights of minors.

The Court has also protected the right of students to refuse to salute the flag or attend high school if this is against their religious beliefs. The question in deciding such cases was whether the government had a compelling interest, one that was great enough to justify limiting the individual's right to the free exercise of religion. For example, the justices considered the government's requiring a student to salute the flag to be an unreasonable attempt to force a student to accept a belief.

Conflicts between the free exercise and establishment clauses

There are times when the free exercise and the establishment clauses come into conflict. For example, consider the following situations:

- Is Congress establishing a religion when it opens its session with prayer led by a chaplain? If it refused to do so, would it be preventing its members from freely exercising their religious beliefs?

- If the government pays to provide for chaplains in the armed forces and in prisons, is it violating the establishment clause? If it failed to provide chaplains, would it be limiting the free exercise of their beliefs by persons serving in the armed forces or in prison?

Should students be excused from public schools to attend religious instruction?

- If public school officials excuse Jewish students from attending classes on Yom Kippur to attend religious services, are they creating a preference for a particular group that violates the establishment clause? If they deny the students the right to be absent, are they prohibiting the right to free exercise?

- On August 11, 1984, the president signed into law the Equal Access Act. This act requires secondary schools to allow student religious groups to hold meetings in school buildings if other groups such as the chess club or social clubs are provided with the same opportunity. If schools do not provide meeting facilities for student religious groups, are they limiting their free exercise? If they do, are they violating the establishment clause?

These are questions upon which reasonable people differ. In our democratic system, it is the right of each person to develop his or her own answers to such questions. Under our system of government, it is the function of the Supreme Court to determine if laws created by the government have violated a person's religious liberty. But such laws would not be passed in the first place if at least some people had not wanted them. Therefore, it is important for each of us to recognize the importance of the religious liberty protected by the First Amendment. If we insist that *everyone's* religious liberty needs to be respected and protected, laws that violate the First Amendment are less likely to be passed.

It is probably worth reminding ourselves that James Madison thought the best protection for religious liberty was to be found in the many different religious faiths that had sprung up in the United States. What was true in the eighteenth century is even more true now. And it is even clearer that we can only live and work together peacefully if we each take the responsibility of insuring that everyone's religious liberty is protected.

Using the Lesson

1. What might be some common problems in protecting religious freedom? Explain how you think they should be dealt with.

2. What are the advantages and disadvantages of religious diversity in society?

3. What criteria should the courts consider when the religious practices of a group conflict with the needs of society?

4. Do you think issues involving religious freedom should be decided in the courts or in the legislative arena?

5. In what ways can individuals take the responsibility of insuring that everyone's religious liberty is protected?

LESSON 21

How Does the First Amendment Protect Your Freedom of Expression?

Purpose of Lesson

The First Amendment says that "Congress shall make no law...abridging the freedom of speech, or of the press, or the right of the people peaceably to assemble, and to petition the Government for a redress of grievances." Together these four rights are considered as one, the right to freedom of expression. They are all different ways to express your ideas and beliefs. All are essential to a free society.

This lesson will discuss what benefits freedom of expression offers to both the individual and society, why it was important to the Founders, and the circumstances under which the government should be able to limit this freedom. In this lesson we will focus on the rights to freedom of speech and press, and in the next lesson on the rights of assembly and petition.

When you have finished this lesson, you should be able to explain the importance of freedom of expression and the historical significance of the First Amendment. You should also be able to discuss considerations useful in deciding when it is reasonable to place limits on freedom of speech and the press. Finally, you should be able to take and defend a position on an issue involving this right.

Terms to Know

time, place, and manner restrictions
Espionage Act of 1918
clear and present danger
libel

Why is protecting the right to freedom of expression important?

The First Amendment was written because the Founders believed that the freedom to express your beliefs is essential in a representative government. As Benjamin Franklin said, "Whoever would overthrow the liberty of a nation must begin by subduing the freeness of speech." The Founders knew from their own experience and from their knowledge of history that freedom of expression needs to be protected from government interference.

It is not easy for many people to tolerate the speech of others with whom they may strongly disagree. It is often especially difficult for people in powerful government positions to tolerate criticisms of their actions. As Justice Oliver Wendell Holmes, Jr., said, "If you have no doubt of your premises or

Why is it important to protect the expression of ideas with which you may disagree?

your powers and want a certain result with all your heart you naturally express your wishes in law and sweep away all opposition." History is filled with examples of government suppression of free expression by people who have had no doubt about their beliefs or powers. Judge Learned Hand has commented on this tendency, stating "The spirit of liberty is the spirit which is not too sure that it is right."

The pressures to suppress freedom of expression are widespread and powerful in any society. To some, it defies common sense for the government to protect the free speech rights of people with obnoxious views. It is important, therefore, to constantly remind ourselves of the important benefits of freedom of expression to the individual and society such as the following:

- **Freedom of expression promotes individual growth and human dignity.** The right to express your ideas and communicate with others contributes to your growth as a person. Human dignity is promoted by allowing you the freedom to say what you think and to hear what others have to say.

- **Freedom of expression is important for the advancement of knowledge.** New and better ideas are more likely to be developed in a community which allows free discussion. As the British philosopher John Stuart Mill (1806-1873) pointed out, an enlightened judgment is only possible if you are willing to consider all facts and ideas, from whatever source, and to test your conclusions against opposing points of view.

- **Freedom of expression is a necessary part of our representative government.** In our system of government, the people are the masters and government is their servant. If people are to perform their role and instruct their government, they must have access to information, ideas, and different points of view. Freedom of expression is crucial both in determining policy and in checking how well the government is carrying out its responsibilities.

- **Freedom of expression is vital to bringing about peaceful social change.** The right to freely express one's ideas provides a "safety valve" for strongly held thoughts and feelings that, if suppressed, may lead to the use of violent means of expressing opposition to laws or policies with which one disagrees. Freedom of expression allows you to try to influence public opinion by persuasion rather than by resorting to violence. We have made many changes in our nation through convincing others of the wisdom of our ideas. The freedom to dissent also makes it easier to accept government decisions, even if you disagree with them.

- **Freedom of expression is essential for the protection of individual rights.** The free expression of ideas and the right to speak against the violation of one's rights by others or by the government are essential for the protection of all rights of the individual.

What are commonly accepted limitations on freedom of expression?

Despite the statement in the First Amendment that "Congress shall make no law...abridging the freedom of speech," few people argue against limiting freedom of expression in certain situations.

Suppose the First Amendment were interpreted to mean that there could be no laws at all limiting speech. If so, people would be able to say anything they wanted at any time they wanted. People could falsely shout "Fire!" in a crowded theater to cause a panic and possible injury or loss of life. People could give military secrets to enemies. They could lie in court and deprive people of their right to a fair trial. People could scream in libraries, give political speeches in the middle of church sermons, or speak though loudspeakers in neighborhoods in the middle of the night.

What limitations, if any, should be placed on freedom of expression?

Most judges, historians, and legal scholars believe the First Amendment should not be interpreted to protect freedom of expression in situations such as those above. In some situations, limiting freedom to speak may actually increase a person's ability to speak and be heard. For example, there are rules governing when someone may talk at a meeting or debate. If there were no rules and everyone was allowed to talk at the same time, it would be difficult for anyone to be heard. Although you have the right to give a speech criticizing the government, you do not have the right to do so in the middle of a math test. You may have the right to protest a government policy you do not like, but you do not have the right to do so with a loudspeaker in a residential area in the middle of the night.

These kinds of limitations on freedom of expression are referred to as **time, place, and manner restrictions**. They govern when, where, and how you can speak, not what you can say. Most people agree that these kinds of limitations do not violate the right to freedom of expression so long as they do not make it very hard or impossible for you to express your ideas to others.

The difficult question is to decide when freedom of expression should be protected and when it should not. An examination of the history of freedom of expression may be useful in learning to deal with this question.

How was freedom of expression protected in the colonies?

In the introductory unit you learned of the British attempts to limit free expression by using seditious libel laws. These laws were also brought over to the American colonies and adopted as part of the state constitutions after the Revolution. However, few colonists were prosecuted or convicted under them.

In reality, if not in law, there was a greater sense of freedom to express political opinions in the colonies than in Great Britain. The trial of printer John Peter Zenger in 1735 had established the idea that truth should be a defense against charges of seditious libel. By the mid-eighteenth century, most Americans believed that the right to express one's political opinions was essential for a free society.

Nowhere is the importance of a free press for Americans better illustrated than during the Revolution. The printing press was an important weapon both in bringing the Revolution about and in its success. The so-called "Pamphlet War" was one of the factors that made it possible for John Adams to claim that the Revolution began long before the war started, having been accomplished in the hearts and minds of the people.

Nevertheless, there is no indication that the Framers intended the Constitution or the Bill of Rights to prevent prosecution for seditious libel. The common view, in both America and Britain, was that no one should be able to make a false or malicious accusation against the government.

Until the end of the eighteenth century, legal protection for speech was limited to legislators speaking in their official capacity. The English Bill of Rights had protected freedom of speech for members of Parliament and this concept was carried over to the colonies, included in the state constitutions, and protected in the Constitution.

The Constitution itself made no mention of a free press because the Framers believed, as Roger Sherman of Connecticut declared, "it is unnecessary. The power of Congress does not extend to the Press." The lack of such protection, however, was one of the criticisms of the new Constitution.

Thomas Jefferson, writing from France, noted the importance of protecting freedom of the press. "Were it left to me to decide whether we should have a government without newspapers or newspapers without a government, I should not hesitate for a moment to prefer the latter."

The Framers' intentions in writing the First Amendment have never been entirely clear. As we have seen, in the eighteenth century free speech was considered to be of more limited scope than we think of today. The passage of the Sedition Act in 1798, by some of the same people who ratified the Bill of Rights, indicates that some Americans still had a narrow view of free expression.

Most people, however, opposed such limitations. One of the reasons the Republicans won the election of 1800 was that they were viewed as the supporters of political freedom, including the freedom to express one's political views. Freedom of speech and press were, at that time, becoming an essential part of a free society.

When has free speech been suppressed?

There has been considerable pressure at different times throughout our history to suppress unpopular ideas. Such restrictions generally have occurred during times of war or when the government has felt threatened. For example, before the Civil War a number of states passed laws that made printing and distributing abolitionist literature a crime. Mobs destroyed printing presses and broke up anti-slavery meetings. In 1837 an Illinois anti-slavery editor, Elijah Lovejoy, was murdered and his printing press destroyed.

Why is it important to protect freedom of the press during a national crisis?

During other difficult periods in our history, attempts also have been made to suppress free expression. The early years of the twentieth century were marked by fears of the growing labor movement, socialism, communism, and anarchy. In 1901 President William McKinley was assassinated by an anarchist and many states responded by passing laws which made it a crime to advocate the forceful overthrow of the government.

America's entry into World War I only increased the feeling that the nation needed to be protected against seditious speech. Both state and federal legislation was passed making it a crime to interfere in any way with the war effort. The federal **Espionage Act of 1918** prohibited anyone from urging resistance to the United States or to the war effort. After the war, thirty-three states passed peacetime sedition laws.

From World War I through the McCarthy era of the 1950s, state and federal governments prosecuted numerous anarchists, socialists, and communists for advocating draft resistance, mass strikes, or overthrow of the government. These actions raised serious questions about the right of free speech and led to a number of Supreme Court cases.

How might government persecution of dissidents, such as took place during the McCarthy era, endanger a free society?

What kinds of actions might be considered forms of expression?

People express their ideas, feelings, and opinions in many different ways. We speak, write, gesture, march in demonstrations, and wear campaign pins, yellow ribbons, and T-shirts with slogans. We may carry picket signs and sing songs with political messages. We may make records or write books, articles, or letters to newspapers. All are forms of expression, and there are many others.

Under most circumstances, all these forms of expression and others are protected by the First Amendment from violation by our federal and state governments. Questions arise when this right conflicts with other important rights, values, and interests.

Critical Thinking Exercise
EVALUATING AND DEVELOPING POSITIONS ON THE SCOPE AND LIMITS OF FREEDOM OF EXPRESSION

Judges and other students of the Constitution such as professors of constitutional law have tried to develop standards that will help us to decide when freedom of expression may be limited. The following are two positions that judges and others have proposed.

Work in small groups to read and discuss the positions and the questions that follow them.

A. **The freedom of expression of groups that advocate anti-democratic ideas may be limited.** People have argued that the rights of certain groups to express their ideas should not be protected by the First Amendment. Typically, these are groups that advocate the overthrow of our government and the establishment of a repressive totalitarian system of government. They may also be groups that express malicious ideas that violate the dignity and feelings of other people in the community.

People argue, for example, that political groups that would eliminate the entire Bill of Rights if they came to power should not be allowed to take advantage of the protections of the First Amendment to express their ideas. People who would deny African Americans and others the equal opportunities protected by the Fourteenth Amendment should not be allowed to express their racist ideas.

People often conclude this position by arguing that only people who agree to abide by the rules of our society, such as those in the Constitution and Bill of Rights, should be allowed to participate in free and open discussion.

B. **All persons should be allowed freedom of expression no matter how obnoxious or dangerous their ideas.** People holding this position say that only under very unusual circumstances should the government be allowed to limit freedom of expression. They claim that even totalitarian, racist, and other obnoxious ideas may serve to make people defend and better understand their own values. To suppress such expression only makes those people who were denied the right to express their ideas become more hostile, eliminates the safety-valve function of free speech, and weakens society.

People also claim that to give government the power to suppress the free expression of ideas that some people find unacceptable is too dangerous. It gives government the power to decide what

What limitations, if any, should be placed on speakers at school assemblies?

beliefs and opinions are acceptable and unacceptable. To make such decisions, the government would have to be given the power to investigate people's beliefs, spy on dissident political groups, and keep files on people holding political opinions considered dangerous.

People supporting this position say the only safe way to protect freedom of expression is to protect it for everyone, no matter how obnoxious the ideas they express may be to other groups or the majority. You may remember the quotation from Voltaire which summarizes this position, "I may disapprove of what you say, but will defend to the death your right to say it."

Examining the Positions

1. What rights, values, and interests of individuals and society might be promoted and endangered by the first position?

2. What rights, values, and interests of individuals and society might be promoted and endangered by the second position?

3. **What do *you* think?** Work with your group to decide which position you prefer. Then be prepared to explain and defend the reasons for your choice.

What considerations has the Supreme Court used to limit freedom of expression?

The Supreme Court has taken the latter position of the two discussed above. It is not clear whether a majority of Americans agree with such a position. Polls have often shown that many Americans do not support the right of members of such groups as the Nazi party or the Ku Klux Klan to speak.

Even advocates of the second position recognize the need to limit the right to freedom of expression in some circumstances. What considerations to use in making such decisions is a continuous matter of discussion and debate among scholars, judges, and other interested citizens.

Over the years, the courts have developed guidelines to use in balancing the right to free expression against other important rights and interests of society. For example, suppose your right to free expression could endanger the public safety or national security. If the danger is considered great enough, the courts will decide that your right to free speech must be limited.

Some judges and historians have argued that the authors of the First Amendment did not intend it to protect all kinds of speech and press. Their belief in the necessity of protecting freedom of expression was based on the idea that the free exchange of political ideas was essential to constitutional democracy. Consequently, speech in the First Amendment only meant political speech or, at the most, speech that was considered to be worthy or valuable. It was not their intention, some believe, to protect speech that was blasphemous, obscene, or libelous.

To some degree the courts still maintain that the speech protections of the First Amendment only apply to certain kinds of speech. Obscenity, for example, is not protected. However, the Supreme Court, in a series of decisions, has made it increasingly difficult to establish what is meant by obscenity. Consequently, while obscene speech does not fall under the protection of the First Amendment, there are fewer and fewer successful prosecutions of free speech because of changing community and legal standards.

The courts have upheld laws prohibiting speech or press that present a **clear and present danger** to others or to society. Examples of such speech include giving away national security secrets, lying under oath, or **libel** (ruining other people's reputation by knowingly spreading lies about them). The courts have also said that you cannot engage in speech which could lead directly to violence or cause a riot. The courts can limit your right to free speech if they believe it poses a clear and present danger to others.

When the rights of free press come into conflict with the right to a fair trial, the courts have generally upheld the right of reporters to cover trials. Judges have been told to find other ways to protect the defendant's right to a fair trial.

In considering cases involving freedom of expression, the courts have had to balance conflicting needs. On the whole, judges have been reluctant to limit any of the fundamental rights of the First Amendment.

How would you define what speech presents a clear and present danger to society?

Critical Thinking Exercise
TAKING AND DEFENDING POSITIONS ON AN ISSUE OF FREEDOM OF EXPRESSION

Read the following description of issues regarding freedom of expression on college and university campuses. Then respond to the questions that follow the selection.

Colleges and universities are supposed to be places where free inquiry, debate, and expression are highly valued. Professors and students are supposed to have great freedom to explore, express, debate, and discuss ideas whether they are popular or not. The ideal of the university is of a place where no ideas are suppressed—all are worthy of exploration.

In years past, most students at major colleges and universities were white. Thanks to such changes as those resulting from the equal protection clause of the Fourteenth Amendment, civil rights legislation, and the work of numerous groups and individuals, today the student bodies of colleges and universities better reflect the diversity of our nation.

Despite the increased appreciation of diversity in the United States, conflicts among students along racial, ethnic, and religious lines have occurred on college campuses. Students have made disparaging and insulting remarks to those who differ from them. As a result, university administrators and student governments have attempted to promote civility and understanding on campus by various means.

Recently, at more than two hundred colleges and universities across the nation, student codes of conduct or "speech codes" were established. They are designed to prevent statements or comments about race, sex, religion, national origin, or sexual preference that might offend some people. The goal of such codes has been to discourage prejudice and create a more comfortable learning environment for all students.

Supporters of the codes explain that "freedom of expression is no more sacred than freedom from intolerance or bigotry." Critics charge that the result has been to violate students' and teachers' right to free expression. They refer to various instances in which students have been suspended or expelled for comments that were offensive to others.

Examining the Issues

1. What issues of freedom of expression are involved in this situation?

2. What values and interests are involved?

3. What arguments might be presented by persons holding the position that the right to free expression by people expressing undemocratic ideas can be limited?

4. What arguments might be presented by persons holding the position that the right to free expression should not

be limited, even for those expressing obnoxious or dangerous ideas?

5. On a typical college campus, a large number of students of relatively diverse backgrounds are thrown together in crowded living conditions. Do you think that these conditions distinguish the college campus from the larger society? If so, do you think this would support the claim that different rules governing speech are needed on campus than those that apply to the society at large? Should any limits be placed on the freedom of expression of professors whose courses are required of all students for graduation?

6. **What do *you* think?** Assume that you and your group are college students asked to determine what policy should be established to deal with this issue. What limitations, if any, would you place on freedom of expression for students on campus? Develop a proposed policy and be prepared to explain and defend it before your class.

Using the Lesson

1. What arguments are given for the importance of freedom of expression?

2. What limitations on freedom of expression are commonly thought reasonable? Do you agree with such limitations? Explain your position.

3. Why have governments often sought to suppress freedom of expression? Give examples from history.

4. What considerations has the Supreme Court used in deciding when freedom of expression can be limited?

5. Would you give government the power to punish people for speech that the government considered might be harmful to society? Explain your answer.

6. Would you give the government the power to punish people for saying things that are profane or indecent even if they do not present a clear and present danger? Explain your answer.

LESSON 22

How Does the First Amendment Protect Your Freedom of Assembly, Petition, and Association?

Purpose of Lesson

The First Amendment states that "Congress shall make no law...abridging...the right of the people peaceably to assemble, and to petition the government for a redress of grievances." This lesson will examine the importance and historical background of these rights. It will also discuss how these rights are protected in our system of government and consider what criteria should be used to limit their exercise.

When you finish this lesson, you should be able to explain the importance of the rights to freedom of assembly, petition, and association. You should also be able to describe their history and in what types of situations they might be limited. Finally, you should be able to take and defend a position on an issue involving these rights.

Terms to Know

redress of grievances
lobby
public forum

What is the importance of the rights to assembly, petition, and association?

The freedom to associate with other people, to assemble in groups, and to petition the government to change its actions and policies are essential parts of the right to freedom of expression. The protection of the right to petition and assembly provided in the First Amendment demonstrates that a free society must accept not only pleasant political discussion but a certain amount of political activism. These rights enable people to work together to promote their political interests by joining political parties and interest groups. They also enable people to achieve their individual and social goals by joining, for example, church groups, professional organizations, social clubs, and community service organizations.

Although the right to freedom of association is not mentioned in the Constitution or Bill of Rights, the courts have recognized it as a basic right. It is one of the unenumerated rights to be studied in Unit Six.

Why were the rights of assembly and petition important to the Founders?

The rights of assembly and petition were part of English common law for hundreds of years and were seen by Americans as fundamental to a constitutional democracy. Historically these rights have been considered together. It appears people thought that the purpose of the right to assemble was in order to petition the government. The right of petition was recognized in the Magna Carta; in fact, the Magna Carta itself was a petition addressed to the king demanding that he correct certain wrongs (**redress of grievances**). Over the centuries, Parliament developed the habit of petitioning the king to get what it wanted. If the king denied its petitions, Parliament denied him the money he requested. A resolution of the House of Commons in 1669 along with the English Bill of Rights of 1689 guaranteed English subjects the right to petition both the House of Commons and the king himself.

How did Parliament use the right to petition against the king?

The American colonists considered the right to petition as a basic right of Englishmen and used it often. Since they could not send representatives to Parliament, they saw the right of petition as an important means of communication with the British government. One of the frustrations of the colonists, in the years before the Revolution, was the feeling that Parliament was ignoring their pleas and petitions.

The royal governors attempted to silence the more radical colonies by shutting down the colonial assemblies. In response, Americans assembled on their own. Numerous committees, conventions, and congresses were formed as the colonists organized to defy Parliament. By the end of 1774, all but three colonies had appointed assemblies on their own without royal approval and the First Continental Congress met in September of that year.

How did the American colonists use the right to petition against Parliament?

The Continental Congress of 1774 protested that the colonists "have a right peaceably to assemble, consider of their grievances, and petition the king; and that all prosecutions, prohibitory proclamations, and commitments for the same, are illegal." When the British ignored the colonists' complaints, they decided it was necessary to free themselves from British rule. The Declaration of Independence listed the king's refusal to pay attention to the colonists' petitions as one of the causes for revolution.

As you can see, the right to petition and assembly, along with freedom of the press, were important weapons in the American Revolution. Indeed, one could argue that the right of assembly marked the beginning of the American colonists acting together against Great Britain. The beginning of the Declaration of Independence reads, "A Declaration by the Representatives of the United States of America, in General Congress Assembled."

Most states protected the rights of assembly and petition, either within their state constitutions or in their state bills of rights. During the ratification debates, a number of states included protections for assembly and petition in their recommended amendments to the Constitution. After little debate, these rights were included in the First Amendment. Since that time, the rights of assembly and petition have been included in all but two of the fifty state constitutions.

How have the rights of assembly and petition been used?

Despite the protection of the right to petition in the federal and state constitutions, it has sometimes been violated by both levels of government. In the 1830s, Congress received numerous petitions urging that slavery be abolished in the District of Columbia. The feeling against abolitionists was so strong that in 1836 Congress succeeded in passing a "gag rule" to prevent debate on all petitions related to slavery. This gag rule not only prevented any discussion of ending slavery, it also limited the ways non-voters could express their views. The use of the right to petition was an important way for women, blacks, and others, denied the right to vote, to communicate with public officials.

Former president John Quincy Adams, a member of Congress at that time, believed the gag rule was fundamentally wrong and should be resisted. He saw in it the same type of tyranny the Founders fought against during the Revolution. During every session of Congress, despite bitter opposition, he fought for its repeal; in 1844 he finally succeeded.

Why was the right to petition so important for people who did not have the right to vote?

In 1894, there was a serious depression in which millions were homeless and out of work. A group of unemployed led by Jacob Coxey marched to Washington to petition the government for some form of public relief. President Grover

Cleveland ordered the leaders of the march to be arrested for stepping on the grass of the Capitol.

During the Great Depression, a "Bonus Army" of World War I veterans marched to the nation's capital to petition Congress for payment of their military bonuses. Congress refused to support the bill they wanted and most marchers returned home. However, several thousand remained in a camp outside the city. President Herbert Hoover ordered General Douglas McArthur and the U.S. Army to drive the veterans out of the camp. He did so with tanks, guns, and tear gas, killing two veterans and wounding several others. Fifteen years earlier the veterans had fought in the same army as the men who now attacked them.

The importance of the right to assemble is nowhere better illustrated than in the civil rights movement of the 1950s and 1960s. Under the leadership of the Reverend Martin Luther King, Jr., thousands marched for "Jobs and Freedom." Dr. King said, "We march in the name of the Constitution, knowing that the Constitution is on our side. The right of the people peaceably to assemble and to petition the Government for a redress of grievances shall not be abridged. That's the First Amendment."

Today, the right to petition is widely used at the local, state, and federal levels. The right to circulate petitions for signatures to create mass pressure on any of the agencies of government may be the most influential way petitions are used today.

However, the right to petition includes much more than formal petitions. Wires, calls, and letters to public officials are also ways of petitioning the government. The right to petition is not limited to people wishing the government to correct wrongs. It is also used by individuals, groups, and corporations to **lobby** government officials to persuade them to adopt policies that will benefit their interests.

What limitations may be placed on the right of assembly?

The rights of free speech and assembly protect the rights of people to march and demonstrate. It is expected that these rights will result in political activities where people express strongly held views on political, economic, and social issues. But, at the same time, the government is responsible for making sure that demonstrations are not only peaceable but also that they do not endanger community safety or unreasonably inconvenience the public.

Public property is owned by the people. It would appear, therefore, that people have a right to assemble on public property to speak and in other ways demonstrate their views on different issues. However, as with all other rights, in some situations it is reasonable and fair to limit this right.

As you might imagine, judges and other students of the Constitution have taken different positions on this question. Some

What limits, if any, should be placed on the right to freedom of assembly?

argue that people should be able to assemble on any public property so long as it does not disrupt the normal use of that property. Others argue that the right to use public property should be limited to only those places, such as street corners and parks, that are traditionally associated with free speech.

Critical Thinking Exercise
DEVELOPING STANDARDS TO USE IN LIMITING FREEDOM OF ASSEMBLY

The following issues raise questions about when people should be able to assemble and demonstrate on public property. Work in small groups to examine the situations and answer the questions that follow them.

A. Should a group be allowed to demonstrate during rush hour on a bridge over a freeway or expressway?

B. Should demonstrators be allowed to march in front of a private home to protest the actions of the homeowner?

C. Should people have the right to assemble and march through a shopping mall? A public school while it is in session?

D. Should pickets be allowed to block the entrance to a place of work? To an abortion clinic?

E. Should a group be allowed to demonstrate by sitting on the floors of the hallways of government buildings such as city halls, universities, or courts? Should they be able to sit in the offices of government officials?

What limits has the Supreme Court placed on freedom of assembly?

Few people would argue that the First Amendment protects the right of a group to demonstrate on a freeway or expressway in the middle of rush hour traffic, to disrupt a courtroom hearing, or to invade a medical clinic. The First Amendment has not been interpreted to protect riots or other violent demonstrations. In general, it has been assumed that the government has a right to impose time, place, and manner restrictions on the right to assemble just as it does on the right to free speech. The courts have said that any regulation must (1) be designed to protect a legitimate government interest and not intended to suppress free speech or assembly and (2) must be applied in a non-discriminatory manner.

The courts have also ruled that the right of assembly extends to meetings held in **public forums** such as streets, parks, and sidewalks. Free access to public property has historically been especially important for people who cannot afford more costly ways to communicate, such as the press or television.

How is the right of association protected?

Although the right of association is not mentioned in either the U.S. or state constitutions, the courts have said that it is implied by the other rights in the First Amendment—in particular, by the rights of free speech and assembly. It has been assumed that the right of association is part of what it means to live in a free society. The government should not interfere with your right to join with others, whether it be in private clubs, college fraternities, political parties, professional organizations, or labor unions.

The first time the Supreme Court dealt with an issue regarding the right of association was in 1958. The state of Alabama had ordered the National Association for the Advancement of

Colored People (NAACP) to disclose its membership lists. During that time, members of the NAACP were engaged in a bitter civil rights struggle. The Supreme Court thought that if the NAACP membership lists were made public, this might lead to hostile reprisals against its members. The Court ruled that freedom of association is protected by the First Amendment and that Alabama's demand for the membership lists violated this right (*NAACP v. Alabama,* 1958).

What is the importance of the right to freedom of association?

About the same time as the Alabama ruling, however, the Court upheld laws which required disclosure of membership lists of the Communist party because the organization advocated the violent overthrow of the government (*Barenblatt v. U.S.,* 1959).

One of the questions that has arisen is whether the right of association also means you have the right not to associate with certain people. Should private organizations be able to prohibit some people from becoming members? For example, should the government be able to require private golf courses to admit blacks or private men's clubs to admit women? This question involves the right of equal protection as well as that of association.

In cases involving this question, the Supreme Court has ruled that the government cannot interfere with whom you wish to associate in your private life. However, it has also ruled that in some situations that go beyond close personal relationships and involve larger social purposes, the government may force private organizations not to discriminate on the basis of race, sex, or ethnic background.

As you can imagine, these issues can be very difficult. The difficulties reflect the tension between two important ideals: (1) the elimination of unfair discrimination in American life and (2) the right of each individual to live his or her own life as free as possible from government interference.

The right to associate can be said to lie at the very heart of the American experiment. One hundred and fifty years ago, Alexis de Tocqueville (1805-1859), the French observer of American life, commented on Americans' unique tendency to come together in groups to solve common problems. The exercise of the right of association was, de Tocqueville thought, one of the outstanding characteristics of American citizenship. It is difficult to imagine the development of American labor unions and political parties, as well as a host of other organizations that play important roles in our civic life, without the protection of this right, as well as those rights of speech, religion, petition, and assembly that are explicitly protected by the First Amendment.

Critical Thinking Exercise
TAKING AND DEFENDING A POSITION ON A FIRST AMENDMENT ISSUE

The following case involves most of the First Amendment rights you have been studying—religion, speech, and association (*Board of Education of the Westside Community Schools v. Mergens,* 1990). Read it and the instructions for holding a simplified moot court hearing.

In 1984 Congress passed the Equal Access Act which prohibits any public secondary school which receives federal funds and provides facilities for various extracurricular organizations from discriminating against student clubs because of their religious or philosophical orientation.

Westside High School is a public school in Omaha, Nebraska, with about 1,500 students. Students have the opportunity to participate in a number of groups and clubs, all of which meet after school on the school's premises. Among these groups are the Creative Writing Club, the Math Club, and the Future Medical Assistants. School board policy requires that each group have a faculty sponsor and none can be sponsored by any organization that denies membership based on race, color, creed, sex, or political belief.

In January 1985 Bridget Mergens met with the Westside principal to request permission to form a Christian club whose purpose would be "to permit students to read and discuss the Bible, to have fellowship, and to pray together." The club would be open to all students, regardless of religious beliefs. There would be no faculty sponsor.

Both the principal and the district superintendent denied the request. They said, first of all, the sponsor requirement was not met. More importantly, permitting the religious club to meet on school property would be unconstitutional. The school board upheld the denial.

Mergens and her parents sued the school for violating the Equal Access Act and the First Amendment protections of free speech, association, and free exercise of religion. The trial judge ruled in favor of the school saying that the Equal Access Act did not apply because all the other clubs at school were related to curriculum and linked to the school's educational function.

The U.S. Court of Appeals reversed the lower court ruling because it said there were other school clubs, such as the chess club or the surfing club, that were not directly related to the school's educational function. The school district appealed to the Supreme Court.

Examining the Issues

1. What First Amendment issues are raised in this case?

2. What values and interests are in conflict in this case?

3. What arguments can you make for allowing the group to meet?

4. What arguments can you make for prohibiting the group from meeting?

5. **What do *you* think?** To complete this exercise your class should be divided into three groups. The first group should develop arguments for Westside High School's position. Group two should develop arguments for the position of Bridget Mergens. The third group should act as judges, listen to both arguments, and decide whether the Christian club should be able to meet after school at Westside. The judges should be able to explain the basis for their decisions and defend them before the class.

Using the Lesson

1. Of all the First Amendment freedoms, only the rights of assembly and petition can be traced back to the Magna Carta. Why do you think these rights are so much older than those of speech, press, or religion?

2. Why did the Founders think the rights of assembly and petition were so important they should be included in the First Amendment?

3. Why is the right of assembly important to groups that lack other means of access to the public?

4. Should the right of association be interpreted to mean that organizations cannot impose any limits on their membership? Explain your position.

Unit Five: What Rights Are Protected by Procedural Due Process of Law?

What rights protect you from unfair imprisonment?

Purpose of Unit

You have studied substantive due process in Unit Three. This unit will deal with the protections of individual rights provided by procedural due process. Substantive due process, as you have seen, limits the degree to which government can interfere with a person's life, liberty, and property. It prohibits, for example, laws such as those which restrict freedom of travel or the right to privacy. Procedural due process, on the other hand, requires government officials to follow fair procedures when interfering with an individual's freedoms.

Certain rights to procedural due process are protected in the body of the Constitution, such as the right to *habeas corpus* and trial by jury in criminal cases. Protections of other rights are found in Amendments Four, Five, Six, and Eight of the Bill of Rights, in the Fourteenth Amendment, and in court decisions. For example, individuals are protected against being searched without a good reason or having to pay an excessive bail in order to be released after being arrested.

Due process is most commonly thought of as limiting the powers of law enforcement agencies and the courts in order to protect both the innocent and the guilty from possible abuses of power. However, the right to due process actually protects individuals from unfair actions by members of all three branches of government at local, state, and federal levels.

This unit will begin by examining the importance of procedural due process. We will then focus specifically on some of the most important provisions of the Fourth, Fifth, Sixth, and Eighth Amendments.

Although the main focus of this unit will be on criminal procedures, it is important to understand that the principles of procedural justice should guide the procedures used by all agencies of government—from school administrations to the president and Congress. The Supreme Court has ruled, for example, that public school students must be given a fair hearing before being suspended from school.

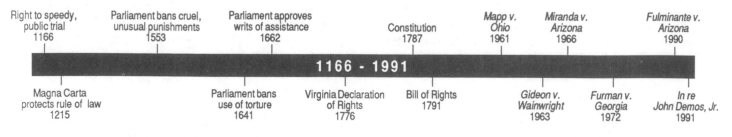

Right to speedy, public trial 1166	Parliament bans cruel, unusual punishments 1553	Parliament approves writs of assistance 1662		Constitution 1787	Mapp v. Ohio 1961	Miranda v. Arizona 1966	Fulminante v. Arizona 1990

1166 - 1991

Magna Carta protects rule of law 1215		Parliament bans use of torture 1641	Virginia Declaration of Rights 1776	Bill of Rights 1791	Gideon v. Wainwright 1963	Furman v. Georgia 1972	In re John Demos, Jr. 1991

LESSON 23

What Is the Importance of Procedural Due Process?

Purpose of Lesson

This lesson will begin our examination of procedural due process by looking at how it protects individuals from possible abuses of power by government. We will examine violations of due process in a contemporary situation. We will then discuss the history of due process and its importance to the Founders.

When you have finished this lesson, you should be able to explain the purpose and importance of procedural due process. You should also be able to identify violations of due process in a specific situation and explain why the Founders believed this right to be so important.

What is the importance of the protections provided by procedural due process?

The individual's right to procedural due process has been called the greatest protection in the Constitution from the abuse of power by government. For this reason, due process has been referred to as the "keystone of liberty" or the "heart of the law." The amendments containing the rights to procedural due process are the most detailed of all the amendments. This is because they were based on centuries of experience in which governments violated these rights. The Framers wanted to make sure these rights were clearly spelled out in the Bill of Rights to protect individuals from such violations.

Many scholars have observed that the degree of procedural justice in a country is a good indication of the respect for human dignity, freedom, and other basic rights that exist in that country. A lack of procedural justice is a common characteristic of authoritarian and totalitarian systems. In such systems, there may be a knock on the door in the middle of the night, police appear and search a home and arrest its occupant, and the person is never heard from again. There may be a secret trial and an immediate execution of persons critical of the government.

The Framers of our Constitution and Bill of Rights believed that individuals must be protected from the government's power to restrict our freedoms. You have seen, for example, how they limited the powers of Congress to make laws respect-

What rights protect you from unfair arrest?

ing freedom of expression. They also realized the importance of limiting the powers of law enforcement agencies and the courts in order to protect individual rights.

Many people question why the Founders placed such importance on rights that are designed to protect individuals accused of breaking the law. As you have read, many Americans before and during the Revolution suffered from the violation of their procedural rights by Great Britain, although these rights were a part of the British constitution. Moreover, the colonists knew that just because a person was accused of a crime did not mean that the person was guilty.

The protection of procedural rights is just as important and difficult today as it was in colonial America. This is why an understanding of the fundamental purposes and principles of due process should be the responsibility of every citizen. However, numerous research studies have shown that many Americans do not understand due process of law or even think it is important unless they have personally suffered a violation of their rights. As a result, public support for many of the rights of due process is lacking, and public debate on issues of due process is often uninformed.

To understand the importance of the complex set of rights that constitutes procedural due process, we will begin this lesson by examining a contemporary criminal case involving some of these rights.

The following situation is based on an actual case that occurred between 1980 and 1990. Fortunately it is not typical of our criminal justice system. However, for such a situation to occur, even infrequently, shows that there is a constant need to insure that all the rights that constitute due process, including the right to basic fairness, are respected.

Critical Thinking Exercise
IDENTIFYING VIOLATIONS OF DUE PROCESS

Read the following situation. Then work in small groups to respond to the questions and instructions that follow it. Be prepared to present and explain your responses to the class.

In 1980 in a small town, a sixteen-year-old white high school girl disappeared while looking for a restroom at a high school. Two custodians later found her body hidden in the loft of the school auditorium. She had been raped and strangled. The community in which this crime occurred was one with a history of racial prejudice and conflict.

The custodians were Jones, a white man, and Smith, an African American. Both were questioned by the police and made to sign statements explaining where they had been and how they had found the body. They were taken to a hospital and were made to give samples of their saliva, blood, and hair. Then a police officer drove them back to the high school. As he dropped them off, he said, "One of you two is gonna hang for this." Then he turned to Smith and said, "Since you're the black, you're elected." One week later, Smith was arrested for raping and murdering the girl. He was tried and convicted by an all-white jury from which qualified blacks had been excluded, and he was sentenced to death. He was twenty-nine years old.

A writ of *habeas corpus* to the state supreme court was filed, and a hearing was held seven years later. The appeals court hearing judge found that the arresting officer and district attorney (DA) did not follow up leads which would have cleared Smith and, in fact, suppressed evidence favorable to him. They had lied and created false testimony in order to have Smith charged and convicted.

At Smith's trial, the medical evidence that would have shown that Smith was innocent was "lost." The medical examiner

What is the importance of the right to an impartial hearing?

What is the importance of the right to appeal?

"forgot" the results of the autopsy, "lost" his notes on his findings, and "lost" the samples he had taken from the victim's body.

A police officer threatened witnesses whose testimony supported Smith's innocence, then coached witnesses to lie in court. The officer also reversed the findings of the lie-detector test that supported Smith's innocence.

The sheriff defied the original trial court's order to release Smith on bail. The judge, rather than enforcing his order, changed it and denied bail. The defense lawyer filed motions forcing the judge to resign, but the judge continued to meet with the next two judges who had taken his place. These judges were also forced to step aside by the defense attorney.

Smith's defense lawyer won two stays of execution, which saved his life while he waited for his case to be heard by the appeals court.

The judge who presided over the 1987 hearing stated in his findings that Smith "did not receive a fair trial, was denied the basic fundamental rights of due process of law, and did not commit the crime for which he now resides on death row."

At the end of the hearing the judge stated, "In the thirty years this court has presided...no case has presented a more shocking scenario of the effects of racial prejudice, perjured testimony, [and] witness intimidation....The continued incarceration of [Smith] under these circumstances is an affront to the basic notions of fairness and justice."

It took two more years for the state supreme court to uphold the order of the appeals court judge and to set Smith free. The court stated: "Due process of law is the cornerstone of a civilized system of justice. Our society wins not only when the guilty are convicted but when criminal trials are fair; our system of justice suffers when an accused is treated unfairly."

Examining the Case

1. In what ways was Smith denied a fundamentally fair trial?

2. In what ways were Smith's rights violated?

3. Although some law enforcement officers and judges appear to have tried to deprive Smith of his rights, the actions of certain people to insure his procedural rights saved his life. What were those procedural rights? Explain your answer.

What do *you* think?

1. What ways can you suggest to prevent the injustices in this case from happening to someone else in the future?

2. What limits, if any, would you put on the number of times a person could use the right to *habeas corpus* to appeal a case to a higher court? Explain your position.

3. What fundamental values and interests of our society were endangered in this situation?

4. Reread the quotation from Judge Learned Hand in Lesson 2. How, if at all, is it relevant to this situation?

How does the rule of law protect the rights of individuals?

Due process includes the basic idea that government officials must obey the law. As you learned earlier, this idea is hundreds of years old. It can be found in the Magna Carta's provision that the loss of life, liberty, and property can only occur according to the "law of the land." Today, no one given the power to create laws, carry them out, enforce them, or interpret them can be excused from obeying the law.

Some of the rights that provide the protections of due process are centuries old, such as the right to *habeas corpus* and trial by jury in criminal cases. Others have been developed in the constant struggle to provide adequate protections for individual rights from government abuse.

The Fourth, Fifth, Sixth, and Eighth Amendments lie at the very heart of the Bill of Rights and the whole theory behind it. They were designed to protect individuals from tyranny at the hands of the federal government. As you have seen, these protections now apply to all levels of government through the incorporation process.

These amendments and the Supreme Court's extension of them distinguish our society from many others. Even Great Britain today does not allow a citizen accused of a crime the full range of rights Americans enjoy—and no totalitarian government could afford to do so even though, in some instances, their constitutions provide them. Also, what distinguishes our form of government is the fact that the power of government is derived from the consent of the people.

Today 95% of all jury trials in the world take place in the United States. No other country has as thorough a system for allowing citizens to appeal decisions in order to expose any possible error which has taken place. It is important that our system allows individuals to challenge actions of law enforcement agencies. This insures that police officers must do their job in a manner acceptable to our notions of fair play.

Although we have not always lived up to the ideal of due process, as Frederick Douglass once said, "There is hope for a people when their laws are righteous, whether for the moment they conform to them or not."

In the next lessons we will examine the procedural due process protections guaranteed by the Bill of Rights. We will focus upon those protections that appear most important and controversial today.

Using the Lesson

1. Why might some people claim that the due process rights are the most important of all? Do you agree? Explain your position.

2. In what ways do the protections of due process limit the powers of the government?

3. In what ways are the protections of due process related to the basic idea of the rule of law?

LESSON 24

How Does the Fourth Amendment Protect You from Unreasonable Searches and Seizures?

Purpose of Lesson

This lesson will focus upon the specific rights contained in the Fourth Amendment. The Fourth Amendment limits the powers of law enforcement officials to enter and search people's houses or to stop and search individuals without reasonable cause. This is important for the protection of our right to be free from unfair and unreasonable interference by the government with our persons or property. It is also necessary for the protection of our right to privacy.

In this lesson, we will examine the history of the Fourth Amendment and the importance of the rights that it protects. Contemporary conflicts over how the amendment should be interpreted and enforced will be explored. The lesson will conclude with an examination of a contemporary issue regarding the Fourth Amendment.

When you have completed the lesson, you should be able to explain the purposes and importance of the Fourth Amendment and some of the problems that arise in enforcing it. You should also be able to take and defend a position on which means of enforcement you would support.

The right of the people to be secure in their persons, houses, papers, and effects, against unreasonable searches and seizures, shall not be violated, and no Warrants shall issue, but upon probable cause, supported by Oath or affirmation, and particularly describing the place to be searched, and the persons or things to be seized.

Although the Fourth Amendment does not specifically state that it protects the **right to privacy**, it has been interpreted to protect this right, which is one of the most significant protections of human freedom and dignity found in the Bill of Rights. The protection of the right to privacy from invasion by government officials is highly valued. It is also important to the right to freedom of conscience, thought, religion, expression, and property. Without the right to privacy, these other valued rights could be violated by government officials. Such a danger is particularly acute today with the advanced surveillance technology and computers available to the government. If people were under constant or periodic observation by government, how free would they be to discuss differing opinions about our political system?

Terms to Know

right to privacy
probable cause
warrant
general warrant
writ of assistance
exclusionary rule

What is the purpose of the Fourth Amendment?

Although the Fourth Amendment originally limited only the powers of the federal government, it has been applied to state and local governments and their agencies by its incorporation into the Fourteenth Amendment. We will begin our examination of the purpose of the Fourth Amendment by looking at the amendment itself. You will see that its intent can be discovered fairly easily by reading it, even though it contains several legal terms and phrases that are not defined and require interpretation.

What is the importance of the right to privacy?

The importance to a free society of the protections against unreasonable searches and seizures was stressed by Justice Robert Jackson soon after he served as a judge at the Nuremberg trials of Nazi war criminals in 1949. He said:

> *Among the deprivations of rights, none is so effective in cowing a population, crushing the spirit of the individual and putting terror in every heart [as] uncontrolled search and seizure. [It] is one of the first and most effective weapons in the arsenal of every arbitrary government.*

The Fourth Amendment prohibits law enforcement officers from searching or seizing people or their property unless there is **probable cause**—a good reason for suspecting a person of breaking a law. The Framers of the Fourth Amendment were not content to allow police officers to decide what constitutes probable cause. They required police officers to present their reasons for a search or seizure to a judge. If the judge agrees there is probable cause to suspect a violation of the law, the law enforcement officer is given a **warrant**—a written document giving permission for a search or seizure.

In some situations law enforcement officers don't have time to get a warrant before searching or arresting a person. The Fourth Amendment has been interpreted to allow searches and arrests without a warrant under certain circumstances that we will discuss later in this lesson.

The Fourth Amendment provides further protections for individuals by limiting the powers of judges to issue warrants. Warrants must specifically describe "the place to be searched and the persons or things to be seized." A judge cannot give law enforcement officers a warrant that enables them to search anything they please. This limitation, like many others, is based on what has been learned from history about the dangers of not placing such limitations on government officials.

In recent times the Fourth Amendment's protections have not been limited to physical intrusions by government upon an individual's person or property. The Fourth Amendment's language does refer only to "persons, houses, papers, and effects," and for many years the Supreme Court gave those words a narrow, literal interpretation. In 1928, for example, the Court held that wiretapping was excluded from the protection of the Fourth Amendment because such eavesdropping involved no physical intrusion upon a person or property (*Olmstead v. United States*).

After many years, however, the Court began to give the Amendment a broader interpretation and extended the Amendment's coverage to wiretapping, "bugging," and other forms of eavesdropping. For example, in 1967, the Supreme Court reversed the conviction of a bookie who had been convicted on the basis of evidence the FBI had acquired by bugging a phone booth from which the bookie regularly made illegal bets. The Court held that before listening to his conversations, the FBI agents should have obtained a warrant authorizing this electronic seizure of evidence (*Katz v. United States*).

What is the history of the Fourth Amendment?

We inherited from British history the saying that "A man's home is his castle." The right to privacy and its importance to a free society have been understood for generations. English common law protected the right to privacy by prohibiting judges from giving law enforcement officials **general warrants** that did not describe in detail the places to be searched and the things or persons to be seized. General warrants have been referred to as open-ended "hunting licenses" authorizing government officials to search people, their businesses, homes, and property indiscriminately.

Despite the common law, royal commissions and Parliament had sometimes authorized the use of general warrants by government officials. At times these searches were directed at violent criminals. But often they were used to harass and persecute individuals who were critical of the government or who dissented from the Church of England.

As early as 1589, in a case involving a general search of Puritans and their property, English lawyers argued that the Magna Carta protected the personal privacy of individuals. Nevertheless, in 1662 Parliament passed a law which permitted general warrants called **writs of assistance**. These writs gave government officials the power to search for goods which had entered the country in violation of custom laws.

What is the importance of the right to be secure in one's home from unreasonable searches and seizures?

Officials did not need to convince a judge that they had reason to suspect an individual of committing a crime or that illegal goods were being hidden in a particular place. Without having to show good reason to suspect that a crime had been committed, unscrupulous government officials found it easy to use the writs of assistance to persecute individuals for their political and religious beliefs, or often, just to seek revenge against someone for personal reasons.

In the eighteenth century, Parliament again passed laws which authorized writs of assistance. These were used by British authorities in the American colonies to enforce the Trade Acts which taxed and limited the colonists' right to trade with other nations. Writs of assistance were generally used to collect taxes and to recover stolen goods, including slaves.

Colonial legislatures tried unsuccessfully to outlaw the writs by requiring warrants specifying who and what was to be searched and why. During the time just before the Revolution, the writs were used more and more frequently against colonists who were critical of British policy. They were also used against those believed to be violating the British restrictions on trade by smuggling tea and other products into Massachusetts and other colonies. The colonists' strong objections to the trade laws and writs of assistance contributed to the American Revolution.

The British were not entirely wrong in suspecting the colonists of smuggling. Some famous Americans violated the trade restrictions. For example, John Hancock's father had made a great deal of money smuggling tea into Boston. A writ of assistance enabled the British to discover that John Hancock himself was smuggling wine. As you can imagine, there was more than one reason why the Founders protested against such general warrants.

After the Revolution, many state declarations of rights outlawed unreasonable searches and seizures. Anti-Federalists later criticized the Constitution for not placing similar limitations on the federal government. A delegate to the Massachusetts ratifying convention said, "There is no provision made in the Constitution to prevent...the most innocent person...[being] taken by virtue of a [general] warrant...and dragged from his home." It was in response to such concerns that the Fourth Amendment was included in the Bill of Rights. Today every state constitution contains a clause similar to the Fourth Amendment.

What controversies are raised in the interpretation and application of the Fourth Amendment?

Three of the most important questions raised by the Fourth Amendment are explained below. We will briefly look at the first two questions. Then we will examine the last question, which has been a constant source of controversy.

1. **When is a warrant not required?** Whenever there is time to do so, law enforcement officers must convince a judge that they have probable cause to justify a search or arrest. In this way, the judge provides a check on the use of power by law enforcement agencies. If the judge accepts the officers' facts and reasoning, he or she will issue a warrant for an arrest, a search, or both.

   However, there are numerous times when law enforcement officers can't wait for a warrant. For example, police may be on the scene of a violent crime or a robbery in progress. If they did not arrest the suspect, the person might injure others or

When should officers be able to arrest people without a warrant?

   escape. Under these emergency circumstances, it is clearly necessary for officers to be able to arrest a person or search property without a warrant. However, after they have gathered the evidence or arrested a person, the officers must convince a judge that they had probable cause to do so and did not have time to obtain a warrant. It is interesting to note that according to a 1980 study conducted in Los Angeles, only 1,000 warrants were issued when about 300,000 searches were actually conducted.

2. **What is probable cause?** What evidence must law enforcement officers have to justify a search or seizure of a person or his property? The criteria used to establish probable cause are difficult to define. Generally, at the moment a law enforcement officer decides to arrest a person, he or she must have reliable knowledge gained from direct contact with the suspect or from a trustworthy source that the suspect either has already committed a crime or was doing so at the time of arrest.

The specific criteria for probable cause are constantly being refined by the courts in the light of experience. This process reveals a commitment to protecting the rights of individuals while at the same time protecting society from those who break the law.

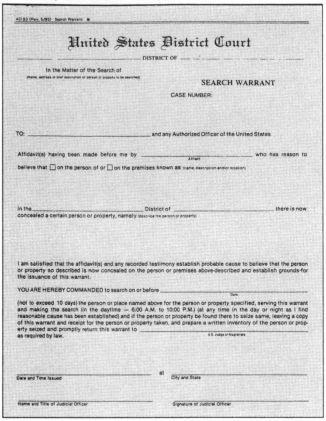

Why are warrants required?

3. **How can the Fourth Amendment be enforced?** What should be done if law enforcement officers break the law and violate individual rights protected by the Fourth Amendment? Suppose officers arbitrarily and unfairly search a person's home or other property or arrest a person without having a good reason for doing so? What can be done to prevent them from violating people's constitutional rights? We will examine this question in the following exercise.

Critical Thinking Exercise
EXAMINING ALTERNATIVE MEANS OF ENFORCING THE FOURTH AMENDMENT

We must give law enforcement officers enough power to protect us from criminals. This means that we must give them the power, in certain situations, to limit our most valuable rights, our rights to our lives, liberty, and property. Let's look at some of the specific powers law enforcement officers have.

Under certain circumstances, law enforcement officers have the power to do the following:

- stop and question us
- use force, if necessary, to restrain us
- search our persons, homes, cars, garbage cans, and other property
- arrest us and place us in jail
- question us while we are being held in jail
- gather evidence to be used in court against us

It is clear these powers must be limited by law to prevent their abuse. The question that arises is how to keep law enforcement officials from violating the law. Below are brief descriptions of several policies that are being used to check the powers of police officers.

Work as an entire class or in small groups to examine each policy and answer the questions that follow. Then be prepared to take and defend a position on which of the policies you would support.

1. **Departmental discipline.** If possible, law enforcement agencies should be required to have a board of officers responsible for investigating claims that an officer has violated a due process right guaranteed by the Constitution and Bill of Rights. The board should conduct a fair hearing and, if it finds the officer guilty, should take appropriate action to prevent that person from breaking the law again. Such action might include, for example, a reprimand, a reduction in rank and pay, dismissal, or submitting the evidence against the person to appropriate authorities for possible criminal prosecution.

2. **Civilian review boards.** Law enforcement agencies should be supervised by a civilian review board appointed by the local government. This board should have the authority to investigate charges against officers accused of breaking the law. It should also have the responsibility to provide the officer a fair hearing. If the board reaches the conclusion that the officer is guilty, it should recommend appropriate action to the law enforcement agency or suggest criminal prosecution.

3. **Civil suits.** Civilians who think their rights have been violated by law enforcement officers should have the right to sue individual officers and the agency for damages in a civil court.

4. **Exclusionary rule.** Any evidence gained by law enforcement officers as a result of breaking the law should not be allowed as evidence in court against the defendant.

What means should be used to discourage officers from violating the law?

Enforcing the Fourth Amendment

Policies such as those you have been discussing are used in numerous places throughout the United States to encourage law enforcement officers to obey the law. Perhaps the most controversial of these policies is the **exclusionary rule.** This rule excludes evidence obtained by law enforcement officers while violating rights protected by the Constitution. The rule

is most often used to exclude evidence gained from illegal searches and seizures. It is also used to exclude evidence obtained in violation of the Fifth Amendment right against self-incrimination and the Sixth Amendment right to counsel, which we will examine in the next lessons.

Even though the term exclusionary rule is a recent one, the idea itself was part of the English common law. Confessions that were obtained by force or torture could not be used in court. The intent of this policy was to prevent law enforcement officers from forcing people to confess by making the results of such action worthless.

The exclusionary rule is not contained in the Constitution and it is not required by the Constitution. It has been created by judges to discourage law enforcement officers from breaking the law. Throughout history, there have been too many examples of officers violating individual rights.

The exclusionary rule has been used since 1914 to limit the powers of federal law enforcement agencies such as the FBI. It was not until 1961 that the Supreme Court ruled that the exclusionary rule must be used in criminal prosecutions at state and local levels (*Mapp v. Ohio*). Since that time there has been continual controversy over its use. Some of the main arguments of those taking opposing positions on this issue are briefly explained below.

1. **Arguments for the exclusionary rule.** Supporters of the exclusionary rule give the following arguments in its defense:

   - **It discourages officials from violating the law.** People argue that the rule is a practical way of discouraging law enforcement officers from violating constitutional rights to gain evidence. If officers know ahead of time that evidence gained illegally cannot be used in court, they are less likely to break the law.

   - **It makes sure that courts obey the law.** If judges were to allow illegally gained evidence in court, they would become accomplices in breaking the law and violating the Constitution.

   - **It rarely results in criminals being set free.** Although there are no comprehensive studies of how many criminals are set free by the exclusionary rule, the number is far lower than most people believe. California has the strictest exclusionary rule in the nation. A study by the National Institute for Justice showed that less than one percent of persons accused of serious crimes in California are not prosecuted because of the rule. Three-fourths of that small percentage were people accused of drug abuse or other drug problems. In the case of the violent crimes of murder, rape, and robbery, only one out of 2,500 persons was set free because of the rule.

Studies in other states show similar results. At the federal level, less than one-half percent of persons accused of serious crimes are released. If the exclusionary rule was abolished, the conviction rate in serious crimes would increase by an even smaller percentage.

- **It makes the point that the government is not above the law.** It provides a means of enforcing rules limiting government power and thus makes it clear that everyone is expected to obey the law. This is the basis for the rule of law—no one is above the law.

2. **Arguments against the exclusionary rule.** Opponents of the exclusionary rule make the following arguments:

- **It is not reasonable to exclude reliable evidence of a crime.** The evidence gained in an illegal search is as reliable as if it had been gained legally. It is unreasonable not to use it to convict guilty persons in order to make police obey the law.

- **There are better ways to make officers obey the law.** In Great Britain, officers are encouraged to obey the law by making them subject to civil or criminal trials when they violate the law. This practice should be used in the United States because it does not require prohibiting the use of illegally obtained evidence in court.

- **The rule encourages police lawlessness.** The rule encourages officers to lie or falsify reports on searches to get around the exclusionary rule.

- **The rule breeds disrespect for the courts.** The public cannot be expected to respect a system that frees criminals just because the evidence against them was gained illegally.

- **Thousands of criminals do go free.** Despite the fact that the percentages are small, so many people are arrested that thousands of guilty people are released each year as a result of the rule.

- **The rule does not protect innocent people.** The worst cases of violations of individual rights are those against innocent people the officers don't intend to arrest in the first place. In such situations the officers may purposely search and seize people illegally and then release them. They may do this to (1) control crimes such as illegal gambling and prostitution, (2) confiscate illegal weapons or stolen property, (3) deter crime, or (4) satisfy public opinion calling for aggressive police action against crime.

Research Exercise

As you probably realize, the use of the exclusionary rule and similar policies raises issues that are constantly being discussed not only in the news media but on television and in motion pictures. You may also expect that the Supreme Court, Congress, and your state government will continue to try to deal with this issue in a way that gives fair protection to the rights of individuals and also serves the interests of society.

You can examine policies used to enforce the Fourth Amendment by seeing how they are treated in the news and by people in your community. If possible, interview citizens, law enforcement officers, judges, and attorneys who specialize in criminal law to learn their perspectives. Then bring what you have learned to class for further discussion.

Using the Lesson

1. What is the purpose of the Fourth Amendment? Whose powers does it limit?

2. What is a warrant, a general warrant, and probable cause? How are these ideas related to the idea of limited government?

3. What are some of the advantages and disadvantages of the exclusionary rule?

4. What are some alternatives to the exclusionary rule used to enforce the Fourth Amendment limitations on law enforcement officers? What are the advantages and disadvantages of each?

5. What effect does the development of modern technology, especially devices that make possible electronic surveillance, have on the Fourth Amendment?

LESSON 25

How Does the Fifth Amendment Protect You Against Self-Incrimination?

Purpose of Lesson

The Fifth Amendment provides several important protections for the rights of individuals. This lesson will focus on the section which protects individuals from being forced to testify against themselves before courts of law, legislative committees, or other government agencies. We will look at the history of the right against self-incrimination and its importance to the Framers. You will have an opportunity to examine and take positions on two cases involving this right. You will also consider common limitations placed upon the right and how they are enforced. Finally, you will look at a current controversy about how the right against self-incrimination should be protected.

After completing the lesson, you should be able to explain the purpose and history of the right against self-incrimination, and take and defend positions on issues it raises.

Terms to Know

right against self-incrimination
perjury
immunity
contempt of court
misdemeanor

What is the purpose of the Fifth Amendment provision against self-incrimination?

No person...shall be compelled in any criminal case to be a witness against himself.

This clause of the Fifth Amendment, which protects against self-incrimination, is probably the most misunderstood and controversial of all the rights in the Constitution and Bill of Rights. Its primary purpose is to protect individuals from being forced by the government to give evidence against themselves. It is intended to prohibit the government from threatening, mistreating, or even torturing people to gain evidence against them or their associates. It reflects the belief that even the worst criminal may not be treated inhumanely, and that to allow official brutality is an affront to human dignity and degrades the entire society.

Refusing to testify by "taking the Fifth" is one of the most familiar provisions of the Bill of Rights. It has become famous through televising the Watergate, Iran-Contra, and other congressional hearings as well as numerous courtroom dramas. It is controversial because many people see the refusal to testify as a way guilty people try to protect themselves. However, the right not to testify against oneself is essential to uphold the principle that a person is presumed innocent until proven guilty beyond a reasonable doubt.

The **right against self-incrimination** is a protection of both the innocent and guilty alike from the potential abuse of government power. Tyrannical governments typically violate this right and force people to confess to crimes in public whether they are guilty or not. During the 1930s in the Soviet Union, critics and opponents of Joseph Stalin's regime were forced to confess in open court and then executed in secret. American prisoners-of-war were forced to confess publicly to "crimes" by their captors in the Korean, Vietnamese, and Persian Gulf Wars.

In addition, the right against self-incrimination further protects the First Amendment rights of freedom of conscience and expression. Throughout history people have been forced to give evidence against themselves as those in power tried to persecute critics of the government and the church. The protection against self-incrimination is also related to the Fourth Amendment right to be secure in one's person and property from illegal searches and seizures. Such searches were commonly used to discover books and writings of a seditious nature to be used as evidence against people.

Why would someone want to refuse to testify at a hearing?

This clause of the Fifth Amendment protects persons accused of crimes. However, it also protects witnesses from being forced to incriminate themselves during civil and criminal trials and in hearings held by the legislative and executive branches of government.

What is the history of the right against self-incrimination?

American ideas about the right against self-incrimination came largely from English common law. The protection against self-incrimination was a major issue in the struggles between the king and Parliament and between the established Anglican church and the Puritans. It was a struggle between the right to freedom of conscience and efforts by the government and church to find and punish political and religious dissenters.

The belief in the protection against self-incrimination developed because of opposition to the use of torture by the government and the established church to force people to confess to crimes. Torture was a practice approved by rulers and the church as far back as Roman times.

People could be forced to appear before the royal High Commission or the Star Chamber to be investigated for crimes. They were asked to take an oath to answer truthfully all questions asked. They would not be told what they were accused of or what evidence there was against them.

What is the importance of the right against self-incrimination?

If a person took the oath, he or she had to answer all questions. For political or religious dissenters to reply truthfully would mean punishment for themselves and their friends whom they were forced to name. To take an oath and then to lie meant to sin against their beliefs and risk being found guilty of **perjury** and punished, often by life imprisonment or death.

Puritans under investigation for their beliefs argued against self-incrimination because of the principle in the Magna Carta that even royal power is limited. This argument was made so many times in later years that people came to believe that the right against self-incrimination was specifically protected by the Magna Carta, even though it was not.

How did protections against self-incrimination develop?

In 1641 Parliament was controlled by Puritans and attorneys trained in the common law. They abolished the High Commission and the Star Chamber. Further, they prohibited church authorities from forcing anyone to "confess or to accuse himself or herself of any crime." However, even after torture was outlawed, the government continued to force people to "bear witness" against themselves.

The right against self-incrimination was first claimed in America in 1637 by John Wheelwright. He was driven out of Massachusetts for his beliefs by the same Puritans who themselves had been persecuted for their beliefs. Almost exactly one hundred years later, Benjamin Franklin criticized a Pennsylvania church for questioning a local minister about the sermons he had written. Franklin said, "It is contrary to the common rights of mankind, no man being obliged to furnish matter of accusation against himself."

In numerous court battles with the king in the years before the Revolution, colonists claimed "a right to silence as the privilege of every Englishman." It was a right included in the Virginia Declaration of Rights and echoed in other state declarations. Delegates to state ratifying conventions later criticized the Constitution for not including this protection.

Although there have been many debates about interpreting this clause since the Bill of Rights was adopted, most scholars agree that the Framers saw it as a ban on torture. Clearly the Framers were not intending to be "soft on criminals" when they included this clause in the Bill of Rights. But they believed that citizens should be able to protect themselves against arbitrary governmental power, particularly in matters of conscience. The prohibition against self-incrimination was one way of doing so.

Contemporary issues about the right against self-incrimination are numerous and frequently reach the Supreme Court. Originally, the right was limited to proceedings during a trial and did not limit the right of law enforcement officers, for example, to question suspects or persons they had arrested. Unfortunately, this allowed the police to force people to confess or give evidence against themselves. One of the most common arguments against forced confessions is that they are unreliable. Almost anyone will confess to anything under enough pressure. If an innocent person confesses, not only does the innocent person suffer injustice, but the guilty person also goes free.

After hearing numerous cases in which the right against self-incrimination had been violated, the Supreme Court ruled that law enforcement officers must give suspects their "Miranda warnings" (*Miranda v. Arizona,* 1966). This is why officers must tell suspects that they may remain silent and that they have the right to have an attorney with them when being questioned. The Court has ruled, however, that the right to remain silent does not mean that officers cannot gather evidence from a suspect, such as blood and hair samples, nor that they cannot take a voluntary statement from the accused.

Should forced confessions be allowed in court?

Critical Thinking Exercise
EXAMINING ISSUES OF SELF-INCRIMINATION

This exercise provides you an opportunity to examine both a historical and a contemporary case involving the right against self-incrimination. Your class should be divided into six groups. Three groups should be assigned to the 1791 case and three to the 1991 case. Students in the first group assigned to each case will play the role of justices. The other two groups assigned for each case will argue for or against the position that the Fifth Amendment prohibition against self-incrimination has been violated. After two-minute oral arguments have been made for each side in each case, the justices should deliberate. Then they should issue their opinions on the question, "Has the self-incrimination clause of the Fifth Amendment been violated?"

Afterward, your entire class should compare the cases and discuss your views using the following questions as a guide:

1. In what ways are the two cases similar or dissimilar?

2. What values and interests are involved in each case?

3. Under what conditions, if any, should the right against self-incrimination be applied and limited? Explain your reasoning.

Commonwealth v. Dillon (1791)

On the 18th of December, Dillon, a twelve-year-old Philadelphia apprentice, was arrested for arson, a crime punishable by death. He was accused of burning several stables containing hay and other goods. According to court records, the boy was visited by his minister, master, and other "respectable citizens." They urged him to confess for the good of his "mortal body and soul." He said he was not guilty.

> *The inspectors of the prison...[then] carried him into the dungeon; they displayed it in all its gloom and horror; they said that he would be confined in it, dark and cold and hungry, unless he made full disclosure [confession]; but if he did...he would be well accommodated with room, fire, and victuals [food], and might expect pity and favour from the court.*

Dillon continued to deny his guilt, even when kept in the dungeon without heat, food, or water. After about forty-eight hours, however, the boy confessed in front of the mayor, his master, and law enforcement officials.

When the case came to trial, Dillon's attorney argued that the charges should be dismissed. He said that the main evidence against Dillon was his confession, which was forced by keeping him in the dungeon, threatening him, and promising him he could expect pity and good treatment by the court. He claimed that such confessions were unreliable and illegal.

The state's attorney, however, argued that the confession was freely made in public. Therefore, it could be used as evidence at his trial. The attorney admitted that the interference of the inspectors at the prison was slightly irregular, but the way in which Dillon was encouraged to confess was not threatening. Therefore, his confession was not forced and should not be excluded at the trial. To do so would be to excuse the fact that he had committed a serious crime. The boy had confessed to a crime which had endangered lives and destroyed the property of others.

The state's attorney said that confessions freely given, as everyone knows, are the best evidence of guilt. The point to be considered was whether Dillon falsely accused himself of a crime. If there was ground even to suspect he had done so, God forbid that he should be executed. But since Dillon had not retracted his statement, he should be found guilty.

What is a forced confession?

Fulminante v. Arizona (1991)

The Arizona police lacked enough evidence to prove that Orestes Fulminante, a convicted child molester, had murdered his eleven-year-old stepdaughter. He was sent to prison on a weapons charge. The murder case, however, remained unsolved. In prison, Fulminante was threatened by several inmates who had heard rumors that he was a child killer. A fellow inmate, with a reputation for mob connections, offered to protect him. But first, the inmate insisted on knowing the details of the murder.

Fearing for his life, Fulminante admitted that he had driven the young girl to the desert. There he abused her, forced her to beg for her life, and then shot her twice in the head.

What Fulminante didn't know was that his fellow inmate was an FBI informer. After being freed on the gun charge, Fulminante was arrested, tried, and convicted of murder. The main evidence against him was his confession to the inmate and a similar confession made to the informant's fiancee at a later date.

Fulminante's attorney appealed the conviction. He argued that the prison confession was forced. Its use to convict Fulminante was a violation of the Fifth Amendment right against self-incrimination. Since the confessions were the only real evidence against Fulminante, he deserved a new trial with a jury that would not hear about the confessions.

The state's attorney argued that even if the first confession was forced, the second was not forced. It was freely made. At most, introducing the confession as evidence should be considered a harmless error, made in good faith by officers and prosecutors in a brutal child sexual assault and murder case.

What are common limitations on the right against self-incrimination?

The right against self-incrimination has generally been interpreted to have some limitations. The following are examples:

1. **A personal right.** Since the right against self-incrimination is intended to protect individuals, it cannot be used to protect organizations such as businesses or trade unions. Nor may someone refuse to testify if the testimony would incriminate a friend or family member. Witnesses, as well as defendants, may refuse to answer questions if their answers might incriminate them personally. Defendants in a criminal case may refuse to take the stand.

2. **Immunity.** Under certain circumstances, a person may be compelled to testify if the court offers **immunity**. For example, if the court states that nothing the person says can be used in a trial against him or her, the person must testify or be charged with **contempt of court**.

How is the right against self-incrimination enforced?

Suppose law enforcement officers break the law and force a suspect to confess to a crime. The evidence that has been gained illegally may not be allowed in court because of the exclusionary rule, the same rule you studied in relation to illegal searches and seizures.

In the past, if a forced confession was used as evidence in a trial and the defendant was found guilty, the verdict would be reversed by an appellate court. In most situations, this would mean that the prosecution would have to try the person again using other evidence.

However, in 1991, the Supreme Court ruled in a 5-4 decision that if a forced confession is used as evidence in court, a guilty verdict will not automatically be reversed. If it is the only evidence used to convict a person, the guilty verdict will be reversed. However, if there was enough other evidence introduced at the trial to convict the person without using the forced confession, the guilty verdict can be upheld (*Fulminante v. Arizona*).

The minority on the Court, however, believed that this ruling radically reduces the protection given individuals by the right against self-incrimination. Once a confession has been introduced in a trial, these justices believe, the effect on jurors is so strong that it may have more of an impact on their decision than any other evidence presented. Law enforcement officials might decide to obtain forced confessions since they can be used in court without automatically resulting in a reversal of a guilty verdict.

What happened to Dillon and Fulminante?

The cases you have examined illustrate how issues involving the right against self-incrimination have been debated for centuries. In 1791, the judge ruled that because arson was a crime punishable by death, benefit of the doubt should be given to twelve-year-old Dillon. The arson charge was dropped and he was retried on a **misdemeanor** charge (a less serious crime). The judge said:

> Though it is the province [of the court] to administer justice, and not to bestow mercy; and though it is better not to err at all...in a doubtful case, error on the side of mercy is safer...than error on the side of rigid justice.

In 1991, the Supreme Court also sent back the Fulminante case for retrial. The majority of justices said that the confession in prison was made under a believable threat of physical violence. Thus it was the product of coercion and was the main evidence against Fulminante. Without the confession, the prosecution probably would not have had enough evidence to get a conviction. Therefore, Fulminante was entitled to a new trial.

The continuing debate over self-incrimination

The debate over the meaning and application of the right against self-incrimination continues. As with other proce- dural rights, we try to balance the need to protect individuals from arbitrary and abusive use of government power while, at the same time, protect society from lawbreakers. In so doing we should always consider the importance of Justice William O. Douglas's statement: "Those who would attach a sinister meaning to the invocation of the Fifth Amendment have forgotten...history. For, from the beginning, the dignity of man cried out against compulsion. If the individual's spirit of liberty is to be kept alive, if government is to be civilized in its relation to the citizen, no form of compulsion should be used to exact evidence from him that might convict him."

Using the Lesson

1. What rights are protected by the Fifth Amendment?

2. What is the purpose of the right against self-incrimination? What historical practices was it intended to prevent?

3. What values and interests are protected by the right against self-incrimination? What values and interests may be endangered by this right?

4. What position would you take on the recent Supreme Court decision that allows forced confessions to be used in court if there is enough other evidence to convict a person? Explain your position.

LESSON 26

How Does the Sixth Amendment Protect Your Right to a Fair Trial?

Purpose of Lesson

This lesson will focus upon the specific rights contained in the Sixth Amendment. This amendment further limits the government when it acts against a person accused of a crime. We will briefly examine all the rights covered by the amendment but will look closely at the right to counsel. Finally, we will examine how Sixth Amendment rights are enforced and look at contemporary issues concerning the right to counsel.

When you have completed this lesson, you should be able to explain the importance of the rights protected by the Sixth Amendment and take and defend positions on contemporary issues raised by the right to counsel.

Terms to Know

adversarial system
inquisitorial system
prosecuting attorney
defense attorney
Gideon v. Wainwright
felony

What limitations does the Sixth Amendment place upon the government?

The Sixth Amendment contains several more of the cluster of procedural rights that constitute due process of law. Almost all the protections of the Sixth Amendment have been incorporated into the Fourteenth Amendment, making them applicable to the states. Let's begin our examination of this amendment by reviewing its provisions:

> *In all criminal prosecutions, the accused shall enjoy the right to a speedy and public trial, by an impartial jury of the State and district wherein the crime shall have been committed; which district shall have been previously ascertained by law, and to be informed of the nature and cause of the accusation; to be confronted with the witnesses against him; to have compulsory process for obtaining witnesses in his favor, and to have the assistance of counsel for his defense.*

You can see that the amendment contains eight clauses or provisions intended to protect the rights of persons accused of crimes to a fair hearing in court. We shall briefly examine each of these provisions before looking at their history and focusing on the right to counsel.

How does the right to a trial by jury provide a check on the power of government?

Critical Thinking Exercise
EXAMINING THE PROCEDURAL RIGHTS OF THE SIXTH AMENDMENT

The following exercise is designed to explore the importance of each of the rights contained in the Sixth Amendment. Your class should be divided into eight groups, each group assigned one of the eight rights. After reading the introduction, read the description of the right assigned to your group. Answer the questions that follow as they apply to your group's right. Be prepared to explain your answers to the class.

Suppose you have been arrested by law enforcement officers for a crime and placed in jail. The following are your rights protected by the Sixth Amendment:

1. **Speedy trial.** The government cannot hold you in jail for a long period of time without bringing you to trial if you demand that the trial be held as soon as possible.

2. **Public trial.** The government cannot try you in secret. Your trial must be open to the public and there must be a public record of the proceedings.

3. **Impartial jury.** The government cannot try you before a jury that is prejudiced against you.

4. **Location of the trial.** The government must try you in the state and district or community where the crime was committed. However, you may have the right to have the trial moved to another place if you can show that the community is prejudiced against you.

5. **Information on charges.** The government cannot arrest you and hold you for trial without telling you why it is doing so. Government lawyers must also present in open court enough evidence to justify holding you for trial. This evidence is important to help you prepare your defense.

6. **Confronting witnesses.** You and your lawyer have the right to confront and cross-examine all witnesses against you. The government cannot present the testimony of secret witnesses against you who do not appear in court.

7. **Favorable witnesses.** The government cannot prevent you from presenting witnesses who might testify in your favor. In fact, if such witnesses do not want to testify and you want them to, the court must force them to appear in court.

8. **Assistance of counsel.** The government cannot prevent you from having a lawyer defend you from the time you have been named as a suspect. If you cannot afford one, the government must provide you one free of charge.

What is the importance of the right to confront and cross-examine witnesses?

Examining Each Right

1. What could happen if you did not have the right?

2. When, if ever, might you want to waive the right?

3. How, if at all, might the right protect you from the majority of the community if it was hostile to you?

4. How might the right help to protect you from the possible abuse of power by government?

5. What values and interests of individuals and society does the right protect?

What is the history of Sixth Amendment rights?

A number of the procedural rights in the Sixth Amendment are found in the Magna Carta and British common law. An early form of the right to trial by jury is even older, dating to ancient European tribal and clan traditions. The right to a speedy and public trial is at least as old as the time of King Henry II who reigned in the twelfth century.

As you have seen in previous units, a number of these rights were protected under the British constitution and such documents as the Petition of Right. Nevertheless, American colonists had often been denied these rights. This was particularly true in the years just before the Revolution when the British took severe measures to suppress rebellion in the colonies. For example, the British denied accused colonists the right to a speedy trial in their communities and took them to England for trial. Jefferson's list of British abuses in the Declaration of Independence contains a number of claimed violations of such procedural rights.

Considering Americans' experiences with British rule, it is not surprising that they included procedural protections in their state declarations of rights. As you have learned, they also included a number of procedural rights in the Constitution.

Anti-Federalists, however, demanded that a more specific list of procedural rights be added in a bill of rights. Since 1791, court rulings and rules of criminal procedure passed by Congress and state legislatures have clarified these rights and extended them to persons and situations they did not apply to in the past. Almost all the due process rights contained in the Constitution and Bill of Rights must now be respected by federal, state, and local governments.

What is the importance of the right to counsel?

In all criminal prosecutions, the accused shall enjoy the right...to have the assistance of counsel for his defense.

The American criminal justice system is an **adversarial system** as opposed to the **inquisitorial system** used in some other countries. In an adversarial system there are two sides that present their positions before an impartial third party—a jury, a judge, or both. The **prosecuting attorney** presents the side of the government; the **defense attorney** presents the side of the defendant. This system assumes that by having each side present and argue its position, the truth is more likely to be discovered and a just decision made. The adversarial system differs from an inquisitorial system in which judges have the primary responsibility to gather evidence and conduct investigations in order to make a decision.

The complexity of our adversarial system, with its rules of procedure and rights of the accused, requires the use of lawyers to represent defendants. Even well-educated people, and many lawyers who do not specialize in criminal law, are not competent to conduct an adequate defense in today's courts. As Justice George Sutherland wrote, a non-lawyer "lacks both the skill and knowledge to adequately prepare his defense, even though he may have a perfect one. He requires the guiding hand of counsel at every step in the proceedings against him."

Justice Sutherland's statement illustrates the importance of the right to counsel to guarantee the protection of all the other procedural rights in the Constitution and Bill of Rights. Suspects ignorant of their rights are protected by an attorney who knows their rights and how to protect them. Government officials are less likely to abuse their powers in front of an attorney who knows the limitations on these powers and what to do if these limitations are violated.

For such reasons, the right of a defendant in a criminal case to the assistance of a lawyer is essential to protect the individual's right to a fair hearing and fair treatment. The right to counsel also helps insure that the procedures used by government are in accord with the basic principles of the rule of law.

What is the history of the right to counsel?

Although the right to counsel dates back over five hundred years, its meaning has changed over time. For example, in the 1500s, the procedures used in felony trials were biased in favor of the Crown and defendants did not have the right to counsel. Only in misdemeanor trials was the accused allowed to have an attorney. It was not until the end of the seventeenth century that people accused of treason had the right to an attorney. Finally, in the nineteenth century, Parliament approved the right to counsel in felony cases.

In America by 1776, the right to counsel was extended far beyond what it was at that time in Britain. Many state declarations included the right to counsel, and it was also included in the Bill of Rights in 1791. For more than one hundred years, this meant you had the right to have a lawyer if you could afford to pay for one. However, in a few states, such as Pennsylvania, the law required that the poor be given attorneys at public expense.

In the twentieth century, the Supreme Court and Congress extended the right to counsel to people to whom it had not been provided in the past. In the case of *Gideon v. Wainwright* (1963), the Court extended the right to free counsel to the poor in all **felony** cases (those involving major crimes). This right is now interpreted to guarantee (1) that every person accused of a felony may have a lawyer and (2) that those too poor to afford to hire a lawyer will have one appointed by the court. The right has also been extended by decisions in such cases as *Miranda v. Arizona* (1966) to apply not only to criminal trials, but to other critical stages in the criminal justice process such as during police questioning of suspects.

Critical Thinking Exercise
EXAMINING CURRENT CONTROVERSIES OVER THE RIGHT TO COUNSEL

A number of issues are currently raised regarding the right to counsel. Two of the most frequently mentioned are discussed below. Read about these issues and develop positions on the questions they raise.

1. **The right to effective counsel.** Wealthy people can afford to hire lawyers of their choice; usually the poor must accept the lawyers assigned to them. Lawyers serving the poor may be excellent, but often they are overworked and do not have sufficient time or the resources to prepare the best defense possible.

    Question: How can the government provide effective counsel to represent the poor? If a poor person is represented ineffectively by a lawyer and found guilty, should this be the basis for a retrial? Explain your position.

2. **Limiting the right to counsel for poor defendants.** The law requires that poor defendants be provided counsel at public expense. Counsel may be attorneys from the community selected by judges to defend the poor. They may also be volunteers or public defenders employed by the government. Sometimes poor defendants appeal their cases numerous times, costing the taxpayers millions of dollars each year.

    Question: Should some limit be placed on how many times or under what circumstances poor people should be provided this assistance? Explain your position.

What are the current guidelines for the right to counsel?

In 1991, the Supreme Court set a new limit on the right of poor defendants to have court-appointed lawyers assist them. The Court ruled that it will no longer routinely accept all appeals filed by those who are too poor to pay for an attorney. Instead, the Court will now reject without consideration "frivolous or malicious" requests for government-paid appeals (*In re John Demos, Jr.*).

The Court has not set very high standards for what constitutes effective representation. In one case, for example, the Court decided a defendant had been fairly represented even though he had only spent a few minutes before trial with his court-appointed lawyer.

The major reason for setting greater limits on the right to counsel is to help eliminate court backlog and reduce costs. However, some fear that these limitations seriously threaten the nation's commitment to justice for all, regardless of wealth or status.

How are the rights in the Sixth Amendment enforced?

Suppose you are tried in a criminal court, found guilty, and imprisoned. You believe that one or more of your Sixth Amendment rights have been violated by the government during your trial. For example, suppose you believe that the jury was prejudiced against you or that the judge conducted the trial unfairly.

The right to appeal your case to a higher court is available to you if any of your procedural rights, guaranteed by the Constitution, may have been violated by a lower court. Each state has a system of appellate courts, and, of course, so does the federal government, with the Supreme Court being the highest court of appeals in the nation. If, after reviewing the trial by a lower court, an appellate court decides the trial has been unfair, it can overturn the lower court's verdict. If that happens, the prosecution can usually choose whether or not to try the case again.

The protection of the innocent versus conviction of the guilty

It is better that ten guilty persons escape than one innocent person suffer.
Sir William Blackstone, 1723-1780

The quotation by the British jurist William Blackstone explains why the rights to criminal due process are pur-

What issues are raised by the right to counsel?

posely designed to make it difficult for the government to convict a person. In the unequal battle between an individual accused of a crime and a powerful government with all the resources to prepare and carry out a prosecution, there is a need to balance the process in favor of the individual. The goal is to help insure that innocent persons are not convicted.

The Founders placed particular importance on procedural due process because they knew that throughout history governments and powerful majorities had violated procedural rights in order to persecute those with whom they disagreed. To allow government to have such powers is to endanger all members of society, not just those guilty of serious crimes.

Critical Thinking Exercise
TAKING AND DEFENDING A POSITION ON THE RIGHT TO COUNSEL

Taking into account the historical background of the rights you have studied, and the need to protect all members of society, answer the following questions.

Examining the Issues

1. Which of the rights in the Fourth, Fifth, and Sixth Amendments appear to favor defendants and make it difficult for government to convict persons of crimes? Explain your answer.

2. What problems might arise from balancing the process in favor of defendants? How should those problems be dealt with? Explain your position.

3. Do you agree with the idea contained in Blackstone's quotation, "It is better that ten guilty persons escape than one innocent person suffer"? Explain your position.

Using the Lesson

1. What are the purposes of the protections of the Sixth Amendment?

2. What are two contemporary issues regarding the right to counsel? What positions would you take on each issue? Explain your position.

3. Why is it argued that individuals need so many procedural protections against the power of the government? Do you agree with the argument? Why or why not?

LESSON 27

How Does the Eighth Amendment Protect You from Excessive Bail and Cruel and Unusual Punishments?

Purpose of Lesson

The Eighth Amendment contains the last group of the procedural rights that are protected by the Bill of Rights. These rights protect people who have been arrested and are being held for trial and persons convicted of crimes from receiving unfair treatment. We will examine the history and purposes of these rights and look at contemporary issues regarding their implementation. Finally, we will examine the continuing controversy over whether the death penalty should be prohibited under the Eighth Amendment.

When you have completed this lesson, you should be able to explain the purposes of the protections included in the Eighth Amendment, their history, and contemporary issues regarding the death penalty. Finally, you should be able to take and defend a position on the use of the death penalty.

Terms to Know

cruel and unusual punishment
bail
capital punishment
retribution
jury nullification
unguided discretion
guided discretion

What limitations does the Eighth Amendment place upon government?

The Eighth Amendment provides the following protections for people accused of crimes and awaiting trial, and people found guilty of crimes:

Excessive bail shall not be required, nor excessive fines imposed, nor cruel and unusual punishments inflicted.

These protections, incorporated by the Fourteenth Amendment, limit the powers of the judicial and legislative branches of federal and state governments in the following ways:

- **Limitations on the judiciary.** Judges usually have the power to decide whether a person arrested for a crime should be held in jail or set free on bail while awaiting trial. They also have the right to decide how much bail should be required. This amendment says that judges cannot require excessive bail.

- **Limitations on the legislature.** Congress and state legislatures establish the range of punishments for breaking laws. This amendment says legislatures cannot pass laws that require excessive fines or the infliction of **cruel and unusual punishments**. The power of judges and juries to decide punishments is limited by the laws passed by the legislatures which, in turn, are limited by the Eighth Amendment.

What are the purposes of the Eighth Amendment rights?

1. **The right to be free on bail pending trial.** Although persons accused of crimes have the right to a speedy trial after they have been arrested, there are inevitable delays while both they and the government prepare for trial. Since a person is presumed innocent until proven guilty in our society, one might argue that suspects should go free until the time of their trial. However, although some suspects can be trusted to appear in court when they are supposed to, others cannot. Some suspects may be dangerous, and it is reasonable to think that those accused of crimes for which there are severe penalties might not appear.

The government's main responsibility in this regard is to make sure suspects appear in court to be tried. This may be accomplished by (1) keeping suspects in jail while awaiting trial or (2) by having them place enough money or property (in the form of **bail**) in the hands of the government to insure that they appear in court rather than forfeit it.

The right to bail allows suspects to be free while preparing their defense which is often difficult to do from jail. It also avoids their being punished by being held in jail before they are found guilty or innocent.

This is particularly important for innocent persons who would otherwise suffer unfair punishment while awaiting trial. The sentencing of persons found guilty takes into account how much time they have spent in jail awaiting a trial.

Problems arising from the implementation of the right to bail include the following:

- **Unfair treatment of the poor.** Wealthy people can afford bail; the poor often cannot. Therefore, the poor are more likely to remain in jail awaiting trial, lose income, and not be able to do as much to prepare their defense.

- **Punishment of innocent poor.** Poor people who are innocent and cannot afford bail are kept in jail and then released after their trial. This means that innocent people are punished by imprisonment and rarely compensated for the time they have lost or the wrongs done to them.

- **Increased chances of conviction and more severe sentences.** Studies have shown that the mere fact that a person has been held in jail prior to trial seems to have a negative influence on judges and juries. It results in a greater possibility of convicting such people of crimes and giving them more severe sentences.

What is the importance of the right to bail?

One remedy to the inequitable aspects of the bail system is to release defendants without bail on their own recognizance, that is, on their promise to return to court for trial. This procedure is being used more and more when defendants have families or other ties to the community which would make it unlikely they would flee. It is used when a suspect's release would not seem to present a danger to the community.

2. **The right to be free from excessive fines.** The purpose of this provision is to require courts to levy fines that are fair and reasonable in relation to whatever crime has been committed. There has never been a Supreme Court case on this issue. However, if a fine was extremely high in proportion to the seriousness of the crime, a person could claim the excessive fine violates his or her rights under the Eighth Amendment.

3. **The right to be free from cruel and unusual punishment.** This right is based on the belief that the law should treat even the most horrible criminal with dignity. Barbarous treatment of criminals degrades the entire system of justice and society itself. Punishments should not violate society's standards of decency.

The question raised by this right is to determine what is meant by the terms "cruel" and "unusual." We will examine this question after looking at the history of the right.

What is the history of the right to be free from cruel and unusual punishments?

One of the earliest prohibitions against cruel and unusual punishments is found in an act of Parliament passed in 1553. The act was based on the idea people should be encouraged to obey the law through a respect for government rather than from fear of severe punishments. The English Bill of Rights also prohibited cruel and unusual punishments as did many of the state declarations of rights adopted at the time of the American Revolution.

The prohibition of cruel and unusual punishments in the English Bill of Rights was a reaction to the cruel treatment of prisoners by the Star Chamber and the inhumane sentences they received. However, even after this act, torture, mutilation, and public humiliation of prisoners was common. According to the standards of the time, these punishments were seen as appropriate for the crime.

By today's standards, the punishments are almost unimaginable. People's arms and legs were tied to oxen which then drew apart until they were torn into four pieces, that is, "drawn and quartered." People were disemboweled, burned, or strangled. Some were mutilated or dismembered by having their hands or ears cut off, their noses slit, or by being branded. Public humiliation included public whipping, the stocks, or the dunking stool.

Such punishments were also common in the American colonies. Highway robbers were branded, imprisoned, and publicly whipped. During the debates over the ratification of the Bill of Rights, one member of Congress stated that "it is sometimes necessary to hang a man, villains often deserve whipping and perhaps having their ears cut off; but are we to be prevented from inflicting punishments because they are cruel?" He then argued that such punishments were necessary to deter crime.

What is cruel and unusual punishment?

Despite this attitude among some of the Founders, the prohibition against cruel and unusual punishment was included in the Bill of Rights. This was due to the strong support from people such as Patrick Henry, who argued at the Virginia ratifying convention that the Constitution should include language similar to that in the Virginia Declaration of Rights: "excessive bail ought not to be required, no excessive fines imposed, nor cruel and unusual punishments inflicted." Henry called for a similar provision in the Constitution to limit the powers of Congress.

Henry lost his battle to include these prohibitions in the body of the Constitution. However, three years later, the provisions from the Virginia Declaration of Rights, drafted by George Mason and borrowed by James Madison, became the Eighth Amendment to the United States Constitution.

What the Framers meant by "cruel and unusual punishments" is not at all clear. Part of the problem is that many punishments the Framers would have approved, we may consider cruel or unusual. Many punishments we might approve today may be considered cruel and unusual in the future. What is considered cruel and unusual has changed gradually over the years. Court decisions and laws passed by legislatures have reflected these changes.

Critical Thinking Exercise
EXAMINING EARLY POSITIONS ON PUNISHMENT

One of the writers who most influenced Americans' views on law and punishment was the French philosopher Montesquieu. Below is a quotation from his writings followed by an excerpt from a letter by Thomas Jefferson. Read them and answer the questions that follow.

Experience shows that in countries remarkable for the leniency of their laws the spirit of the inhabitants is as much affected by slight penalties as in other countries by severer punishments....Mankind must not be governed with too much severity...if we inquire into the cause of all human corruptions, we shall find that they proceed from the impunity [exemption from punishment] *of criminals, and not from the moderation of punishments....It is* [also] *an essential point, that there should be a certain proportion in punishments....It is a great abuse amongst us to condemn to the same punishment a person that only robs on the highway and another who robs and murders.*

Baron de Montesquieu (1689-1755)

Baron de Montesquieu, "Of the Power of Punishments," *The Spirit of the Laws,* 1748

The fantastical idea of virtue and the public good being sufficient security to the state against the commission of crimes, which you say you have heard insisted on by some, I assure you was never mine. It is only the sanguinary [bloodthirsty] *hue of our penal laws which I meant to object to. Punishments I know are necessary, and I would provide them, strict and inflexible, but proportioned to the crime....Let mercy be the character of the law-giver, but let the judge be a mere machine. The mercies of the law will be dispensed equally and impartially to every description of men.*

Thomas Jefferson to Edmund Pendleton, August 26, 1776

Examining the Positions

1. What position does Montesquieu take on the effects of lenient and severe punishments?

2. What does Montesquieu say is a major cause of crime?

3. In what ways do Montesquieu and Jefferson appear to be in agreement?

4. What idea is contained in Jefferson's statement that is not in Montesquieu's?

5. **What do *you* think?** Do you agree or disagree with the positions stated by Montesquieu and Jefferson? Explain your position.

What is the history of capital punishment in the United States?

The most controversial issue involving the prohibition on cruel and unusual punishment is the issue of **capital punishment**, that is, the death penalty. The main argument for the use of the death penalty is that it deters crime. It is also seen as a means of **retribution**, of punishing a person for committing a terrible crime such as murder. This idea may be seen in the Old Testament notion of requiring "an eye for an eye, a tooth for a tooth." For such reasons the death penalty has been used for thousands of years.

The Constitution's language clearly appears to accept the legitimacy of the death penalty. For example, both the Fifth and Fourteenth Amendments forbid the government of depriving a person of life without due process of law. These clauses at least suggest that if due process is provided, people who have been convicted of serious crimes may be deprived of their lives by the government. Similarly, the provisions of the Fifth Amendment granting the right to a grand jury in capital cases and forbidding double jeopardy "of life and limb" appear to sanction capital punishment at least under certain circumstances. Finally, the protection against cruel and unusual punishments in the Eighth Amendment has not been interpreted by a majority of the Supreme Court to prohibit the death penalty. In recent years, however, dissenting justices and some scholars claim that because of evolving standards of decency it should be so interpreted.

The death penalty has been used in the United States from early colonial times to the present. For most of that time the states were left free to develop their own standards for the use of the death penalty. During this period, execution was, in many states, the automatic penalty for anyone convicted of murder or several other serious felonies (major crimes). This meant that if a judge or jury believed a person guilty of such a crime, they had no legal power to save the person from death. Gradually, states developed laws that classified different degrees of murder. There was a difference between a person who killed another in a fit of vengeful passion and one who committed a premeditated murder. A prosecutor had to convict a person of the most serious kind of murder, murder in the first degree, in order to obtain a death penalty. Again, in those states that did not allow a judge or jury to grant leniency, once convicted, the penalty was automatic and no jury could modify it.

Eventually, in the latter part of the nineteenth century, state legislatures began to reject the practice of using automatic death penalties. Some argued that such laws were too harsh and did not give judges or juries the discretion to show mercy to those who deserved it. Others argued that the laws resulted in juries being too lenient; juries that believed a person was guilty but did not deserve the death penalty would refuse to find the person guilty. When a jury refuses to apply a law, the process is called **jury nullification**. When juries chose to do this, murderers could go free. In some cases jury nullification could be supported as achieving just results. In other cases, the process resulted in great injustices. For example, in the South, all-white juries often refused to convict white murderers of black people.

By the early twentieth century, most states had developed new laws that gave juries the discretion to decide between life and death when they found a person guilty of a capital crime. However, they were given no legal standards to use in making such decisions. Further, juries rarely had any information on a defendant's background, character, or previous criminal record. Decisions made by such juries could not be changed. The **unguided discretion** policy was common throughout the states until 1972.

Should the death penalty be considered cruel and unusual punishment?

What is the basis for opposition to the death penalty?

Executions of murderers and rapists were common in the United States up to the 1960s when moral and political opposition developed because of a number of factors:

- Studies did not confirm the belief that capital punishment deterred crime.

- Information on how the death penalty was decided upon revealed that juries often acted randomly and capriciously in deciding who should be executed and who should not. People convicted of similar crimes were treated differently with some being executed and others given lesser sentences.

- Studies showed that the race of the defendant and the victim appeared to be the most important factors in whether a jury inflicted the death penalty. Blacks were sentenced to death more often than whites. People who committed crimes against whites were executed far more often than those who committed crimes against blacks.

- Also, some argued that the expense of execution, after all the appeals that are allowed for a convicted person, cost society much more money than placing that person in prison for life.

What issues are involved in allowing capital punishment?

Studies revealing such unfairness in the imposition of the death penalty led to widespread debate and increasing opposition to its use. The courts and legislatures faced growing pressure to develop clear, reasonable, and fair standards to be used by juries in making their decisions.

In the case of *McGautha v. California* (1971), Judge John Marshall Harlan warned that because of the moral complexity and subjectivity of the issue of capital punishment, it was impossible to develop and implement rational, formal legal standards to use in imposing the penalty. He said:

> *To identify before the fact those characteristics of criminal homicides and their perpetrators which call for the death penalty and to express these characteristics in language which can be fairly understood and applied by the sentencing authority, appear to be tasks which are beyond present human ability.*

Despite this warning, since 1972 the Supreme Court and legislatures have been attempting to develop such standards. This process resulted from a decision made by the Court in the case of *Furman v. Georgia* (1972). A five-to-four majority struck down a statute giving juries absolute discretion in the imposition of the death penalty.

The *Furman* decision did not result in the prohibition of the death penalty. Only two justices wrote opinions arguing that the death penalty violated the prohibition against cruel and unusual punishments. The majority, however, argued that while the death penalty is constituional, state laws permitting unguided discretion were unconstitutional. The result was that states wishing to impose the death penalty had to develop more fair and rational standards for doing so.

The result of this decision was that all executions in the United States were suspended. State legislatures were faced with the task of developing new laws containing rational standards which would avoid the discriminatory imposition of the penalty characteristic of the past.

Some states attempted to solve the problem by going back to the practice of automatic death penalties for certain serious crimes. Others developed new **guided discretion** laws. These laws called for juries or judges to decide whether to impose life or death sentences at a hearing held for this purpose after the trial in which a person was found guilty. The problem remained, however, to determine what information should be considered and what standards should be used in deciding whether to grant the death penalty.

In 1976, the Supreme Court heard five cases on the new state laws. It upheld the new practice of guided discretion and declared the automatic sentencing laws unconstitutional. Thus, the Court upheld the constitutionality of the death penalty once again. However, no clear standards were set to implement the policy of guided discretion. As a result, the courts have been flooded with appeals of death penalty sentences claiming unfair standards have been used in the imposition of the penalty.

Recent studies have found that, despite the efforts of state legislatures and the courts to develop fair and reasonable standards, the system may still result in inconsistent and racially biased sentences. Murderers of whites are far more likely to be sentenced to death than murderers of blacks. Such studies have given new impetus to the question of the constitutionality of the death penalty. The courts continue to struggle with the problem.

It is important to note that whether or not the Supreme Court says the Constitution prohibits the death penalty is an altogether different issue from the question of whether or not society ought to execute individuals who have committed certain kinds of crimes. Even if the death penalty is constitutional, legislatures are free to abolish it. It is quite possible to argue that while the Constitution does not prevent the government from imposing the death penalty, the government should not do so. Chief Justice Warren Burger has said, for example, that if he were a legislator, he would vote against the death penalty, but as a member of the Court he believes the death penalty is allowed under the Constitution.

Procedural justice and government

The requirement that the government use fair procedures in dealing with individuals applies to all branches and levels of government, not just to our system of criminal justice. Procedural justice refers to the means used by government agencies to gather information and to make decisions. Gathering information is a responsibility of law enforcement officers investigating crimes, of environmental protection agencies looking into causes of pollution and possible remedies, and congressional committees holding hearings to determine how best to assist in improving public education. Making decisions is not only the responsibility of the courts, but also of legislative and executive agencies.

The right to procedural due process requires government to use fair means to achieve its goals. The hearings held by government agencies must be impartial. People must be allowed to present their positions, often with the assistance of counsel and witnesses supporting them. Privacy must be respected and people treated with dignity. Above all, the actions of government must be limited by the rule of law.

Using the Lesson

1. What position would you take on the constitutionality of the death penalty? Explain your position.

2. Even if the death penalty is constitutional, do you think it should be used? Explain your position.

3. What values would you use in your arguments for or against the death penalty in the war on drugs?

4. What branches or agencies of government are limited by the Eighth Amendment?

5. What are the purposes of the right to bail? What problems have arisen about this right? What solutions would you propose?

6. What are some early positions on the prohibition against cruel and unusual punishments?

7. What is the history of the death penalty in the United States? How has the Supreme Court dealt with this issue?

8. What are some contemporary problems regarding the use of the death penalty? What solutions have been proposed?

Unit Six: Who Should Be Responsible for Preserving and Extending Our Heritage of Individual Rights?

What responsibility should you take to protect individual rights?

Purpose of Unit

The rights we have today are the heritage of over two hundred years of our nation's history. The expansion of the meaning of these rights and their extension to those deprived of them in the past has been a result of efforts by Americans of both sexes and all races, ethnic backgrounds, and beliefs. Over the past two hundred years, the gap has been narrowed between the ideals of liberty and justice for all and the reality of unfair discrimination and injustice.

In this final unit, we will examine the unenumerated rights referred to in the Ninth Amendment, but not listed in the Bill of Rights or the Constitution itself. We will look at the role of

the Supreme Court in identifying and establishing these rights and the controversies that have resulted. We will also deal with the role played by Congress and the executive branch in establishing and protecting individual rights.

We will examine the Universal Declaration of Human Rights and compare the rights it contains with those in our own basic documents. Finally, we will examine the ideas of prominent leaders of the past concerning the role of citizens in promoting a free society, dedicated both to the rights of the individual and the common welfare.

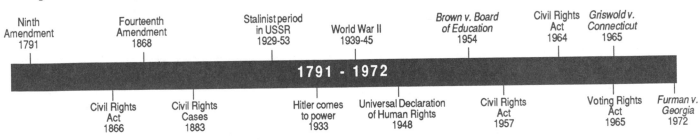

Ninth Amendment 1791 — Fourteenth Amendment 1868 — Stalinist period in USSR 1929-53 — World War II 1939-45 — Brown v. Board of Education 1954 — Civil Rights Act 1964 — Griswold v. Connecticut 1965

1791 - 1972

Civil Rights Act 1866 — Civil Rights Cases 1883 — Hitler comes to power 1933 — Universal Declaration of Human Rights 1948 — Civil Rights Act 1957 — Voting Rights Act 1965 — Furman v. Georgia 1972

LESSON 28

How Have Unenumerated Rights Been Identified and Protected by the Supreme Court?

Purpose of Lesson

In this lesson we will examine the question of unenumerated rights and how they are identified and protected. We will look at the history of the Ninth and Tenth Amendments. We will then focus on issues raised by the power of the Court to identify and define rights not specifically listed in the Constitution and Bill of Rights.

When you have completed this lesson, you should be able to describe the history of the Ninth and Tenth Amendments and discuss problems raised by the idea of unenumerated rights and how they are identified.

Terms to Know

penumbra
emanations

What is the history of the Ninth Amendment?

You have learned that the Framers of the Constitution did not include a bill of rights because they believed it was not only unnecessary but could be dangerous. Alexander Hamilton argued that the Constitution did not give the federal government the power to interfere with rights such as freedom of religion and speech. Thus there was no reason to limit powers it did not have. If a bill of rights were developed, it could not possibly enumerate (list) all the rights of the people. Leaving some rights unenumerated (unlisted) would appear to imply that they did not exist and, therefore, that government might have the power to interfere with them. It could also be interpreted to mean such rights were not important.

As you know, the Anti-Federalists did not accept these arguments and insisted on a bill of rights. The Federalists promised to add one after the adoption of the Constitution. To fulfill this promise, Madison drafted the Bill of Rights. It is likely that the Ninth Amendment was a direct response to the fears raised by Hamilton and others that to list only certain rights might be interpreted to mean that any unlisted rights did not exist or were not important. Thus Madison drafted the following amendment:

The enumeration in the Constitution of certain rights shall not be construed to deny or disparage others retained by the people.

This amendment assures people that they have all the rights that a free society takes for granted, not just the rights listed in the Constitution and Bill of Rights. Beyond this general purpose, however, it is unclear what particular rights the Framers meant to protect.

Some justices and scholars believe Madison and others meant the amendment to be a broad protection of individual rights from both federal and state governments. At the other extreme, Justice Hugo Black said it meant nothing more than that the powers of the federal government were limited, and that the amendment did not apply to the states.

For over 150 years the Ninth Amendment was not the basis of any argument presented to the Supreme Court. This is hardly surprising since the Bill of Rights did not play an important role until relatively recently. In recent years, however, there has been an increased interest in the Ninth Amendment. It has occasionally been referred to in opinions written by the Supreme Court to justify the claim that an unlisted right is included among those protected from government interference. However, the Ninth Amendment still has not been used as a primary justification for protecting any right not specifically listed in the Constitution.

Why was the Tenth Amendment included in the Bill of Rights?

The powers not delegated to the United States by the Constitution, nor prohibited by it to the States, are reserved to the States respectively, or to the people.

One of the major fears of the Anti-Federalists was that the Constitution would create a federal government that would overwhelm, and perhaps even destroy, the state governments. The Tenth Amendment is a response to those fears. In addition, of course, it repeats the basic doctrine that all government power comes from "We the People." Consequently, the Tenth Amendment is not simply a means of protecting the power of the states from the federal government. It is also a means of emphasizing the limitations on the federal government that are spelled out in the first eight amendments.

What problems
arise from using
the idea of
natural rights?

What problems arise from using the idea of natural rights to identify and justify unenumerated rights?

Some people argue that the Ninth Amendment should be interpreted to provide a constitutional guarantee of natural rights. As you remember, eighteenth-century Americans believed that we can determine what these rights are by asking ourselves, "What are the things that all people need and seek, no matter what they believe, no matter when and how they live?" Americans have generally believed that natural rights include the right to life, liberty, and property. It is our right to liberty, for example, that provides the foundation for our claim to liberty of conscience, for if liberty means anything, it must mean the right to believe what we wish.

According to this philosophy, then, individuals have certain natural rights that do not depend on government. Some of them are mentioned in the Constitution, but that is not why we have them. They are mentioned in the Constitution because they are natural. Reason and religion tell us human beings should have these rights. They are the rights, Thomas Jefferson said, to which we are entitled by "the Laws of Nature and of Nature's God." And just because certain rights are not specifically mentioned in the Constitution does not mean we do not possess them.

An example will help make this clear. In the mid-nineteenth century the Supreme Court used a natural rights argument to protect a right not specifically listed in the Constitution or Bill of Rights—the right to travel (*Crandall v. Nevada*, 1868). The Court claimed that a law made by the state of Nevada which restricted travel between states violated a "right that is in its nature independent of the will of the state." Note that the Court did not argue that the Nevada law violated the Ninth Amendment even though this right is not enumerated in the Constitution or Bill of Rights. Instead the Court relied on the older

argument of the natural rights philosophy. Thus, the Ninth Amendment continued to be overlooked as a source of protection for unenumerated rights.

The problem with using the idea of natural law as a source of unlisted rights is that people disagree about what natural rights are. Defenders of slavery, for example, claimed that they had a natural right to own slaves. Abolitionists claimed slavery violated the unalienable right to liberty that Jefferson proclaimed in the Declaration of Independence.

What problems arise from using the idea of substantive due process to identify and justify unenumerated rights?

After the ratification of the Fourteenth Amendment the Supreme Court used the idea of substantive due process to protect rights not listed in the Constitution. As you remember, substantive due process defined situations or areas in which the government could not interfere. At first this interpretation was used to protect the freedom of individuals, business, and industry to use their property as they wished. This included the right to enter into contracts and operate business and industry without interference from government. This interpretation of due process had earlier been used to justify the right of individuals to own slaves.

Later the Court switched its emphasis from using substantive due process to protect property rights, to the protection of individual liberty. This interpretation focused on the right to marry, to establish a home and raise children, and to work in any occupation one chooses. Then, in the 1960s, the Court began to use the due process clause energetically to justify unenumerated rights not supported before, such as the right to privacy.

Critics argue that the idea of substantive due process is so subjective that the Court can use it one day to include certain rights and the next day to deny them. To support this charge, critics point to the Court's changing views on the use of substantive due process—first to support property rights, then liberty rights. Such subjectivity appears to violate the very idea that the powers of the Court are limited.

Before 1965, the Ninth Amendment had not been used to justify unenumerated rights. This may have been because to do so would have been just as subjective as using the idea of substantive due process. As a result, we have been left with many unanswered questions such as those raised in the following exercise.

Critical Thinking Exercise
EXAMINING ISSUES RAISED BY THE CONCEPT OF UNENUMERATED RIGHTS

Unenumerated rights are just that—rights that are not listed. Yet the Framers wanted to be sure that rights Americans took for granted, other than those listed in the Constitution and Bill of Rights, would be protected. This raises the following questions:

1. What rights do you take for granted that are not listed in the Constitution or Bill of Rights? You may wish to consider rights related to the way you live your life, what freedoms you should have, and how you will make your living and use your property. List and be prepared to explain those rights.

---

2. What are the advantages and disadvantages of each of the following means of protecting the rights you have identified? Should they be protected by

   ■ the Ninth Amendment as unenumerated rights?

   ■ substantive due process?

   ■ laws passed by state legislatures or Congress?

   ■ education promoting an understanding of the purposes of the rights and their importance?

   ■ custom and mutual consent of the people?

   ■ other means not listed above?

3. What are the advantages and disadvantages of giving the Supreme Court the power to identify and establish rights not enumerated in the Constitution?

4. Should legislatures pass laws to define unenumerated rights in order to avoid confusion over the ambiguity of the Ninth Amendment? Explain your answer.

5. If state legislatures pass laws defining unenumerated rights, should the Supreme Court have the power to declare such laws unconstitutional if the Court believes they violate the Constitution? Explain your answer.

6. What would be the advantages and disadvantages of using the process of constitutional amendments to clarify unenumerated rights?

Who should have the power to identify unenumerated rights?

Who should have the power to identify unenumerated rights?

Who should decide what is an unenumerated right protected by the Constitution? There are great differences of opinion on how this question should be answered. At issue is a basic principle of constitutional government which requires that the powers of all agencies of government be limited by law.

The Supreme Court has the power, among other things, to decide whether a legislative act or an order of the executive branch violates a right protected by the Constitution. This task is difficult enough with issues involving rights explicitly listed in the Constitution such as the rights to due process, freedom of speech, and the prohibition against the establishment of religion. The task becomes even more difficult when the issue involves rights not specifically listed in the Constitution. What standard, if any, can the Court use to avoid reading its own prejudices into the Constitution?

Critics of the Court often refer to the language of the majority opinion in *Griswold v. Connecticut* (1965) written by Justice William O. Douglas. The case involved a Connecticut law that prohibited the use of contraceptives in all circumstances. A doctor from a birth control clinic had been arrested for giving information on contraception to a married couple. Douglas's opinion claimed the Connecticut law violated the right of marital privacy. This right is not specifically referred to anywhere in the Constitution or Bill of Rights. Douglas, speaking for the majority, claimed it was protected by "**penumbras**, formed by **emanations**" from other enumerated rights, specifically the First, Third, Fourth, and Fifth Amendments. By this, he apparently meant that other provisions of the Bill of Rights implied a right to marital privacy. The Ninth Amendment was mentioned, but the Court decided to justify its opinion as being supported by substantive due process.

As you might imagine, critics have claimed that anyone can find any right they want in the shadows of the Constitution's emanations. To allow such latitude gives the Court almost unlimited power, not only to interpret the law but in doing so, to create new law. The result is that a majority of the justices serving on the Court at any particular time can interpret the Constitution to protect any values those justices hold. Changing justices on the Court will result in changing the opinions of the Court. The majority of the Court may be liberal for one period and conservative the next.

Shortly after the decision in *Griswold*, the appointment of new members to the Court gave it a more conservative majority. Decisions began to reflect a less expansive interpretation of the Court's role in extending the protection of individual rights. Greater responsibility was given to Congress and state legislatures to protect individual rights. This philosophy was expressed by Chief Justice Warren E. Burger in his opinion in the case of *Furman v. Georgia* (1972). One of the claims of attorneys appealing death sentences was that the death penalty was a violation of the prohibition against cruel and unusual punishment. Chief Justice Burger stated that the Eighth Amendment cannot be interpreted to prohibit the death penalty, whatever one's personal views about capital punishment might be. He said:

> *If we were possessed of legislative power, I would either join with Mr. Justice Brennan and Mr. Justice Marshall [in voting to abolish the death penalty] or, at the very least, restrict the use of capital punishment to a small category of heinous crimes. Our constitutional inquiry, however, must be divorced from personal feelings as to the morality and efficacy of the death penalty and be confined to the meaning and applicability of the uncertain language of the Eighth Amendment....[O]f all our fundamental guarantees, the ban on "cruel and unusual punishment" is one of the most difficult to translate into judicially manageable terms....it is essential to our role as a court that we not seize upon the enigmatic [puzzling] character of the guarantee as an invitation to enact our personal predilections [preferences] into law.*

> *[I]n a democratic society legislatures, not courts, are constituted to respond to the will and consequently the moral values of the people....[P]unishments such as branding and cutting off of ears, which were commonplace at the time of the adoption of the Constitution, passed from the penal scene without judicial intervention because they became basically offensive to the people and the legislatures responded to this sentiment....*

> *There are no obvious indications that capital punishment offends the conscience of society to such a degree that our traditional deference to the legislative judgement must be abandoned.*

Supporters of this position conclude that it is far better to place greater limitations on the discretionary powers of the Court and to rely, instead, upon using the political process to influence legislators to pass laws that protect rights. This is wiser, they say, than relying upon nine justices, appointed for life, who are not directly answerable to the people.

Whatever the appropriate limits, the Court has always had a special role to play in the identification, definition, and protection of individual rights. In *Federalist* No.78, Alexander Hamilton spoke of the Court's role in the protection of individual rights against the government. As long ago as *Marbury v. Madison* (1803), Chief Justice John Marshall argued that the courts, the traditional interpreters of law, are the proper branch of government to make the final decisions about what the Constitution means.

There are those who claim that such decisions must include the interpretation of the unenumerated rights mentioned in the Ninth Amendment as well as the enumerated rights mentioned in other parts of the Constitution. Moreover, they hold that the courts have some degree of latitude in interpreting the provisions of the Constitution and applying them to current circumstances. Justice William J. Brennan, Jr., for example, held a broader view of the Court's role in expanding rights than did Chief Justice Burger. He once said:

> We current Justices read the Constitution in the only way that we can: as Twentieth Century Americans. We look to the history of the time of framing and to the intervening history of interpretation. But the ultimate question must be, what do the words of the text mean in our time? For the genius of the Constitution rests not in any static meaning it might have had in a world that is dead and gone, but in the adaptability of its great principles to cope with current problems and current needs.

Justices and others have noted that our rights are embedded in the Constitution. Therefore, in order for us to remain a nation obedient to law, it is necessary for the courts to play an ever vigilant role. This will insure that these rights are not only protected, but that they will grow and adapt to modern needs and the changing values of society.

Using the Lesson

1. Why was the Ninth Amendment created?

2. What problems are raised by the idea of natural law? How might they be solved?

3. How has the Supreme Court used the idea of substantive due process to identify rights not specifically listed in the Constitution or Bill of Rights?

4. What issues have been raised by the Court's use of the idea of substantive due process?

5. What issue is raised by finding rights in "penumbras formed by emanations"?

6. Why do you suppose the Court has not used the Ninth Amendment as a primary means of justifying unenumerated rights?

7. Do you think the Court or Congress should take the primary responsibility for identifying and protecting unenumerated rights? Explain your position.

8. If state and federal legislatures fail to protect our rights, are the courts justified in "legislating from the bench"?

LESSON 29

What Have Been the Roles of Congress and the Executive Branch in Protecting and Expanding Rights?

Purpose of Lesson

This lesson will examine how Congress and the executive branch of the federal government have expanded the protection of individual rights. It will focus on the continuing controversy over the roles of Congress, the president, and the Supreme Court in protecting individual rights.

When you have finished this lesson, you should be able to describe the history of congressional legislation and presidential actions to protect individual rights. You should also be able to explain the controversy that has arisen over these measures and the responsibilities of each branch of government in protecting rights.

Terms to Know

Civil Rights Cases of 1883
civil rights movement
Civil Rights Act of 1957
Civil Rights Act of 1964
commerce clause
Voting Rights Act of 1965

Congress as a protector of individual rights

In recent years the Supreme Court has played such an important role in protecting individual rights that we tend to overlook what the other branches of government have done. As originally written, the Constitution does not appear to give Congress the responsibility to pass laws protecting individual rights, nor does it prohibit Congress from doing so. However, the Thirteenth, Fourteenth, and Fifteenth Amendments all contain the provision that "Congress shall have the power to enforce this article by appropriate legislation." This provision may also be found in the other amendments protecting civil rights, specifically, the Nineteenth, Twenty-third, Twenty-fourth, and Twenty-sixth Amendments.

These amendments clearly give Congress the power to create laws to protect individual rights. However, as you have seen,

What branch of government was responsible for the desegregation of the armed forces?

this power has sometimes had very little effect. The Civil Rights Act of 1866 was an attempt by the federal government to take responsibility for protecting the rights of the newly freed slaves from violations by state governments. This act reversed the earlier practice of leaving the protection of individual rights up to the states. Although the Civil Rights Act of 1866 failed to achieve its goals, since that time the federal government has increasingly assumed the responsibility for setting national standards for the protection of individual rights.

The power of Congress to give the federal government the responsibility for protecting individual rights was almost destroyed by the Supreme Court decisions in the **Civil Rights Cases of 1883**. Congress had passed civil rights legislation intended to enforce the protection of rights given to blacks by the Thirteenth and Fourteenth Amendments. Despite the fact that the Fourteenth Amendment clearly gave Congress the power to pass such laws, the Supreme Court declared them unconstitutional. For over fifty years, this decision crippled the power of the federal government to protect rights and left such responsibility up to the states.

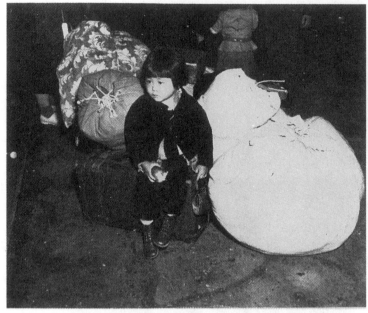

What impact did World War II have on the civil rights movement?

Federal courts and the civil rights movement

World War II had a significant impact on the development of a powerful **civil rights movement** in the United States. This was partly because African Americans, Native Americans, Mexican Americans, Japanese Americans, and members of other groups which had suffered discrimination for years, served in the armed forces. Members of these groups fought bravely for their country, and many gave their lives in the cause of freedom. Ironically, the armed forces were segregated during the war. Minority servicemen sacrificed their lives for a country where they could not sit on a bus or in a restaurant next to a white soldier, or even fight next to one on the battlefield.

After the war, a greater awareness of the problems of racial and ethnic discrimination strengthened the civil rights movement working to protect and promote individual rights. In July 1948, President Harry S. Truman ordered the desegregation of the armed forces. In the years that followed, civil rights organizations such as the NAACP looked primarily to the federal courts for help in gaining protection for their rights. They did not feel they could get help from their state legislatures or from Congress. Racial prejudice was too strong among many members of these state legislatures and even among some members of Congress. The federal courts, however, were less subject to racial prejudice. Federal judges were appointed, not elected, and were less influenced by political pressures. Therefore they played an increasingly important role in protecting the constitutional rights of minorities.

Help from the executive branch

The leaders of the civil rights movement also looked to the executive branch for help in the enforcement of civil rights legislation. In 1941, President Franklin D. Roosevelt created a Fair Employment Practices Commission to promote equal opportunity in employment. After Roosevelt's death, President Truman asked Congress to make this commission permanent. When Congress, dominated by Southerners, refused to do so, Truman established the presidential Committee on Civil Rights. This committee recommended that Congress pass legislation to eliminate poll taxes and to provide equal opportunity in education, housing, and jobs. Once again, Congress refused to respond.

Help from the Supreme Court

In 1954 the decision of the Supreme Court in *Brown v. Board of Education* established the principle that the equal protection clause of the Fourteenth Amendment prohibited racial segregation in public schools. Any federal, state, or local laws or actions that did so could be challenged in court and prohibited. This decision resulted in greatly increased activity by the civil rights movement throughout the nation.

Civil rights legislation passed by Congress

Civil rights leaders, such as the Rev. Martin Luther King, Jr., embarked on an extensive campaign of demonstrations, sit-ins, petitioning, and picketing. They hoped to change the

How did Martin Luther King, Jr., and other leaders work to promote fair treatment for women and minorities?

opinions and positions of the general public and the state legislatures. They also tried to get more favorable representation in Congress and their state legislatures by conducting extensive voter registration campaigns and voting drives.

Congress responded to the demands for racial equality by passing the **Civil Rights Act of 1957**. This law created a Civil Rights Commission with limited powers to investigate violations of individual rights. It also authorized the Justice Department to file suits in court to protect voting rights. Three years later Congress passed laws giving greater federal protection for voting rights and appointed federal officials to help blacks register and vote in safety.

President John F. Kennedy abolished segregation in federally funded housing, but knew he needed more effective laws to protect the rights of blacks and other minorities. Consequently, he proposed the bill that became the **Civil Rights Act of 1964**. This act is the most extensive civil rights law ever passed by Congress. Even today it is the basis for many protections of individual rights. It has been used to promote equal rights in education, public accommodations, and voting.

Congress has also used the clause in the Constitution that gives it the power to regulate interstate commerce (the **commerce clause**) to pass laws prohibiting racial discrimination in public and private agencies and businesses that deal with people traveling between states. This has resulted in laws preventing discrimination in restaurants, hotels, and gasoline stations.

These laws have also protected the rights of minorities to use public parks and public swimming pools and to attend events in public stadiums.

Civil rights legislation has also protected the rights of women. Congress has enacted laws requiring equal pay for equal work, regardless of one's sex, race, or ethnic background. Colleges and universities that receive federal funding are required to provide equal facilities and programs for men and women.

Despite these laws and actions of the federal government, discrimination against black voters has continued in some areas of the nation. The **Voting Rights Act of 1965** gave the federal government greater powers to prevent this problem. Federal officers were sent to any part of the nation where voter registration was lower than 50% and given the power to remedy any unfairness that existed. Congress has extended both the Civil Rights and Voting Rights Acts to the present time. Although there is still unfair discrimination in some places, these acts have been effective in protecting the right of blacks and other minorities to vote.

Although there have been a series of cases challenging the constitutionality of the Civil Rights and Voting Rights Acts, they have been upheld by the Supreme Court. The Court upheld the right of Congress to pass these laws as granted by the commerce clause, the equal protection clause, and the provision of the Fourteenth Amendment that gives Congress the power to make laws enforcing it.

Why were the armed forces needed to protect the rights of minorities?

What should be the responsibilities of government in the protection of rights?

Over the years all three branches of the federal government have taken a more active role in the protection of individual rights. Our system of government, with its separation of powers and checks and balances, provides more than one avenue for citizens to seek protection of their rights. People may turn to the courts, Congress, or the executive branch—whichever they feel will be most responsive to their needs.

It is clear that the courts have a central role in insuring that the government does not overstep the limits defined by the Constitution and Bill of Rights. The importance of this role in the protection of individual rights is indisputable. We have seen, however, that the other branches of government have also played an important role. We must be careful not to underestimate the part played the Congress and the president in passing civil rights acts and issuing executive orders that provide further protection for the rights of all citizens.

State governments, as well as the federal government, may also be a source of protection for individual rights. Although state governments have often been guilty of persecuting minorities, many states and even some local governments have passed very strong laws protecting individual rights. In fact, some state constitutions go even farther than the United States Constitution in protecting individual rights. Some, for example, contain provisions explicitly protecting the right to privacy from government interference.

"We have met the enemy, and it is us," a character in a popular comic strip called *Pogo* used to cry. And so it is. Unless citizens are vigilant in the protection of their rights, it is not likely that the actions of the courts, Congress, or the president will be of much avail. The future of the Bill of Rights is insecure without the efforts of citizens who watch and make sure that the laws passed by government are protective of the rights of everyone. Unless people are prepared to take action when they see rights violated, no court can save the Bill of Rights.

Senator Everett Dirksen of Illinois, speaking of the 1964 Civil Rights Act, said, "Every denial of freedom, every denial of equal opportunity for a livelihood, for an education, for the right to participate in representative government diminishes me. There is the moral basis of our cause."

Using the Lesson

1. What effect did the Court's decision in the Civil Rights Cases have on the ability of the federal government to protect individual rights?

2. Why do you suppose leaders of the civil rights movement looked to the courts for help instead of their state legislatures or Congress?

3. What were some of the major steps taken by Congress and the executive branch to protect individual rights in the period after World War II?

4. Why do you suppose there has been such great progress in promoting individual rights since World War II?

5. What do you think should be the responsibilities of the various branches of government in protecting individual rights?

6. What responsibilities should citizens assume in protecting individual rights? Explain your position.

7. In your opinion, what appear to be the most important contemporary issues regarding individual rights currently being discussed in the United States? Explain these issues and the position you might take on them.

LESSON 30

What Can Be Learned from an International Perspective on Human Rights?

Purpose of Lesson

In this lesson we will examine one of the most important international documents about rights, the Universal Declaration of Human Rights. We will examine the similarities and differences between this document and our Bill of Rights and look at the problem of enforcing rights on an international scale.

When you have finished this lesson, you should be able to explain the major differences between the Universal Declaration and the Bill of Rights. You should understand the problems involved in enforcing human rights on an international level. You should also be able to take and defend a position on what rights, if any, from the Universal Declaration should be established in the United States.

Terms to Know

Universal Declaration of Human Rights
United Nations
totalitarian government

What historical events and experiences influenced the Universal Declaration of Human Rights?

As you have learned, our Constitution and Bill of Rights reflect the Founders' knowledge of history and government as well as their own experiences. In much the same way, the **Universal Declaration of Human Rights**, adopted by the **United Nations** in 1948, reflects the history and experiences of its time. It was strongly influenced by the fall of democratic governments and the rise of **totalitarian governments**. Totalitarian governments possess greater power and exercise far more extensive control over the lives of their subjects than even the worst tyrannies of the past. These governments were guilty of many of the abuses of rights that occurred in the first half of the twentieth century, especially during World War II (1939-1945).

During World War II, the United States and the allied nations fought against the Axis Powers of Germany, Italy, and Japan. Nazi Germany had become one of the worst violators of individual rights in history. People throughout the United States were aware of the means by which the Nazis had overthrown a democratic government and come to power in Germany. In 1933, within months after gaining power, the Nazi government opened Dachau, its first concentration camp. Dachau and other camps were soon filled with members of opposition political parties and other opponents of the Nazi regime.

In addition to destroying their political opponents, the Nazis also embarked on a program of systematic racial persecution of Jews, Gypsies, and other groups they believed were racially impure and should be eliminated as "undesirable elements." According to orders of the security police, the following categories of people were to be sought out and destroyed:

> *Communists, Marxists, Jews, politically-active churches, freemasons, politically dissatisfied people (grumblers), members of the national opposition, reactionaries, members of the Black Front, economic saboteurs, common criminals, abortionists and homosexuals, traitors and those guilty of high treason.*

By the time the Nazi regime was defeated, over twelve million people had been killed. Many of those were political opponents, but over six million were killed merely because they were Jews. As many as a quarter of a million Gypsies were murdered as well as tens of thousands of homosexuals and "mental defectives."

What abuses of rights during World War II led to the Declaration of Human Rights?

The best-known violations of human rights during this period were those committed by Nazi Germany and its allies, especially Japan. However, although not widely known at the time, some of the worst abuses occurred in the Soviet Union under Joseph Stalin. Government repression of dissent and the use of suicidal tactics in warfare were responsible for the death of over thirty million people, mostly Soviet citizens.

In addition to the unprecedented scale of abuses of human rights, several other factors influenced the development of the Declaration of Human Rights. These were the following:

1. **Worldwide depression.** During the 1930s an economic depression affected most of the nations of the world. Millions of people could not find work. Poverty, hunger, and early death were widespread. Many people argue that this condition was a major cause of World War II.

2. **Post-war devastation.** Nations in Europe, Northern Africa, and Asia were devastated by World War II. Millions of people lacked decent jobs, adequate housing, sufficient food, and medical care.

3. **Rise of socialism.** At the end of the World War II, many countries in Europe and Asia adopted socialist-type governments. These governments exercised strict control over their economies in an effort to protect individuals against such hardships as the loss of income and the lack of goods and services. These governments also attempted to guarantee that all people had access to certain goods and services that in the past had only been available to those who could afford them.

Critical Thinking Exercise
EXAMINING THE UNIVERSAL DECLARATION OF HUMAN RIGHTS

Review the Universal Declaration of Human Rights found in the Appendix and answer the following questions:

1. What rights does the Declaration contain that are in our Constitution and Bill of Rights?

2. What rights in our Constitution and Bill of Rights are not included in the Declaration? Why do you suppose they are not included?

3. What appear to be the purposes of the rights contained in the Declaration that are not protected by our Constitution or Bill of Rights?

4. How do the rights listed in the Declaration appear to reflect the history and experiences of the time in which it was written?

5. **What do *you* think?**

   a. Examine each of the rights contained in the Declaration that is not protected specifically in our Constitution. Is the right you have identified protected in our nation by another means of protecting rights, such as the following:

      ■ civil rights legislation

      ■ civil or criminal law

      ■ contracts between private parties such as labor and management agreements on employment benefits, vacation pay, and sick leave

      ■ custom or tradition

      ■ other means not listed above

   b. What rights, if any, contained in the Universal Declaration should be established in the United States? How should they be established? Explain your position.

What power does the United Nations have to protect the rights contained in the Universal Declaration?

Differences between the documents

As you have seen, there are several rights in the Bill of Rights that are not in the Universal Declaration. One of the most interesting of these is the First Amendment's prohibition against the establishment of religion. In many parts of the world even today, there are established, state-supported religions. These member nations of the United Nations do not see this as a violation of individual rights as we do.

What makes the Declaration interesting is the many rights it contains that are not in our Bill of Rights. As you have undoubtedly discovered, these include an explicit statement regarding equal rights for women as well as numerous economic and social rights for all people. For example, the Declaration includes the right to work, to an adequate standard of living, to medical care and retirement benefits, and to rest and leisure.

An important difference between the statements of rights in the Universal Declaration and our Bill of Rights is that there is no international government with the power to protect or guarantee the rights listed in the Declaration. Its rights are "a common standard of achievement for all peoples." The listing of these rights does not place any legal obligation on the member nations to provide or protect them. Furthermore, the member nations have not given the United Nations the authority to force governments to protect the rights listed in the Declaration. The decision whether or not to protect the rights contained in the Declaration is left up to each member nation.

Perhaps the most important difference between the Universal Declaration of Human Rights and the United States Constitution is to be seen in their respective views of rights. In the natural rights tradition, which provides the foundation for the United States Constitution, rights are seen as restraints on the power of government. The Bill of Rights, as you have seen, generally requires the government *not* to act. For example, the First Amendment says, "Congress shall pass no law...." While the Universal Declaration also mentions rights that are to be protected from government interference, it also speaks of many rights, such as jobs, vacations, and decent standards of living, that require government intervention on behalf of certain desired social ends. While the Bill of Rights generally prohibits or limits government action, the Universal Declaration, in addition to limiting government action, requires government to act.

Some people argue that governments have a moral obligation to protect the rights listed in the Declaration. One way to do this, of course, is for the people of a nation to require their government to pass laws establishing such rights as legal rights to which all citizens are entitled. Another way would be for a nation to include these rights in its constitution.

Our history and the history of other nations clearly reveal that the existence of a written constitution or a bill of rights does not mean that citizens actually have the rights they contain. Neither does the existence of civil and criminal laws guarantee that the rights of citizens will actually be protected. On the other hand, the Ninth Amendment demonstrates that just because rights are not explicitly stated does not necessarily mean that they do not exist or are not protected.

Using the Lesson

1. What were the most important influences on the development of the Universal Declaration? Explain your answer.

2. What are the advantages and disadvantages of the different ways rights can be established in a nation?

3. What are the primary values and interests promoted by the Declaration?

4. What contemporary issues involve rights contained in the Declaration? Explain what position you would take on these issues.

5. What means might our government use to stop other governments from violating human rights? Which means have been used recently? Explain the advantages and disadvantages of each of the means you identify.

LESSON 31

What Responsibilities Do People Have in Preserving and Extending Rights?

Purpose of Lesson

In this concluding lesson, we will examine the importance of the character and commitment of citizens in a free society to the preservation and extension of individual rights and justice. We will begin by examining some of the ideas of the Founders. Then we will look at what a number of thoughtful people have had to say about the subject.

When you have completed this lesson, you should be able to take and defend a position on the role of individuals in preserving and expanding rights and promoting the ideals of justice.

What is the importance of the character of the people?

I know of no safe depository of the ultimate powers of the society but the people themselves; and if we think them not enlightened enough to exercise their control with a wholesome discretion, the remedy is not to take it from them, but to inform their discretion.
Thomas Jefferson, 1820

When Jefferson wrote these words he was stating a basic idea of constitutional government. Students of politics have long realized that a constitutional democracy, more than any other form of government, depends upon an enlightened and responsible citizenry.

Some of the Founders, such as James Madison and Alexander Hamilton, emphasized the importance of the separation of powers, checks and balances, and the federal system to protect the rights of individuals. But others, like Thomas Jefferson and John Adams, saw that even the best designed constitutions and institutions of government require the support of an enlightened citizenry possessing civic virtue.

The experience of the past two hundred years confirms the Founders' belief that even the most carefully designed political institutions are ultimately dependent on the character of the people and those whom they select for public office. To conclude our study of the Bill of Rights, let's examine the thoughts of some leaders from the past concerning the rights and responsibilities of citizens.

Critical Thinking Exercise
EXAMINING MESSAGES FROM THE PAST

Examine each of the following statements and discuss the position it expresses, either explicitly or implicitly, about rights and responsibilities. Then answer the questions that follow.

1.

No man is an island, entire of itself; every man is a piece of the continent, a part of the main; if a clod be washed away by the sea, Europe is the less, as well as if a promontory were, as well as if a manor of thy friend's or of thine own were; any man's death diminishes me, because I am involved in mankind; and therefore never send to know for whom the bell tolls; it tolls for thee.
John Donne, *Devotions Upon Emergent Occasions*, 1631

2.

I deny the right of the people...either by themselves or by their government...to control the expression of opinion....If all mankind minus one were of one opinion and only one person were of contrary opinion, mankind would be no more justified in silencing that one person, than he, if he had the power, would be in silencing mankind. Were an opinion a personal possession of no value except to the owner; if to be obstructed in the enjoyment of it were simply a private injury, it would make some difference whether the injury was inflicted only on a

few persons or on many. But the peculiar evil of silencing the expression of an opinion is, that it is robbing the human race: posterity as well as the existing generation; those who dissent from the opinion, still more than those who hold it. If the opinion is right, they are deprived of the opportunity of exchanging error for truth: if wrong, they lose, what is almost as great a benefit, the clearer perception and livelier impression of truth, produced by its collision with error.

John Stuart Mill, *On Liberty*, 1859

3.

We hold these Truths to be self-evident, that all Men are created equal, that they are endowed by their Creator with certain unalienable Rights, that among these are Life, Liberty, and the Pursuit of Happiness—That to secure these Rights, Governments are instituted among Men, deriving their just Powers from the Consent of the Governed, that whenever any Form of Government becomes destructive of these Ends it is the Right of the People to alter or abolish it, and to institute new Government, laying its Foundation on such Principles, and organizing its Powers in such Form, as to them shall seem most likely to effect their Safety and Happiness.

Declaration of Independence, July 4, 1776

4.

I come before you to declare that my sex is entitled to the inalienable right to life, liberty, and the pursuit of happiness....All I ask is justice. I believe in the equality of sexes. I believe in government of men and women, instead of government of men and women run by men alone. Equal rights to all and special privileges to none should be the foundation of all governments.

Marilla Ricker, attorney, denied the right to run for governor of New Hampshire, 1910

5.

I often wonder whether we do not rest our hopes too much upon constitutions, upon laws and courts. These are false hopes; believe me, these are false hopes. Liberty lies in the hearts of men; when it dies there, no constitution, no law, no court can save it; no constitution, no law, no court can even do much to help it. While it lies there it needs no constitution, no law, no court to save it.

Judge Learned Hand, to the graduating class at Yale University, 1941

6.

In Germany the Nazis came first for the Communists, and I didn't speak up because I wasn't a Communist. Then they came for the Jews, and I didn't speak up because I wasn't a Jew. Then they came for the trade unionists, and I didn't speak up because I wasn't a trade unionist. Then they came for the Catholics, and I didn't speak up because I was a Protestant. Then they came for me, and by that time no one was left to speak up.

Attributed to Martin Niemoeller (1892-1984)

7.

I have a dream that one day on the red hills of Georgia the sons of former slaves and the sons of former slave owners will be able to sit down together at the table of brotherhood....I have a dream that my four little children will one day live in a nation where they will not be judged by the color of their skin, but by the content of their character.

Martin Luther King, Jr., Civil Rights March on Washington, D.C., August 28, 1963

8.

Let the word go forth from this time and place, to friend and foe alike, that the torch has been passed to a new generation of Americans, born in this century, tempered by a war, disciplined by a hard and bitter peace, proud of our ancient heritage and unwilling to witness or permit the slow undoing of those human rights to which this nation has always been committed, and to which we are committed today at home and around the world. Let every nation know, whether it wishes us well or ill, that we shall pay any price, bear any burden, meet any hardship, support any friend, oppose any foe to assure the survival and success of liberty.

President John F. Kennedy,
Inaugural Address, January 20, 1961

What do *you* think?

1. What responsibilities of individuals and government are implied in each statement?

2. What is the importance of fulfilling these responsibilities in order to preserve a free and just society?

Conclusion

We hope that with the guidance of your teacher you have found the material in this lesson and the entire text interesting and useful. The understanding and skills you have gained from studying the Constitution and Bill of Rights should provide a sound foundation for dealing with contemporary issues of individual rights in our society. In 1822, James Madison wrote of the importance of an educated citizenry:

A popular Government, without popular information, or the means of acquiring it, is but a Prologue to a Farce or a Tragedy; or perhaps both. Knowledge will forever govern ignorance: And a people who mean to be their own Governors, must arm themselves with the power which knowledge gives.

You are about to assume the highest political office in our constitutional democracy, the office of citizen. In our tradition, we, the citizens, are the masters of our government, not its servants. It is up to us to decide what must be done to make the goal of liberty and justice for all a reality.

Appendix

Virginia Declaration of Rights
June 12, 1776

A DECLARATION OF RIGHTS made by the Representatives of the good people of VIRGINIA, assembled in full and free Convention; which rights do pertain to them and their posterity, as the basis and foundation of Government.

1. That all men are by nature equally free and independent, and have certain inherent rights, of which, when they enter into a state of society, they cannot, by any compact, deprive or divest their posterity; namely, the enjoyment of life and liberty, with the means of acquiring and possessing property, and pursuing and obtaining happiness and safety.

2. That all power is vested in, and consequently derived from, the People; that magistrates are their trustees and servants, and at all times amenable to them.

3. That Government is, or ought to be, instituted for the common benefit, protection, and security of the people, nation, or community;—of all the various modes and forms of Government that is best which is capable of producing the greatest degree of happiness and safety, and is most effectually secured against the danger of mal-administration;—and that, whenever any Government shall be found inadequate or contrary to these purposes, a majority of the community hath an indubitable, unalienable, and indefeasible right, to reform, alter, or abolish it, in such manner as shall be judged most conducive to the publick weal.

4. That no man, or set of men, are entitled to exclusive or separate emoluments and privileges from the community, but in consideration of publick services; which, not being descendible, neither ought the offices of Magistrate, Legislator, or Judge, to be hereditary.

5. That the Legislative and Executive powers of the State should be separate and distinct from the Judicative; and, that the members of the two first may be restrained from oppression, by feeling and participating the burdens of the people, they should, at fixed periods, be reduced to a private station, return into that body from which they were originally taken, and the vacancies be supplied by frequent, certain, and regular elections, in which all, or any part of the former members, to be again eligible, or ineligible, as the law shall direct.

6. That elections of members to serve as Representatives of the people, in Assembly, ought to be free; and that all men, having sufficient evidence of permanent common interest with, and attachment to, the community, have the right of suffrage, and cannot be taxed or deprived of their property for publick uses without their own consent or that of their Representative so elected, nor bound by any law to which they have not, in like manner, assented, for the publick good.

7. That all power of suspending laws, or the execution of laws, by any authority, without consent of the Representatives of the people, is injurious to their rights, and ought not to be exercised.

8. That in all capital or criminal prosecutions a man hath a right to demand the cause and nature of his accusation, to be confronted with the accusers and witnesses, to call for evidence in his favour, and to a speedy trial by an impartial jury of his vicinage, without whose unanimous consent he cannot be found guilty, nor can he be compelled to give evidence against himself; that no man be deprived of his liberty except by the law of the land, or the judgment of his peers.

9. That excessive bail ought not to be required, nor excessive fines imposed, nor cruel and unusual punishments inflicted.

10. That general warrants, whereby any officer or messenger may be commanded to search suspected places without evidence of a fact committed, or to seize any person or persons not named, or whose offence is not particularly described and supported by evidence, are grievous and oppressive, and ought not to be granted.

11. That in controversies respecting property, and in suits between man and man, the ancient trial by Jury is preferable to any other, and ought to be held sacred.

12. That the freedom of the Press is one of the greatest bulwarks of liberty, and can never be restrained but by despotick Governments.

13. That a well-regulated Militia, composed of the body of the people, trained to arms, is the proper, natural, and safe defence of a free State; that Standing Armies, in time of peace, should be avoided as dangerous to liberty; and that, in all cases, the military should be under strict subordination to, and governed by, the civil power.

14. That the people have a right to uniform Government; and, therefore, that no Government separate from, or independent of, the Government of *Virginia*, ought to be erected or established within the limits thereof.

15. That no free Government, or the blessing of liberty, can be preserved to any people but by a firm adherence to justice, moderation, temperance, frugality, and virtue, and by frequent recurrence to fundamental principles.

16. That Religion, or the duty which we owe to our Creator, and the manner of discharging it, can be directed only by reason and conviction, not by force or violence; and, therefore, all men are equally entitled to the free exercise of religion, according to the dictates of conscience; and that it is the mutual duty of all to practice Christian forbearance, love, and charity, towards each other.

Declaration of Independence

IN CONGRESS, JULY 4, 1776.

A DECLARATION

BY THE **REPRESENTATIVES** OF THE

UNITED STATES OF AMERICA,

IN GENERAL CONGRESS ASSEMBLED

WHEN in the Course of human Events, it becomes necessary for one People to dissolve the Political Bands which have connected them with another, and to assume among the Powers of the Earth, the separate and equal Station to which the Laws of Nature and of Nature's God entitle them, a decent Respect to the Opinions of Mankind requires that they should declare the causes which impel them to the Separation.

We hold these Truths to be self-evident, that all Men are created equal, that they are endowed by their Creator with certain unalienable Rights, that among these are Life, Liberty, and the Pursuit of Happiness—That to secure these Rights, Governments are instituted among Men, deriving their just Powers from the Consent of the Governed, that whenever any Form of Government becomes destructive of these Ends it is the Right of the People to alter or to abolish it, and to institute new Government, laying its Foundation on such Principles, and organizing its Powers in such Form, as to them shall seem most likely to effect their Safety and Happiness. Prudence, indeed, will dictate that Governments long established should not be changed for light and transient Causes; and accordingly all Experience hath shewn, that Mankind are more disposed to suffer, while Evils are sufferable, than to right themselves by abolishing the Forms to which they are accustomed. But when a long Train of Abuses and Usurpations, pursuing invariably the same Object, evinces a Design to reduce them under absolute Despotism, it is their Right, it is their Duty, to throw off such Government, and to provide new Guards for their future Security. Such has been the patient Sufferance of these Colonies; and such is now the Necessity which constrains them to alter their former Systems of Government. The History of the present King of Great-Britain is a History of repeated Injuries and Usurpations, all having in direct Object the Establishment of an absolute Tyranny over these States. To prove this, let Facts be submitted to a candid World.

He has refused his Assent to Laws, the most wholesome and necessary for the public Good.

He has forbidden his Governors to pass Laws of immediate and pressing Importance, unless suspended in their Operation till his Assent should be obtained; and when so suspended, he has utterly neglected to attend to them.

He has refused to pass other Laws for the Accommodation of large Districts of People, unless those People would relinquish the Right of Representation in the Legislature, a Right inestimable to them, and formidable to Tyrants only.

He has called together Legislative Bodies at Places unusual, uncomfortable, and distant from the Depository of their public Records, for the sole Purpose of fatiguing them into Compliance with his Measures.

He has dissolved Representative Houses repeatedly, for opposing with manly Firmness his Invasions on the Rights of the People.

He has refused for a long Time, after such Dissolutions, to cause others to be elected; whereby the Legislative Powers, incapable of Annihilation, have returned to the People at large for their exercise; the State remaining in the mean time exposed to all the Dangers of Invasions from without, and Convulsions within.

He has endeavored to prevent the Population of these States; for that Purpose obstructing the Laws for Naturalization of Foreigners; refusing to pass others to encourage their Migrations hither, and raising the Conditions of new Appropriations of Lands.

He has obstructed the Administration of Justice, by refusing his Assent to Laws for establishing Judiciary Powers.

He has made Judges dependent on his Will alone, for the Tenure of their Offices, and the Amount and Payment of their Salaries.

He has erected a Multitude of new Offices, and sent hither Swarms of Officers to harass our People and eat out their Substance.

He has kept among us, in Times of Peace, Standing Armies, without the consent of our Legislatures.

He has affected to render the Military independent of and superior to the Civil Power.

He has combined with others to subject us to a Jurisdiction foreign to our Constitution, and unacknowledged by our Laws; giving his Assent to their Acts of pretended Legislation:

For quartering large Bodies of Armed Troops among us:

For protecting them, by a mock Trial, from Punishment for any Murders which they should commit on the Inhabitants of these States:

For cutting off our Trade with all Parts of the World:

For imposing Taxes on us without our Consent:

For depriving us, in many Cases, of the Benefits of Trial by Jury:

For transporting us beyond Seas to be tried for pretended Offenses:

For abolishing the free System of English Laws in a neighbouring Province, establishing therein an Arbitrary Government, and enlarging its Boundaries, so as to render it at once an Example and fit Instrument for introducing the same absolute Rule into these Colonies:

For taking away our Charters, abolishing our most valuable Laws, and altering fundamentally the Forms of our Governments:

For suspending our own Legislatures, and declaring themselves invested with Power to legislate for us in all Cases whatsoever.

He has abdicated Government here, by declaring us out of his Protection and waging War against us.

He has plundered our Seas, ravaged our Coasts, burnt our Towns, and destroyed the Lives of our People.

He is, at this Time, transporting large Armies of foreign Mercenaries to compleat the Works of Death, Desolation, and Tyranny, already begun with circumstances of Cruelty and Perfidy, scarcely paralleled in the most barbarous Ages, and totally unworthy the Head of a civilized Nation.

He has constrained our fellow Citizens taken Captive on the high Seas to bear Arms against their Country, to become the Executioners of their Friends and Brethren, or to fall themselves by their Hands.

He has excited domestic Insurrections amongst us, and has endeavoured to bring on the Inhabitants of our Frontiers, the merciless Indian Savages, whose known Rule of Warfare, is an undistinguished Destruction, of all Ages, Sexes and Conditions.

In every stage of these Oppressions we have Petitioned for Redress in the most humble Terms: Our repeated Petitions have been answered only by repeated Injury. A Prince, whose Character is thus marked by every act which may define a Tyrant, is unfit to be the Ruler of a free People.

Nor have we been wanting in Attentions to our British Brethren. We have warned them from Time to Time of Attempts by their Legislature to extend an unwarrantable Jurisdiction over us. We have reminded them of the Circumstances of our Emigration and Settlement here. We have appealed to their native Justice and Magnanimity, and we have conjured them by the Ties of our common Kindred to disavow these Usurpations, which, would inevitably interrupt our Connections and Correspondence. They too have been deaf to the Voice of Justice and of Consanguinity. We must, therefore, acquiesce in the Necessity, which denounces our Separation, and hold them, as we hold the rest of Mankind, Enemies in War, in Peace, Friends.

We, therefore, the Representatives of the UNITED STATES OF AMERICA, in GENERAL CONGRESS, Assembled, appealing to the Supreme Judge of the World for the Rectitude of our Intentions, do, in the Name, and by Authority of the good People of these Colonies, solemnly Publish and Declare, That these United Colonies are, and of Right ought to be, FREE AND INDEPENDENT STATES; that they are absolved from all Allegiance to the British Crown, and that all political Connection between them and the State of Great-Britain, is and ought to be totally dissolved; and that as FREE AND INDEPENDENT STATES, they have full Power to levy War, conclude Peace, contract Alliances, establish Commerce, and to do all other Acts and Things which INDEPENDENT STATES may of right do. And for the support of this Declaration, with a firm Reliance on the Protection of divine Providence, we mutually pledge to each other our Lives, our Fortunes, and our sacred Honor.

Signed by ORDER and in BEHALF of the CONGRESS,
JOHN HANCOCK, PRESIDENT.

Signers of the Declaration of Independence

New-Hampshire
Josiah Bartlett,
Wm. Whipple,
Matthew Thornton.

Massachusetts-Bay
Saml. Adams,
John Adams,
Robt. Treat Paine,
Elbridge Gerry.

Rhode-Island and Providence, &c.
Step. Hopkins,
William Ellery.

Connecticut
Roger Sherman,
Saml. Huntington,
Wm. Williams,
Oliver Wolcott.

New-York
Wm. Floyd,
Phil. Livingston,
Frans. Lewis,
Lewis Morris.

New-Jersey
Richd. Stockton,
Jno. Witherspoon,
Fras. Hopkinson,
John Hart,
Abra. Clark.

Pennsylvania
Robt. Morris,
Benjamin Rush,
Benja. Franklin,
John Morton,
Geo. Clymer,
Jas. Smith,
Geo. Taylor,
James Wilson,
Geo. Ross.

Delaware
Casar Rodney,
Geo. Read,
(Tho M:Kean.)

Maryland
Samuel Chase,
Wm. Paca,
Thos. Stone,
Charles Carroll, of Carrollton.

Virginia
George Wythe,
Richard Henry Lee,
Ths. Jefferson,
Benja. Harrison,
Thos. Nelson, Jr.
Francis Lightfoot Lee,
Carter Braxton.

North-Carolina
Wm. Hooper,
Joseph Hewes,
John Penn.

South-Carolina
Edward Rutledge,
Thos. Heyward, Junr.
Thomas Lynch, Junr.
Arthur Middleton.

Georgia
Button Gwinnett,
Lyman Hall,
Geo. Walton.

According to the authenticated list printed by order of Congress of January 18, 1777.
Spelling, and abbreviations of names conform to original printed list.

The Constitution of the United States of America

Preamble

We the People of the United States, in Order to form a more perfect Union, establish Justice, insure domestic tranquility, provide for the common defence, promote the general Welfare, and secure the Blessings of Liberty to ourselves and our Posterity, do ordain and establish this Constitution for the United States of America.

ARTICLE I.

The Legislative Branch

Section 1.

All legislative Powers herein granted shall be vested in a Congress of the United States, which shall consist of a Senate and House of Representatives.

Section 2.

House of Representatives: Organization and Power of Impeachment

1. The House of Representatives shall be composed of Members chosen every second Year by the People of the several States, and the Electors in each State shall have the Qualifications requisite for Electors of the most numerous Branch of the State Legislature.

2. No Person shall be a Representative who shall not have attained to the Age of twenty five Years, and been seven Years a Citizen of the United States, and who shall not, when elected, be an Inhabitant of that State in which he shall be chosen.

3. [Representatives and direct Taxes shall be apportioned among the several States which may be included within this Union, according to their respective Numbers, which shall be determined by adding to the whole Number of free Persons, including those bound to Service for a Term of Years, and excluding Indians not taxed, three fifths of all other Persons.]* The actual Enumeration shall be made within three Years after the first Meeting of the Congress of the United States, and within every subsequent Term of ten Years, in such Manner as they shall by Law direct. The number of Representatives shall not exceed one for every thirty Thousand, but each State shall have at Least one Representative; and until such enumeration shall be made, the State of New Hampshire shall be entitled to choose three, Massachusetts eight, Rhode Island and Providence Plantations one, Connecticut five, New York six, New Jersey four, Pennsylvania eight, Delaware one, Maryland six, Virginia ten, North Carolina five, South Carolina five, and Georgia three.

4. When vacancies happen in the Representation from any State, the Executive Authority thereof shall issue Writs of Election to fill such Vacancies.

5. The House of Representatives shall choose their Speaker and other Officers; and shall have the sole Power of Impeachment.

Section 3.

The Senate, Organization and
Powers of Impeachment

1. The Senate of the United States shall be composed of two Senators from each State, [chosen by the Legislature thereof,]** for six Years; and each Senator shall have one Vote.

---

* Changed by section 2 of the Fourteenth Amendment.
** Changed by the Seventeenth Amendment.

2. Immediately after they shall be assembled in Consequence of the first Election, they shall be divided as equally as may be into three Classes. The seats of the Senators of the first Class shall be vacated at the Expiration of the second Year, of the second Class at the Expiration of the fourth Year, and of the third Class at the Expiration of the sixth Year, so that one third may be chosen every second Year; [and if Vacancies happen by Resignation, or otherwise, during the Recess of the Legislature of any State, the Executive thereof may make temporary Appointments until the next Meeting of the Legislature, which shall then fill such Vacancies.]*

3. No Person shall be a Senator who shall not have attained to the Age of thirty Years, and been nine Years a Citizen of the United States, and who shall not, when elected, be an Inhabitant of that State for which he shall be chosen.

4. The Vice President of the United States shall be President of the Senate, but shall have no Vote, unless they be equally divided.

5. The Senate shall choose their other officers, and also a President pro tempore, in the Absence of the Vice President, or when he shall exercise the Office of President of the United States.

6. The Senate shall have the sole Power to try all Impeachments. When sitting for that Purpose, they shall be on Oath or Affirmation. When the President of the United States is tried, the Chief Justice shall preside: And no person shall be convicted without the Concurrence of two thirds of the Members present.

7. Judgment in Cases of Impeachment shall not extend further than to removal from Office, and disqualification to hold and enjoy any Office of honor, Trust or Profit under the United States; but the Party convicted shall nevertheless be liable and subject to Indictment, Trial, Judgment and Punishment, according to Law.

Section 4.
Elections and Meeting of Congress

1. The Times, Places and Manner of holding Elections for Senators and Representatives shall be prescribed in each State by the Legislature thereof; but the Congress may at any time by Law make or alter such Regulations, except as to the Places of choosing Senators.

2. The Congress shall assemble at least once in every Year, and such Meeting shall be [on the first Monday in December,]** unless they shall by Law appoint a different Day.

Section 5.
Congress's Rules of Procedure, Powers, Quorum, Journals, Meetings, Adjournments

1. Each House shall be the Judge of the Elections, Returns and Qualifications of its own Members, and a Majority of each shall constitute a Quorum to do Business; but a smaller Number may adjourn from day to day, and may be authorized to compel the Attendance of absent Members, in such Manner, and under such Penalties as each House may provide.

2. Each House may determine the Rules of its Proceedings, punish its members for disorderly Behavior, and, with the Concurrence of two thirds, expel a Member.

3. Each House shall keep a Journal of its Proceedings, and from time to time publish the same, excepting such Parts as may in their Judgment require Secrecy; and the Yeas and Nays of the Members of either House on any question shall, at the Desire of one fifth of those Present, be entered on the Journal.

4. Neither House, during the Session of Congress, shall, without the Consent of the other, adjourn for more than three days, nor to any other Place than that in which the two Houses shall be sitting.

* Changed by the Seventeenth Amendment.
** Changed by section 2 of the Twentieth Amendment.

Section 6.
Pay, Privileges, Limitations

1. The Senators and Representatives shall receive a Compensation for their Services, to be ascertained by Law, and paid out of the Treasury of the United States. They shall in all cases, except Treason, Felony and Breach of the Peace, be privileged from Arrest during their Attendance at the Session of their respective Houses, and in going to and returning from the same; and for any Speech or Debate in either House, they shall not be questioned in any other Place.

2. No Senator or Representative shall, during the Time for which he was elected, be appointed to any civil Office under the Authority of the United States, which shall have been created, or the Emoluments whereof shall have been increased during such time; and no Person holding any Office under the United States, shall be a Member of either House during his Continuance in Office.

Section 7.
Procedure in Passing Bills,
President's Veto Power

1. All Bills for raising Revenue shall originate in the House of Representatives; but the Senate may propose or concur with Amendments as on other Bills.

2. Every Bill which shall have passed the House of Representatives and the Senate, shall, before it becomes a Law, be presented to the President of the United States; if he approve he shall sign it, but if not he shall return it, with his Objections, to that House in which it shall have originated, who shall enter the Objections at large on their Journal, and proceed to reconsider it. If after such Reconsideration two thirds of that House shall agree to pass the Bill, it shall be sent, together with the Objections, to the other House, by which it shall likewise be reconsidered, and if approved by two thirds of that House, it shall become a Law. But in all such Cases the Votes of both Houses shall be determined by yeas and nays, and the Names of the Persons voting for and against the Bill shall be entered on the Journal of each House respectively. If any Bill shall not be returned by the President within ten Days (Sundays excepted) after it shall have been presented to him, the Same shall be a Law, in like Manner as if he had signed it, unless the Congress by their Adjournment prevent its Return, in which Case it shall not be a Law.

3. Every Order, Resolution, or Vote to which the Concurrence of the Senate and House of Representatives may be necessary (except on a question of Adjournment) shall be presented to the President of the United States; and before the Same shall take Effect, shall be approved by him, or being disapproved by him, shall be repassed by two thirds of the Senate and House of Representatives, according to the Rules and Limitations prescribed in the Case of a Bill.

Section 8.
Powers Delegated to Congress

The Congress shall have Power

1. To lay and collect Taxes, Duties, Imposts and Excises, to pay the Debts and provide for the common Defence and general Welfare of the United States; but all Duties, Imposts and Excises shall be uniform throughout the United States;

2. To borrow Money on the credit of the United States;

3. To regulate Commerce with foreign Nations, and among the several States, and with the Indian Tribes;

4. To establish an uniform Rule of Naturalization, and uniform Laws on the subject of Bankruptcies throughout the United States;

5. To coin Money, regulate the Value thereof, and of Foreign Coin, and fix the Standard of Weights and Measures;

6. To provide for the Punishment of counterfeiting the Securities and current Coin of the United States;

7. To establish Post Offices and post Roads;

8. To promote the Progress of Science and useful Arts, by securing for limited Times to Authors and Inventors the exclusive Right to their respective Writings and Discoveries;

9. To constitute Tribunals inferior to the supreme Court;

10. To define and punish Piracies and Felonies committed on the high Seas, and Offenses against the Law of Nations;

11. To declare War, grant Letters of Marque and Reprisal, and make Rules concerning Captures on Land and Water;

12. To raise and support Armies, but no Appropriation of Money to that Use shall be for a longer Term than two Years;

13. To provide and maintain a Navy;

14. To make Rules for the Government and Regulation of the land and naval Forces;

15. To provide for calling forth the Militia to execute the Laws of the Union, suppress Insurrections and repel Invasions;

16. To provide for organizing, arming, and disciplining the Militia, and for governing such Part of them as may be employed in the Service of the United States, reserving to the States respectively, the Appointment of the Officers, and the Authority of training the Militia according to the discipline prescribed by Congress;

17. To exercise exclusive Legislation in all Cases whatsoever, over such District (not exceeding ten Miles square) as may, by Cession of particular States, and the Acceptance of Congress, become the Seat of the Government of the United States, and to exercise like Authority over all Places purchased by the Consent of the Legislature of the State in which the Same shall be, for the Erection of Forts, Magazines, Arsenals, dock-Yards and other needful Buildings;—And

18. To make all Laws which shall be necessary and proper for carrying into Execution the foregoing powers, and all other Powers vested by this Constitution in the Government of the United States, or in any Department or Officer thereof.

Section 9.
Powers Denied to Congress

1. The Migration or Importation of such Persons as any of the States now existing shall think proper to admit, shall not be prohibited by the Congress prior to the Year one thousand eight hundred and eight, but a Tax or duty may be imposed on such Importation, not exceeding ten dollars for each Person.

2. The Privilege of the Writ of Habeas Corpus shall not be suspended, unless when in Cases of Rebellion or Invasion the public Safety may require it.

3. No Bill of Attainder or ex post facto Law shall be passed.

4. [No Capitation, or other direct, Tax shall be laid, unless in Proportion to the Census or Enumeration herein before directed to be taken.]*

5. No Tax or Duty shall be laid on Articles exported from any State.

* Changed by the Sixteenth Amendment.

6. No Preference shall be given by any Regulation of Commerce or Revenue to the Ports of one State over those of another: nor shall Vessels bound to, or from, one State, be obliged to enter, clear, or pay Duties in another.

7. No Money shall be drawn from the Treasury, but in Consequence of Appropriations made by Law; and a regular Statement and Account of the Receipts and Expenditures of all public Money shall be published from time to time.

8. No Title of Nobility shall be granted by the United States: And no Person holding any Office of Profit or Trust under them, shall, without the Consent of the Congress, accept of any present, Emolument, Office, or Title, of any kind whatever, from any King, Prince, or foreign State.

Section 10.

Restrictions on States' Powers

1. No State shall enter into any Treaty, Alliance, or Confederation; grant Letters of Marque and Reprisal; coin Money; emit Bills of Credit; make any Thing but gold and silver Coin a Tender in Payment of Debts; pass any Bill of Attainder, ex post facto Law, or Law impairing the Obligation of Contracts, or grant any Title of Nobility.

2. No State shall, without the Consent of the Congress, lay any Imposts or Duties on Imports or Exports, except what may be absolutely necessary for executing its inspection Laws: and the net Produce of all Duties and Imposts, laid by any State on Imports or Exports, shall be for the Use of the Treasury of the United States; and all such Laws shall be subject to the Revision and Control of the Congress.

3. No State shall, without the Consent of Congress, lay any Duty of Tonnage, keep Troops, or Ships of War in time of Peace, enter into any Agreement or Compact with another State, or with a foreign Power, or engage in War, unless actually invaded, or in such imminent Danger as will not admit of delay.

ARTICLE II.

The Executive Branch

Section 1.

President and Vice-President: Election, Qualifications, and Oath

1. The executive Power shall be vested in a President of the United States of America. He shall hold his Office during the term of four Years, and, together with the Vice President, chosen for the same Term, be elected, as follows.

2. Each State shall appoint, in such Manner as the Legislature thereof may direct, a Number of Electors, equal to the whole Number of Senators and Representatives to which the State may be entitled in the Congress: but no Senator or Representative, or Person holding an Office of Trust or Profit under the United States, shall be appointed an Elector.

3. [The Electors shall meet in their respective states, and vote by Ballot for two Persons, of whom one at least shall not be an Inhabitant of the same State with themselves. And they shall make a List of all the Persons voted for, and of the Number of Votes for each; which List they shall sign and certify, and transmit sealed to the Seat of the Government of the United States, directed to the President of the Senate. The President of the Senate shall, in the Presence of the Senate and House of Representatives, open all the Certificates, and the Votes shall then be counted. The Person having the greatest Number of Votes shall be the President, if such Number be a Majority of the whole Number of Electors appointed; and if there be more than one who have such Majority, and have an equal Number of Votes, then the House of Representatives shall immediately choose by Ballot one of them for President; and if no Person have a Majority, then from the five highest on the List the said House shall in like manner choose the President. But in choosing the President, the Votes shall be taken by States, the Representation from each State having one Vote; A quorum for this Purpose shall consist of a Member or Members from two thirds of the States, and a Majority of all the States shall be necessary to a Choice. In every Case, after the Choice of the President, the Person having the greatest Number of Votes of the Electors shall be the Vice President. But if there should remain two or more who have equal Votes, the Senate shall choose from them by Ballot the Vice President.]*

4. The Congress may determine the Time of choosing the Electors, and the day on which they shall give their Votes; which Day shall be the same throughout the United States.

5. No Person except a natural born Citizen, or a Citizen of the United States at the time of the Adoption of this Constitution, shall be eligible to the Office of the President; neither shall any person be eligible to that Office who shall not have attained to the Age of thirty five Years, and been fourteen Years a Resident within the United States.

6. [In Case of the Removal of the President from Office, or of his Death, Resignation, or Inability to discharge the Powers and Duties of the said Office, the Same shall devolve on the Vice President, and the Congress may by Law provide for the Case of Removal, Death, Resignation or Inability, both of the President and Vice President, declaring what Officer shall then act as President, and such Officer shall act accordingly, until the Disability be removed, or a President shall be elected.]**

7. The President shall, at stated Times, receive for his Services, a Compensation, which shall neither be increased nor diminished during the Period for which he shall have been elected, and he shall not receive within that Period any other Emolument from the United States, or any of them.

8. Before he enter the Execution of his Office, he shall take the following Oath or Affirmation:—"I do solemnly swear (or affirm) that I will faithfully execute the Office of President of the United States, and will to the best of my Ability, preserve, protect, and defend the Constitution of the United States."

Section 2.

Powers of the President

1. The President shall be Commander in Chief of the Army and Navy of the United States, and of the Militia of the several States, when called into the actual Service of the United States; he may require the Opinion, in writing, of the principal Officer in each of the executive Departments, upon any Subject relating to the Duties of their respective Offices, and he shall have Power to grant Reprieves and Pardons for Offenses against the United States, except in Cases of Impeachment.

2. He shall have Power, by and with the Advice and Consent of the Senate, to make Treaties, provided two thirds of the Senators present concur; and he shall nominate, and by and with the Advice and Consent of the Senate, shall appoint Ambassadors, other public Ministers and Consuls, Judges of the supreme Court, and all other Officers of the United States, whose Appointments are not herein otherwise provided for, and which shall be established by Law: but the Congress may by Law vest the Appointment of such inferior Officers, as they think proper, in the President alone, in the Courts of Law, or in the Heads of Departments.

3. The President shall have Power to fill up all Vacancies that may happen during the Recess of the Senate, by granting Commissions which shall expire at the End of their next Session.

Section 3.

Duties of the President

He shall from time to time give to the Congress Information of the State of the Union, and recommend to their Consideration such Measures as he shall judge necessary and expedient; he

* Changed by the Twelfth Amendment.
** Changed by the Twenty-fifth Amendment.

may, on extraordinary Occasions, convene both Houses, or either of them, and in Case of Disagreement between them, with Respect to the Time of Adjournment, he may adjourn them to such Time as he shall think proper; he shall receive Ambassadors and other public Ministers; he shall take Care that the Laws be faithfully executed, and shall Commission all the Officers of the United States.

Section 4.

Impeachment and Removal from Office for Crimes

The President, Vice President and all civil Officers of the United States, shall be removed from Office on Impeachment for, and Conviction of, Treason, Bribery, or other high Crimes and Misdemeanors.

ARTICLE III.

The Judicial Branch

Section 1.

Federal Courts, Tenure of Office

The judicial Power of the United States, shall be vested in one supreme Court, and in such inferior Courts as the Congress may from time to time ordain and establish. The Judges, both of the supreme and inferior Courts, shall hold their Offices during good Behavior, and shall, at stated Times, receive for their Services a Compensation, which shall not be diminished during their Continuance in Office.

Section 2.

Jurisdiction of Federal Courts

1. The judicial Power shall extend to all Cases, in Law and Equity, arising under this Constitution, the Laws of the United States, and Treaties made, or which shall be made, under their Authority;— to all Cases affecting Ambassadors, other public Ministers and Consuls;—to all Cases of admiralty and maritime Jurisdiction;—to Controversies to which the United States shall be a Party;—to Controversies between two or more States; [between a State and Citizens of another State;] between Citizens of different States;—between Citizens of the same State claiming Lands under Grants of different States;—[and between a State, or the Citizens thereof, and foreign States, Citizens or Subjects.]*

2. In all Cases affecting Ambassadors, other public Ministers and Consuls, and those in which a State shall be Party, the supreme Court shall have original Jurisdiction. In all the other Cases before mentioned, the supreme Court shall have appellate Jurisdiction, both as to Law and Fact, with such Exceptions, and under such Regulations as the Congress shall make.

3. The Trial of all Crimes, except in Cases of Impeachment, shall be by Jury; and such Trial shall be held in the State where said Crimes shall have been committed; but when not committed within any State, the Trial shall be at such Place or Places as the Congress may by Law have directed.

Section 3.

Treason: Conviction Of and Punishment For

1. Treason against the United States shall consist only in levying War against them, or in adhering to their Enemies, giving them Aid and Comfort. No Person shall be convicted of Treason unless on the Testimony of two Witnesses to the same overt Act, or on Confession in open Court.

---

* Changed by the Eleventh Amendment.

2. The Congress shall have Power to declare the Punishment of Treason, but no Attainder of Treason shall work Corruption of Blood, or Forfeiture except during the Life of the Person attainted.

ARTICLE IV.

Relations Among the States

Section 1.

Full Faith and Credit

Full Faith and Credit shall be given in each State to the public Acts, Records, and judicial Proceedings of every other State; And the Congress may by general Laws prescribe the manner in which such Acts, Records and Proceedings shall be proved, and the Effect thereof.

Section 2.

Rights of State Citizens; Right of Extradition

1. The Citizens of each State shall be entitled to all Privileges and Immunities of Citizens in the several States.

2. A Person charged in any State with Treason, Felony, or other Crime, who shall flee from Justice, and be found in another State, shall on Demand of the executive Authority of the State from which he fled, be delivered up, to be removed to the State having Jurisdiction of the Crime.

3. [No person held to Service or Labour in one State, under the Laws thereof, escaping into another, shall, in Consequence of any Law or Regulation therein, be discharged from such Service or Labour, but shall be delivered up on Claim of the Party to whom such Service or Labour may be due.]*

Section 3.

Admission of New States

1. New States may be admitted by the Congress into this Union; but no new State shall be formed or erected within the Jurisdiction of any other State; nor any State be formed by the Junction of two or more States, or parts of States, without the Consent of the Legislatures of the States concerned as well as of the Congress.

2. The Congress shall have Power to dispose of and make all needful Rules and Regulations respecting the territory or other Property belonging to the United States; and nothing in this Constitution shall be so construed as to Prejudice any Claims of the United States, or of any particular State.

Section 4.

Republican Government Guaranteed

The United States shall guarantee to every State in this Union a Republican Form of Government, and shall protect each of them against Invasion; and on Application of the Legislature, or of the Executive (when the Legislature cannot be convened) against domestic Violence.

* Changed by the Thirteenth Amendment.

ARTICLE V.

Amendment Procedures

The Congress, whenever two thirds of both Houses shall deem it necessary, shall propose Amendments to this Constitution, or, on the Application of the Legislatures of two thirds of the several States, shall call a Convention for proposing Amendments, which, in either Case, shall be valid to all Intents and Purposes, as Part of this Constitution, when ratified by the Legislatures of three fourths of the several States, or by Conventions in three fourths thereof, as the one or the other Mode of Ratification may be proposed by the Congress; Provided that no Amendment which may be made prior to the Year One thousand eight hundred and eight shall in any Manner affect the first and fourth Clauses in the Ninth Section of the first Article; and that no State, without its Consent, shall be deprived of its equal Suffrage in the Senate.

ARTICLE VI.

Supremacy of the Constitution and Federal Laws

1. All debts contracted and Engagements entered into, before the Adoption of this Constitution, shall be as valid against the United States under this Constitution, as under the Confederation.

2. This Constitution, and the Laws of the United States which shall be made in Pursuance thereof; and all Treaties made, or which shall be made, under the Authority of the United States, shall be the supreme Law of the Land; and the Judges in every State shall be bound thereby, any Thing in the Constitution or Laws of any State to the Contrary notwithstanding.

3. The Senators and Representatives before mentioned, and the Members of the several State Legislatures, and all executive and judicial Officers, both of the United States and of the several States, shall be bound by Oath or Affirmation, to support this Constitution; but no religious Test shall ever be required as a Qualification to any Office or public Trust under the United States.

ARTICLE VII.

Ratification

The Ratification of the Conventions of nine States, shall be sufficient for the Establishment of this Constitution between the States so ratifying the Same.

Done in Convention by the unanimous consent of the States present the seventeenth day of September in the year of our Lord one thousand seven hundred and eighty seven and of the Independence of the United States of America the Twelfth. In witness whereof we have hereunto subscribed our Names,

George Washington—President
and deputy from Virginia

This constitution was adopted on September 17, 1787, by the Constitutional Convention, and was declared ratified on July 2, 1788.

Signers of the Constitution

New Hampshire
John Langdon
Nicholas Gilman

Massachusetts
Nathaniel Gorham
Rufus King

Connecticut
William Samuel Johnson
Roger Sherman

New York
Alexander Hamilton

New Jersey
William Livingston
David Brearley
William Paterson
Jonathan Dayton

Pennsylvania
Benjamin Franklin
Thomas Mifflin
Robert Morris
George Clymer
Thomas Fitzsimons
Jared Ingersoll
James Wilson
Gouverneur Morris

Delaware
George Read
Gunning Bedford, Jr.
John Dickinson
Richard Bassett
Jacob Broom

Maryland
James McHenry
Daniel of St. Tho. Jenifer
Daniel Carrol

Virginia
John Blair
James Madison, Junior

North Carolina
William Blount
Richard Dobbs Spaight
Hugh Williamson

South Carolina
John Rutledge
Charles Cotesworth Pinckney
Charles Pinckney
Pierce Butler

Georgia
William Few
Abraham Baldwin

Attest *William Jackson*
Secretary

Amendments to the Constitution

Since 1787, twenty-six amendments have been proposed by the Congress and ratified by the several states, pursuant to Article Five of the original Constitution. The first ten amendments are known as the Bill of Rights.

Amendment I.

Freedom of Religion and Expression

Congress shall make no law respecting an establishment of religion, or prohibiting the free exercise thereof; or abridging the freedom of speech, or of the press, or the right of the people peaceably to assemble, and to petition the Government for a redress of grievances. (Ratified December, 1791.)

Amendment II.

Right to Bear Arms

A well regulated Militia, being necessary to the security of a free State, the right of the people to keep and bear Arms, shall not be infringed. (Ratified December, 1791.)

Amendment III.

Quartering of Soldiers

No Soldier shall, in time of peace be quartered in any house, without the consent of the Owner, nor in time of war, but in a manner to be prescribed by law. (Ratified December, 1791.)

Amendment IV.

Security From Unreasonable Searches and Seizures

The right of the people to be secure in their persons, houses, papers, and effects, against unreasonable searches and seizures, shall not be violated, and no Warrants shall issue, but upon probable cause, supported by Oath or affirmation, and particularly describing the place to be searched, and the persons or things to be seized. (Ratified December, 1791.)

Amendment V.

Rights of Due Process of Law

No person shall be held to answer for a capital, or otherwise infamous crime, unless on a presentment or indictment of a Grand Jury, except in cases arising in the land or naval forces, or in the Militia, when in actual service in time of War or public danger; nor shall any person be subject for the same offence to be twice put in jeopardy of life or limb, nor shall be compelled in any criminal case to be a witness against himself, nor be deprived of life, liberty, or property, without due process of law; nor shall private property be taken for public use without just compensation. (Ratified December, 1791.)

Amendment VI.

Right to a Fair Trial

In all criminal prosecutions, the accused shall enjoy the right to a speedy and public trial, by an impartial jury of the State and district wherein the crime shall have been committed; which district shall have been previously ascertained by law, and to be informed of the nature and cause of the accusation; to be confronted with the witnesses against him; to have compulsory process for obtaining witnesses in his favor, and to have the assistance of counsel for his defence. (Ratified December, 1791.)

Amendment VII.
Trial by Jury

In Suits at common law, where the value in controversy shall exceed twenty dollars, the right of trial by jury shall be preserved, and no fact tried by a jury shall be otherwise re-examined in any Court of the United States, than according to the rules of the common law. (Ratified December, 1791.)

Amendment VIII.
Fair Bail and Punishments

Excessive bail shall not be required, nor excessive fines imposed, nor cruel and unusual punishments inflicted. (Ratified December, 1791.)

Amendment IX.
Rights Retained by the People

The enumeration in the Constitution of certain rights shall not be construed to deny or disparage others retained by the people. (Ratified December, 1791.)

Amendment X.
Powers Reserved to States and People

The powers not delegated to the United States by the Constitution, nor prohibited by it to the States, are reserved to the States respectively, or to the people. (Ratified December, 1791.)

Amendment XI.
Limitations on Federal Courts

The Judicial power of the United States shall not be construed to extend to any suit in law or equity, commenced or prosecuted against one of the United States by Citizens of another State, or by Citizens or Subjects of any Foreign State. (Ratified February, 1795.)

Amendment XII.
Election of President

The Electors shall meet in their respective states, and vote by ballot for President and Vice President, one of whom, at least, shall not be an inhabitant of the same state with themselves; they shall name in their ballots the person voted for as President, and in distinct ballots the person voted for as Vice-President, and they shall make distinct lists of all persons voted for as President, and of all persons voted for as Vice-President, and of the number of votes for each, which lists they shall sign and certify, and transmit sealed to the seat of the government of the United States, directed to the President of the Senate;—The President of the Senate shall, in the presence of the Senate and House of Representatives, open all the certificates and the votes shall then be counted;—The person having the greatest number of votes for President, shall be the President, if such number be a majority of the whole number of Electors appointed; and if no person have such majority, then from the persons having the highest numbers not exceeding three on the list of those voted for as President, the House of Representatives shall choose immediately, by ballot, the President. But in choosing the President, the votes shall be taken by states, the representation from each state having one vote; a quorum for this purpose shall consist of a member or members from two-thirds of the states, and a majority of all the states shall be necessary to a choice. [And if the House of Representatives shall not choose a President whenever the right of choice shall devolve upon them, before the fourth day of March next following, then the Vice-President shall act as President, as in the case of the death or other constitutional disability of the President—]* The person having the

---

* Superseded by section 3 of the Twentieth Amendment.

greatest number of votes as Vice-President, shall be the Vice-President, if such number be a majority of the whole number of Electors appointed, and if no person have a majority, then from the two highest numbers on the list, the Senate shall choose the Vice-President; a quorum for the purpose shall consist of two-thirds of the whole number of Senators, and a majority of the whole number shall be necessary to a choice. But no person constitutionally ineligible to the office of President shall be eligible to that of Vice-President of the United States. (Ratified June, 1804.)

The Civil War Amendments

Amendment XIII.

Slavery Abolished

Section 1. Neither slavery nor involuntary servitude, except as a punishment for crime whereof the party shall have been duly convicted, shall exist within the United States, or any place subject to their jurisdiction.

Section 2. Congress shall have power to enforce this article by appropriate legislation. (Ratified December, 1865.)

Amendment XIV.

Equal Protection and Due Process; Citizenship Defined and Guaranteed

Section 1. All persons born or naturalized in the United States and subject to the jurisdiction thereof, are citizens of the United States and of the State wherein they reside. No State shall make or enforce any law which shall abridge the privileges or immunities of citizens of the United States; nor shall any State deprive any person of life, liberty, or property, without due process of law; nor deny to any person within its jurisdiction the equal protection of the laws.

Section 2. Representatives shall be apportioned among the several States according to their respective numbers, counting the whole number of persons in each State, excluding Indians not taxed. But when the right to vote at any election for the choice of electors for President and Vice President of the United States, Representatives in Congress, the Executive and Judicial officers of a State, or the members of the Legislature thereof, is denied to any of the male inhabitants of such State, being twenty-one years of age, and citizens of the United States, or in any way abridged, except for participation in rebellion, or other crime, the basis of representation therein shall be reduced in the proportion which the number of such male citizens shall bear to the whole number of male citizens twenty-one years of age in such State.

Section 3. No person shall be a Senator or a Representative in Congress, or elector of President and Vice President, or hold any office, civil or military, under the United States, or under any State, who, having previously taken an oath, as a member of Congress, or as an officer of the United States, or as a member of any State legislature, or as an executive or judicial officer of any State, to support the Constitution of the United States, shall have engaged in insurrection or rebellion against the same, or given aid or comfort to the enemies thereof. But Congress may by a vote of two-thirds of each House, remove such disability.

Section 4. The validity of the public debt of the United States, authorized by law, including debts incurred for payment of pensions and bounties for services in suppressing insurrection or rebellion, shall not be questioned. But neither the United States nor any State shall assume or pay any debt or obligation incurred in aid of insurrection or rebellion against the United States, or any claim for the loss or emancipation of any slave; but all such debts, obligations and claims shall be held illegal and void.

Section 5. The Congress shall have power to enforce, by appropriate legislation, the provisions of this article. (Ratified July, 1868.)

Amendment XV.

Blacks' Right to Vote

Section 1.   The right of citizens of the United States to vote shall not be denied or abridged by the United States or by any State on account of race, color, or previous condition of servitude.

Section 2.   The Congress shall have power to enforce this article by appropriate legislation. (Ratified February, 1870.)

Amendment XVI.

Power to Tax Incomes

The Congress shall have power to lay and collect taxes on incomes, from whatever source derived, without apportionment among the several States, and without regard to any census or enumeration. (Ratified February, 1913.)

Amendment XVII.

Popular Election of Senators

The Senate of the United States shall be composed of two Senators from each State, elected by the people thereof, for six years; and each Senator shall have one vote. The electors in each State shall have the qualifications requisite for electors of the most numerous branch of the State legislatures.

When vacancies happen in the representation of any State in the Senate, the executive authority of such State shall issue writs of election to fill such vacancies: Provided, That the legislature of any State may empower the executive thereof to make temporary appointments until the people fill the vacancies by election as the legislature may direct.

This amendment shall not be so construed as to affect the election or term of any Senator chosen before it becomes valid as part of the Constitution. (Ratified April, 1913.)

Amendment XVIII.

Prohibition of Alcoholic Beverages

[Section 1.   After one year from the ratification of this article the manufacture, sale, or transportation of intoxicating liquors within, the importation thereof into, or the exportation thereof from the United States and all territory subject to the jurisdiction thereof for beverage purposes is hereby prohibited.

Section 2.   The Congress and the several States shall have concurrent power to enforce this article by appropriate legislation.

Section 3.   This article shall be inoperative unless it shall have been ratified as an amendment to the Constitution by the legislatures of the several States, as provided in the Constitution, within seven years from the date of the submission hereof to the States by the Congress.]* (Ratified January, 1919.)

Amendment XIX.

Female Suffrage

The right of citizens of the United States to vote shall not be denied or abridged by the United States or by any State on account of sex.

Congress shall have power to enforce this article by appropriate legislation. (Ratified August, 1920.)

---

* Repealed by the Twenty-first Amendment.

Amendment XX.

Changes in Terms of President and Congress

Section 1.   The terms of the President and Vice President shall end at noon on the 20th day of January, and the terms of Senators and Representatives at noon on the 3d day of January, of the years in which such terms would have ended if this article had not been ratified; and the terms of their successors shall then begin.

Section 2.   The Congress shall assemble at least once in every year, and such meeting shall begin at noon on the 3d day of January, unless they shall by law appoint a different day.

Section 3.   If, at the time fixed for the beginning of the term of the President, the President elect shall have died, the Vice President elect shall become President. If a President shall not have been chosen before the time fixed for the beginning of his term, or if the President elect shall have failed to qualify, then the Vice President elect shall act as President until a President shall have qualified; and the Congress may by law provide for the case wherein neither a President elect nor a Vice President elect shall have qualified, declaring who shall then act as President, or the manner in which one who is to act shall be selected, and such person shall act accordingly until a President or Vice President shall have qualified.

Section 4.   The Congress may by law provide for the case of the death of any of the persons from whom the House of Representatives may choose a President whenever the right of choice shall have devolved upon them, and for the case of the death of any of the persons from whom the Senate may choose a Vice President whenever the right of choice shall have devolved upon them.

Section 5.   Sections 1 and 2 shall take effect on the 15th day of October following the ratification of this article.

Section 6.   This article shall be inoperative unless it shall have been ratified as an amendment to the Constitution by the legislatures of three-fourths of the several States within seven years from the date of its submission. (Ratified January, 1933.)

Amendment XXI.

Repeal of Alcohol Prohibition

Section 1.   The eighteenth article of amendment to the Constitution of the United States is hereby repealed.

Section 2.   The transportation or importation into any State, Territory, or possession of the United States for delivery or use therein of intoxicating liquors, in violation of the laws thereof, is hereby prohibited.

Section 3.   This article shall be inoperative unless it shall have been ratified as an amendment to the Constitution by conventions in the several States, as provided in the Constitution, within seven years from the date of the submission hereof to the States by the Congress. (Ratified December, 1933.)

Amendment XXII.

President Limited to Two Terms

Section 1.   No person shall be elected to the office of the President more than twice, and no person who has held the office of President, or acted as President, for more than two years of a term to which some other person was elected President shall be elected to the office of the President more than once. But this Article shall not apply to any person holding the office of President when this Article was proposed by the Congress, and shall not prevent any person who may be holding the office of President, or acting as President, during the term within which this Article becomes operative from holding the office of President or acting as President during the remainder of such term.

Section 2.   This article shall be inoperative unless it shall have been ratified as an amendment to the Constitution by the legislatures of three-fourths of the several States within seven years from the date of its submission to the States by the Congress. (Ratified February, 1951.)

Amendment XXIII.

Presidential Suffrage for District of Columbia

Section 1.   The District constituting the seat of Government of the United States shall appoint in such manner as the Congress may direct:

A number of electors of President and Vice President equal to the whole number of Senators and Representatives in Congress to which the District would be entitled if it were a State, but in no event more than the least populous State; they shall be in addition to those appointed by the States, but they shall be considered, for the purposes of the election of President and Vice President, to be electors appointed by a State; and they shall meet in the District and perform such duties as provided by the twelfth article of amendment.

Section 2.   The Congress shall have power to enforce this article by appropriate legislation. (Ratified March, 1961.)

Amendment XXIV.

Poll Tax Forbidden

Section 1.   The right of citizens of the United States to vote in any primary or other election for President or Vice President, for electors for President or Vice President, or for Senator or Representative in Congress, shall not be denied or abridged by the United States or any State by reason of failure to pay any poll tax or other tax.

Section 2.   The Congress shall have power to enforce this article by appropriate legislation. (Ratified January, 1964.)

Amendment XXV.

Procedures for Presidential Succession

Section 1.   In case of the removal of the President from office or of his death or resignation, the Vice President shall become President.

Section 2.   Whenever there is a vacancy in the office of the Vice President, the President shall nominate a Vice President who shall take office upon confirmation by a majority vote of both Houses of Congress.

Section 3.   Whenever the President transmits to the President pro tempore of the Senate and the Speaker of the House of Representatives his written declaration that he is unable to discharge the powers and duties of his office, and until he transmits to them a written declaration to the contrary, such powers and duties shall be discharged by the Vice President as Acting President.

Section 4.   Whenever the Vice President and a majority of either the principal officers of the executive departments or of such other body as Congress may by law provide, transmit to the President pro tempore of the Senate and the Speaker of the House of Representatives their written declaration that the President is unable to discharge the powers and duties of his office, the Vice President shall immediately assume the powers and duties of the office as Acting President.

Thereafter, when the President transmits to the President pro tempore of the Senate and the Speaker of the House of Representatives his written declaration that no inability exists, he shall resume the powers and duties of his office unless the Vice President and a majority of either the principal officers of the executive department or of such other body as Congress may by law provide, transmit within four days to the President pro tempore of the Senate and the Speaker of the House of Representatives their written declaration that the President is unable to discharge the powers and duties of his office. Thereupon Congress shall decide the issue, assembling within forty-eight hours for that purpose if not in session. If the Congress, within twenty-one days after receipt of the latter written declaration, or, if Congress is not in session, within twenty-one days after Congress is required to assemble, determines by two-thirds vote of both Houses that the President is unable to discharge the powers and duties of his office, the Vice President shall continue to discharge the same as Acting President; otherwise, the President shall resume the powers and duties of his office. (Ratified February, 1967.)

Amendment XXVI.

Voting Age Lowered to Eighteen

Section 1. The right of citizens of the United States, who are eighteen years of age or older, to vote shall not be denied or abridged by the United States or by any State on account of age.

Section 2. The Congress shall have power to enforce this article by appropriate legislation. (Ratified July, 1971.)

This is the original text and section numbers. Descriptive headings have been added by editors. Passages in brackets indicate that they were changed by Amendments.

Universal Declaration of Human Rights [1948]

Preamble

Whereas recognition of the inherent dignity and of the equal and inalienable rights of all members of the human family is the foundation of freedom, justice and peace in the world,

Whereas disregard and contempt for human rights have resulted in barbarous acts which have outraged the conscience of mankind, and the advent of a world in which human beings shall enjoy freedom of speech and belief and freedom from fear and want has been proclaimed as the highest aspiration of the common people,

Whereas it is essential, if man is not to be compelled to have recourse, as a last resort, to rebellion against tyranny and oppression, that human rights should be protected by the rule of law,

Whereas it is essential to promote the development of friendly relations between nations,

Whereas the peoples of the United Nations have in the Charter reaffirmed their faith in fundamental human rights, in the dignity and worth of the human person and in the equal rights of men and women and have determined to promote social progress and better standards of life in larger freedom,

Whereas Member States have pledged themselves to achieve, in co-operation with the United Nations, the promotion of universal respect for and observance of human rights and fundamental freedoms,

Whereas a common understanding of these rights and freedoms is of the greatest importance for the full realization of this pledge,

Now, therefore,

The General Assembly

Proclaims this Universal Declaration of Human Rights as a common standard of achievement for all peoples and all nations, to the end that every individual and every organ of society, keeping this Declaration constantly in mind, shall strive by teaching and education to promote respect for these rights and freedoms and by progressive measures, national and international, to secure their universal and effective recognition and observance, both among the peoples of Member States themselves and among the peoples of territories under their jurisdiction.

Article 1

All human beings are born free and equal in dignity and rights. They are endowed with reason and conscience and should act towards one another in a spirit of brotherhood.

Article 2

Everyone is entitled to all the rights and freedoms set forth in this Declaration, without distinction of any kind, such as race, colour, sex, language, religion, political or other opinion, national or social origin, property, birth or other status.

Furthermore, no distinction shall be made on the basis of the political, jurisdictional or international status of the country or territory to which a person belongs, whether it be independent, trust, non-self-governing or under any other limitation of sovereignty.

Article 3

Everyone has the right to life, liberty and the security of person.

Article 4

No one shall be held in slavery or servitude; slavery and the slave trade shall be prohibited in all their forms.

Article 5

No one shall be subjected to torture or to cruel, inhuman or degrading treatment or punishment.

Article 6

Everyone has the right to recognition everywhere as a person before the law.

Article 7

All are equal before the law and are entitled without any discrimination to equal protection of the law. All are entitled to equal protection against any discrimination in violation of this Declaration and against any incitement to such discrimination.

Article 8

Everyone has the right to an effective remedy by the competent national tribunals for acts violating the fundamental rights granted him by the constitution or by law.

Article 9

No one shall be subjected to arbitrary arrest, detention or exile.

Article 10

Everyone is entitled in full equality to a fair, and public hearing by an independent and impartial tribunal, in the determination of his rights and obligations and of any criminal charge against him.

Article 11

1. Everyone charged with a penal offence has the right to be presumed innocent until proved guilty according to law in a public trail at which he has had all the guarantees necessary for his defence.

2. No one shall be held guilty of any penal offence on account of any act or omission which did not constitute a penal offence, under national or international law, at the time when it was committed. Nor shall a heavier penalty be imposed than the one that was applicable at the time the penal offence was committed.

Article 12

No one shall be subjected to arbitrary interference with his privacy, family, home or correspondence, nor to attacks upon his honour and reputation. Everyone has the right to the protection of the law against such interference or attacks.

Article 13

1. Everyone has the right to freedom of movement and residence within the borders of each State.

2. Everyone has the right to leave any country, including his own, and to return to his country.

Article 14

1. Everyone has the right to seek and to enjoy in other countries asylum from persecution.

2. This right may not be invoked in the case of prosecutions genuinely arising from non-political crimes or from acts contrary to the purposes and principles of the United Nations.

Article 15

1. Everyone has the right to a nationality.

2. No one shall be arbitrarily deprived of his nationality nor denied the right to change his nationality.

Article 16

1. Men and women of full age, without any limitation due to race, nationality or religion, have the right to marry and to found a family. They are entitled to equal rights as to marriage, during marriage and at its dissolution.

2. Marriage shall be entered into only with the free and full consent of the intending spouses.

3. The family is the natural and fundamental group unit of society and is entitled to protection by society and the State.

Article 17

1. Everyone has the right to own property alone as well as in association with others.

2. No one shall be arbitrarily deprived of his property.

Article 18

Everyone has the right to freedom of thought, conscience and religion; this right includes freedom to change his religion or belief, and freedom, either alone or in community with others and in public or private, to manifest his religion or belief in teaching, practice, worship and observance.

Article 19

Everyone has the right to freedom of opinion and expression; this right includes freedom to hold opinions without interference and to seek, receive and impart information and ideas through any media and regardless of frontiers.

Article 20

1. Everyone has the right to freedom of peaceful assembly and association.

2. No one may be compelled to belong to an association.

Article 21

1. Everyone has the right to take part in the government of his country, directly or through freely chosen representatives.

2. Everyone has the right of equal access to public service in his country.

3. The will of the people shall be the basis of the authority of government; this will shall be expressed in periodic and genuine elections which shall be by universal and equal suffrage and shall be held by secret vote or by equivalent free voting procedures.

Article 22

Everyone, as a member of society, has the right to social security and is entitled to realization, through national effort and international co-operation and in accordance with the organization and resources of each State, of the economic, social and cultural rights indispensable for his dignity and the free development of his personality.

Article 23

1. Everyone has the right to work, to free choice of employment, to just and favourable conditions of work and to protection against unemployment.

2. Everyone, without any discrimination, has the right to equal pay for equal work.

3. Everyone who works has the right to just and favourable remuneration ensuring for himself and his family an existence worthy of human dignity, and supplemented, if necessary, by other means of social protection.

4. Everyone has the right to form and to join trade unions for the protection of his interests.

Article 24

Everyone has the right to rest and leisure, including reasonable limitation of working hours and periodic holidays with pay.

Article 25

1. Everyone has the right to a standard of living adequate for the health and well-being of himself and of his family, including food, clothing, housing and medical care and necessary social services, and the right to security in the event of unemployment, sickness, disability, widowhood, old age or other lack of livelihood in circumstances beyond his control.

2. Motherhood and childhood are entitled to special care and assistance. All children, whether born in or out of wedlock, shall enjoy the same social protection.

Article 26

1. Everyone has the right to education. Education shall be free, at least in the elementary and fundamental stages. Elementary education shall be compulsory. Technical and professional education shall be made generally available and higher education shall be equally accessible to all on the basis of merit.

2. Education shall be directed to the full development of the human personality and to the strengthening of respect for human rights and fundamental freedoms. It shall promote understanding, tolerance and friendship among all nations, racial or religious groups, and shall further the activities of the United Nations for the maintenance of peace.

3. Parents have a prior right to choose the kind of education that shall be given to their children.

Article 27

1. Everyone has the right freely to participate in the cultural life of the community, to enjoy the arts and to share in scientific advancement and its benefits.

2. Everyone has the right to the protection of the moral and material interests resulting from any scientific, literary or artistic production of which he is the author.

Article 28

Everyone is entitled to a social and international order in which the rights and freedoms set forth in this Declaration can be fully realized.

Article 29

1. Everyone has duties to the community in which alone the free and full development of his personality is possible.

2. In the exercise of his rights and freedoms, everyone shall be subject only to such limitations as are determined by law solely for the purpose of securing due recognition and respect for the rights and freedoms of others and of meeting the just requirements of morality, public order and the general welfare in a democratic society.

3. These rights and freedoms may in no case be exercised contrary to the purposes and principles of the United Nations.

Article 30

Nothing in this Declaration may be interpreted as implying for any State, group or person any right to engage in any activity or to perform any act aimed at the destruction of any of the rights and freedoms set forth herein.

Glossary

GLOSSARY OF MAJOR TERMS AND CONCEPTS

The following terms are defined as used in this textbook. Some of the words are specialized legal terms which may have other meanings in other contexts.

abolitionists. People who advocated the end of slavery in the United States.

abridge. Take away; reduce; diminish.

absolute. Without limits.

Adamson v. California (1947). A case in which the Supreme Court ruled that not all the protections of the Bill of Rights were part of due process and therefore were not incorporated into the Fourteenth Amendment as limitations on the states.

adversarial system. The trial system in which opposing parties are given full opportunity to present and establish their evidence, and cross-examine the evidence presented by their adversaries. All this is done under established rules of procedure before an impartial judge and/or jury.

advocate. To speak or write in favor or support of something.

affirmative action. A policy, or a requirement imposed by law or administrative regulation, that an organization take positive steps to increase the number or proportion of women and minorities in its membership.

aggressive recruitment programs. A form of affirmative action in which extensive efforts are made to notify and solicit applications from underrepresented groups.

amendment. A change in or addition to a document.

Anti-Federalists. The political leaders who were against ratification of the Constitution because they thought it gave too much power to the federal government and did not protect the political rights of the people.

appeal. A request for review by a higher court of a lower court's decision.

appellate court. A judicial body that hears appeals from a lower court.

Articles of Confederation. The first constitution of the newly independent states, adopted by Congress in 1781 and replaced by the United States Constitution, ratified in 1788.

authority. The right to control or direct the actions of others, in accordance with law, morality, or custom.

bail. Money or other security given to obtain a person's release from custody, which may be forfeited if the person subsequently fails to appear before the court for trial.

Barron v. Baltimore (1833). An early Supreme Court case which established that the Bill of Rights did not apply to actions of the state governments.

bear witness. Give testimony.

bill of attainder. An act of the legislature that inflicts punishment on a named individual or group without a judicial trial.

Bill of Rights. The first ten amendments to the Constitution which restrict the federal government's power to interfere with certain basic rights of the people.

black codes. Regulations passed by southern state governments during Reconstruction to prohibit blacks from voting. See poll tax, literacy test, and grandfather clause.

British constitution. The framework for running the British government. The British constitution is unwritten, consisting of the common law, acts of Parliament, and political customs and traditions.

Brown v. Board of Education (1954). The Supreme Court case which declared that "separate-but-equal" educational facilities are inherently unequal and therefore a violation of the equal protection of the laws guaranteed by the Fourteenth Amendment.

cabinet. The heads of the departments of the executive branch who advise the president.

capital offense. A crime punishable by death.

capital punishment. The infliction of the death penalty.

capitalism. An economic system in which the means of producing and distributing goods are privately owned and operated for profit in a competitive market.

censorship. The act of examining materials in order to suppress or delete anything considered objectionable.

checks and balances. The distribution and balancing of power among different branches of government so that no one branch is able to dominate the others.

citizenship. The status of being a member of a state, one who owes allegiance to the government and is entitled to its protection and to political rights.

civic virtue. The dedication of citizens to the common welfare above their own individual interests.

civil law. The body of law which deals with the private rights of individuals, as distinguished from the criminal law.

civil rights. Fundamental rights belonging to every member of a society.

Civil Rights Act of 1866. An act of Congress which attempted to protect the rights of African Americans following the Civil War. The act was ineffective because the president refused to enforce it and the Supreme Court refused to hear cases about it.

Civil Rights Act of 1875. An act of Congress which gave the federal government the power to enforce the protections of citizens' rights under the Fourteenth Amendment. The act was not enforced by the president and was declared unconstitutional by the Supreme Court.

civil rights laws. Laws passed by Congress or state legislatures designed to protect the rights of individuals to fair treatment by private persons, groups, organizations, businesses, and government.

civil rights movement. A movement which sought to guarantee civil rights to all members of society. The movement gained momentum following World War II and strengthened in the 1960s.

Civil War Amendments. The Thirteenth, Fourteenth, and Fifteenth Amendments, passed following the Civil War, which freed the slaves, granted them citizenship, and guaranteed them the rights of citizens.

class system. A system in which members of social classes are prevented from moving into other classes.

classical republicanism. The theory of government that holds that the best kind of government is one that promotes the common welfare instead of the interests of only one class of citizens. The Roman Republic was thought by the Founders to be one of the best examples of a society living under this theory of government.

clear and present danger. A standard used to justify limitations on speech which will lead directly to harm to others.

codes of conduct. Rules designed to regulate such behavior as prejudicial speech and action.

colonial charters. The documents under which the original colonies were granted authority by the British.

commerce clause. The clause in the Constitution which gives Congress the power "to regulate commerce with foreign nations and among the several States." The clause has been used to regulate organizations which are engaged in interstate relations by, for example, prohibiting them from engaging in racial discrimination.

commission. An organization set up by Congress and given limited power and authority.

common law. The body of unwritten law developed in England from judicial decisions, which constitutes the basis of the English legal system and became part of American law.

common welfare. The good of the community as a whole. Also referred to as the common good.

compelling state interest. A state interest that takes precedence over individual rights.

competitive market. A situation in which the buying and selling of goods and services is governed by competition among buyers and sellers.

compromise. A way to settle differences by each side agreeing to give up some of what it wants.

Confederacy. The league of eleven southern states that seceded from the United States at the beginning of the Civil War.

conflict of interest. A situation in which a person cannot fulfill one responsibility or obligation without violating another.

Congress. The legislature of the United States consisting of the Senate and the House of Representatives.

consent of the governed. An agreement by the people to set up and live under a government. According to the natural rights philosophy, all legitimate government must rest on the consent of the governed.

constitution. A set of customs, traditions, rules, and laws that sets forth the way a government is organized and operated.

constitutional. A law or act that is in accord with and does not violate the constitution.

constitutional government. A system of government in which the powers of the government are limited by a constitution.

contempt of court. Willful disobedience of a judge's command or of an official court order.

counsel. A person who gives legal advice and represents those accused of crimes; attorney; lawyer.

covenant. A binding agreement made by two or more persons or parties; compact.

criminal justice system. The ways in which crimes are investigated and accused persons are brought to trial and, if found guilty, are punished.

criminal law. The branch of law which deals with the enforcement of laws and the punishment of persons who, by breaking laws, commit crimes.

criteria. Standards or rules on which a judgment or decision can be based.

cruel and unusual punishments. A clause in the Eighth Amendment which prohibits treatment of criminals that is not in accord with the moral standards of a humane and compassionate society.

damages. Money awarded by a court to a person for loss or damage for which another person is liable.

death penalty. A sentence calling for the execution of a criminal.

declaration of rights. A statement of the rights of people which must be protected in a given jurisdiction. Most of the state constitutions written prior to the U.S. Constitution began with a declaration of rights.

defense attorney. The lawyer who presents the side of the defendant (the accused) in a criminal trial.

delegate. A person chosen to act for or represent others, as at a convention.

deterrence. A means of preventing or discouraging an action, such as a criminal act.

discretion. Freedom to decide or act on one's own.

dispossessed. Being deprived of the possession of something, especially property.

dissent. To disagree with the majority or prevailing viewpoint on an issue. Also, an opinion of a Supreme Court justice that is in disagreement with the Court's decision in a case.

diversity. Variation among the members of a society, for example, in their property ownership and wealth, religious or moral beliefs, race, or ethnicity.

divine right of kings. The theory of government that holds that a monarch receives the right to rule directly from God and not from the people.

domestic tranquility. Internal peacefulness; lack of disturbance within a country.

double jeopardy. The provision in the Fifth Amendment that one may not be tried twice for the same crime, "be twice put in jeopardy of life or limb."

Dred Scott v. Sanford (1857). A Supreme Court case which held that blacks were not citizens and had no right to sue in federal courts.

due process clause. As interpreted by the courts, this clause in the Fifth and Fourteenth Amendments requires that a person be treated fairly by the government.

due process of law. The principle that every person is entitled to fair treatment by the government. For example, a person accused of a crime is entitled to a fair trial. Both fair laws and fair procedures must be used to judge the person.

electoral vote. The official vote for president cast by the electoral college, a group of presidential electors chosen by the states. Each state has a number of electors equal to the total of its members in the Senate and House of Representatives.

emanate. To come from, or out of, a source.

emancipation. Freedom from slavery.

Emancipation Proclamation (1863). President Lincoln's official statement that as of January 1, 1863, all slaves in the states that were under Confederate control would be freed.

England. One of the three countries which make up the island of Great Britain. England was united with Scotland and Wales in 1707 to form Great Britain.

English Bill of Rights. An act passed by Parliament in 1689 which limited the power of the monarch. This document established Parliament as the most powerful branch of the English government.

enumeration. The specific listing of something.

equal opportunity. An equal chance; for example, for men and women to be equally eligible for a job.

equal protection clause. The clause in Section 1 of the Fourteenth Amendment that prohibits states from denying "any person...the equal protection of the laws."

equal protection of the laws. The idea that no individual or group may receive special privileges nor be unjustly discriminated against by the law.

equality of condition. Equality in all aspects of life, such as personal possessions, living standards, medical care, and working conditions.

Espionage Act of 1918. An act of Congress during World War I that prohibited anyone from urging resistance to the United States or to the war effort. An example of suppression of freedom of speech.

established church. An established religion.

established religion. An official, state-sponsored religion.

establishment clause. The clause in the First Amendment that says the government may not set up, or establish, an official religion.

ex post facto **law.** A law that declares an act a crime, even though it was not a crime when committed. *Ex post facto* laws are forbidden by the Constitution (Article I, Sections 9 and 10).

exclusionary rule. The rule, established by the Supreme Court, that evidence unconstitutionally gathered by law enforcement officers may not be used against a defendant in a trial.

factions. Groups, according to James Madison, that seek to promote their own special interests regardless of the common welfare.

federal government. The United States government, as established by the Constitution, exercising control over the entire nation, as distinguished from state and local governments.

federalism. A form of political organization in which governmental power is divided between a central government and territorial subdivisions—in the United States, among the federal and state governments.

Federalist, The. A series of articles written in 1787-1788 by Alexander Hamilton, James Madison, and John Jay, urging the adoption of the Constitution and supporting the need for a strong federal government.

Federalists. The people who supported the ratification of the Constitution and advocated a strong federal government.

felony. A crime, such as murder or rape, considered more serious than a misdemeanor and subject to more stringent punishment.

feudalism. A political and economic system in which a king or queen shared power with the nobility, who required services from the common people in return for allowing them to use the noble's land.

Founders. The people who played important roles in the development of the national government of the United States.

Framers. The delegates to the Philadelphia Convention held in 1787 and those who wrote and ratified the Bill of Rights.

free exercise clause. The clause in the First Amendment that says the government shall make no law prohibiting the free practice of religious beliefs.

freedom of assembly. The freedom of people to gather together in public.

freedom of conscience. The freedom of belief. Many consider freedom of conscience an absolute right, one that has no limitations.

freedom of expression. The freedoms of speech, press, assembly, and petition that are protected by the First Amendment.

freedom of petition. The freedom to present requests to the government without reprisal.

freedom of press. The freedom to print or publish.

freedom of religion. The freedom to worship as one pleases.

freedom of speech. The freedom to express oneself, either verbally or non-verbally (e.g., symbolically).

fundamental rights. Rights considered to be essential.

gag rule. A rule limiting discussion or debate on a particular issue.

general warrant. A legal warrant that does not describe in detail the places to be searched and the things or persons to be seized.

general welfare. The good of society in general. Common welfare.

Gideon v. Wainright (1963). A Supreme Court case which declared that every defendant in a felony case is entitled to a lawyer. Those defendants too poor to hire a lawyer must be provided one by the court.

Gitlow v. New York (1925). A Supreme Court case in which the rights of free speech and the press were incorporated into the Fourteenth Amendment and therefore protected against interference by state government.

Glorious Revolution (1688). The struggle that overthrew King James II and established Parliament's supremacy in the English government.

good faith. With the intent to do the proper thing.

grandfather clauses. The laws, in many southern states, that allowed whites who could not pass a literacy test to vote if their grandfathers had been eligible to vote.

Great Awakening. Religious revivals in the eighteenth century during which a number of new Protestant churches began.

Great Britain. The island consisting of England, Scotland, and Wales. Today, Great Britain is part of the United Kingdom of Great Britain and Northern Ireland.

guided discretion. The freedom of juries in capital cases to decide whether to impose life sentences or death sentences under standards dictated by the court.

guilds. Medieval associations or societies of merchants, craftsmen, or artisans.

habeas corpus, **writ of.** A Latin term meaning "you shall have the body." It is an order commanding that a prisoner be brought to court to be told the reason for being held.

immunity. Exemption from prosecution.

impartial. Not prejudiced or biased.

impeachment. Charging a public official with a crime in office.

incorporation. The process by which the Supreme Court interpreted the Fourteenth Amendment to extend the Bill of Rights to include protections against actions of the state governments.

individual rights. Rights possessed by individuals as opposed to those rights which belong to groups such as the nobility or tradesmen.

inherent rights. Rights that all people have because they are human. Also called natural rights.

inquisitorial system. A trial system in which a single person acts as both prosecutor and judge, questioning witnesses, examining evidence, and reaching a verdict.

interest group. A group of people that is organized to promote the interests of its members.

Judeo-Christian. Beliefs and practices which have their historical roots in Judaism and Christianity.

judgment of his peers. A phrase in the Magna Carta establishing the accountability of an accused man to others in society besides the king. It did not, however, refer to trial by jury as we understand it today.

judicial review. The power of the courts to declare laws and actions of the local, state, or federal government invalid if the courts decide they violate the Constitution.

jurisdiction. The power to interpret and apply the law; the territory within which that power may be exercised.

jury nullification. A situation in which the jury refuses to apply a law and renders a verdict contrary to the facts in order to achieve a desired result.

knight. A medieval tenant giving military service to a feudal landholder.

laissez faire. An economic theory that government should not interfere in business, industry, or commerce.

law of the land. A phrase in the Magna Carta establishing the rule of law; that is, that no man, even the king, is above the law.

legislative supremacy. A system of government, such as that set forth in the early state constitutions, in which most of the power is given to the legislature.

leniency. Lack of harshness; mercy.

libel. Published words or pictures that falsely and maliciously defame a person.

limited government. According to the natural rights philosophers, a government restricted to protecting natural rights and which does not interfere with other aspects of life.

literacy test. A test given to people to prove they were able to read and write as a qualification for voting. In the South, these tests were used to keep blacks from voting.

lobby. To represent a special interest group in trying to influence legislatures.

Loyalist. An American who supported Great Britain in the Revolutionary War.

Magna Carta. A contract between King John and his nobles signed in 1215. The agreement established that the king must obey the law and it protected certain rights of the nobles.

Marbury v. Madison **(1803).** A case in which the Supreme Court held that it had the power of judicial review over acts of Congress and the president.

Massachusetts Body of Liberties (1641). A document that described the rights of citizens and the authority of public officials.

Mayflower Compact. A document drawn up by the Pilgrims in 1620 that provided a legal basis for self-government.

Middle Ages. A period, lasting from the fifth century to the fourteenth century, during which the political, economic, and military structure was characterized by feudalism. The term "medieval" describes that which occurred during the Middle Ages.

Miranda v. Arizona **(1966).** A Supreme Court case that said the right to be represented by a lawyer applied not only to criminal trials, but also to other critical stages in the criminal justice process, such as during police questioning of suspects.

misdemeanor. A crime less serious than a felony.

moral education. According to classical republicanism, education which is required to instill civic virtue among the members of society. Moral education stressed the importance of individual participation in the political life of the society.

National Association for the Advancement of Colored People (NAACP). An interracial group founded in 1909 to advocate the rights of African Americans.

natural rights. Those rights that are so much a part of human nature that they cannot be taken away or given up, as opposed to rights conferred by law.

Nineteenth Amendment. The amendment to the Constitution, ratified in 1920, guaranteeing women the right to vote.

Ninth Amendment. This amendment states, in effect, that the Bill of Rights is only a partial listing of the people's rights.

nobility. A group of persons having titles, usually of a hereditary nature, who compose the aristocracy in a society. In Great Britain, the nobility is represented in the House of Lords.

Northwest Ordinance of 1787. One of the great accomplishments of the U.S. government under the Articles of Confederation. This law provided for the settlement of the western lands and for their admission into the Union.

null and void. Of no legal or binding force; invalid.

Parliament. The British legislature, made up of two houses, the House of Lords and the House of Commons.

parliamentary supremacy. The principle that the parliament, or legislative body, has ultimate sovereignty, or control, in a state.

penumbra. A partial shadow, as in an eclipse, between regions of complete shadow and complete light. Refers to unenumerated rights implied or suggested within the boundaries of other, enumerated, rights.

perjury. The deliberate giving of false, misleading, or incomplete testimony under oath.

petition. A document making a formal written request, usually accompanied by the signatures of a number of citizens. The right to petition the government is specifically protected by the First Amendment.

Petition of Right (1628). A document which limited the English king's power to tax people without the consent of Parliament and which also guaranteed English subjects certain rights.

Philadelphia Convention. The meeting held in Philadelphia in 1787 at which the U.S. Constitution was written.

Plessy v. Ferguson (1896). A case in which the Supreme Court ruled that "separate-but-equal" public facilities for blacks and whites were permissible under the Constitution.

poll taxes. Taxes that voters in many southern states were required to pay before they could vote. They were used to prevent blacks from voting.

popular sovereignty. The idea that government is based on the consent of the people.

preamble. An introduction to a formal document that explains its purpose.

preferential treatment programs. A form of affirmative action in which underrepresented groups are given preferred treatment in gaining jobs and entrance to colleges and universities. These programs are designed to make up for the effects of past discrimination.

prejudice. An adverse or hostile opinion formed without just cause; an unreasonable bias against persons of another race or religion.

prior restraint. A form of censorship in which the government requires approval of materials for publication or broadcast before they can be printed (or taped) and distributed.

private property. Property belonging to a particular person or persons as opposed to the public or the government.

privileges and immunities clause. A clause of the Fourteenth Amendment which was intended to require that each state recognize the civil liberties and rights protected by the federal Constitution and Bill of Rights.

probable cause. A good reason for suspecting a person of breaking a law. Required in cases in which a law enforcement officer needs to conduct a search or seizure and cannot, for practical purposes, obtain a search warrant.

procedural due process. Refers to those clauses in the Constitution that protect individuals from unreasonable and unfair governmental procedures.

prosecuting attorney. The lawyer who presents the side of the government in a criminal trial.

provision. A qualification or clause in a document or agreement.

public forums. Public places in the community, such as streets, parks, and sidewalks, where people can express their viewpoints.

Puritans. A group of English Protestants who in the sixteenth and seventeenth centuries advocated strict religious discipline and simplification of the ceremonies and creeds of the Church of England.

ratified. Formally approved.

ratifying conventions. Meetings held in the states to approve the Constitution.

recognizance. A promise or obligation entered into before a court or magistrate to appear for trial.

redress of grievances. Correction of complaints. The First Amendment protects the right to petition the government to obtain a remedy for a claimed wrong.

Reformation. A great religious reform movement in Europe in the 1500s that led to the establishment of Protestant churches.

regulation. A rule designed to govern behavior.

religious test. A requirement that a person swear to a belief in God or belong to a particular religion in order, for example, to qualify for office or to vote.

remedial programs. A form of affirmative action in which special education programs are provided to help people gain the basic skills they need to succeed in the job market.

Renaissance. The great revival of art and learning in Europe during the fourteenth through seventeenth centuries.

representative government. A system of government in which power is held by the people and exercised indirectly through elected representatives.

retribution. Something demanded in repayment, such as punishment for crime.

reverse discrimination. The argument that preferential treatment affirmative action programs discriminate against majority groups.

right against self-incrimination. The constitutional right of people to refuse to give testimony against themselves that could subject them to criminal prosecution. The right is guaranteed in the Fifth Amendment.

right to counsel. The right to be represented by a lawyer.

right to know. The right of members of a society to receive information about the actions of their government.

right to privacy. The right to be free from intrusion into one's private life by government officials.

right to property. The right of individuals to own and control property free from government intervention.

right to silence. The right against self-incrimination, that is, not to be forced to give testimony which might incriminate oneself.

rights of Englishmen. Basic rights, established over time, that all subjects of the English monarch were understood to have. They included the right not to be kept in prison without a trial and the right to a trial by a jury.

rights of groups. The rights of people as members of their group or class, such as the nobility, the clergy, tradesmen, or craftsmen. These rights contrast with the rights of people as individuals.

Roman Republic. A society, dating from 509 B.C. to 27 B.C., which served as the model for the theory of classical republicanism.

royalty. The king or other royal persons. It can also mean that part of the government that represents the monarch.

rule of law. The principle that every member of a society, even a ruler, must follow the law.

safety valve. An outlet for the release of tension or anger. Many argue that allowing freedom of speech, even when repugnant or obnoxious, serves as a safety valve to prevent the build-up of hostility in those who hold such viewpoints.

Scottsboro cases (1932). Supreme Court cases which established the right of persons accused of capital crimes in state courts to have the right to an attorney.

Sedition Act (1798). An act of the Federalist-controlled Congress which made it a crime to criticize the government. It was an early violation of freedom of speech and press.

seditious libel. Printed language which seeks to convince others to engage in the overthrow of the government.

segregation. The separation or isolation of a race, class, or ethnic group from the rest of society.

self-incrimination. Giving evidence or answering questions which might subject oneself to criminal prosecution.

separate-but-equal doctrine. The argument, once upheld by the Supreme Court, that separate public facilities for blacks and whites were constitutional if the facilities were of equal quality.

separation of church and state. The concept that religion and government should be separate; the basis for the establishment clause of the First Amendment.

separation of powers. The division of powers among different branches of government; in the United States, among a legislative, executive, and judicial branch.

Shays's Rebellion. An uprising by Massachusetts farmers in 1786 that convinced many people that the Articles of Confederation needed to be changed.

Slaughterhouse Cases (1873). A group of Supreme Court cases in which the Court refused to use the privileges and immunities clause of the Fourteenth Amendment to protect the rights listed in the Bill of Rights from violation by state government.

social contract. An agreement among all the people in a society to give up part of their freedom to a government in return for protection of their natural rights. A theory developed by Locke to explain the origin of legitimate government.

sovereignty. The ultimate, supreme power in a state; in the United States, sovereignty rests with the people.

speech codes. Rules designed to limit certain types of speech, such as racially or sexually offensive speech, on college campuses.

Star Chamber. A fifteenth-to-seventeenth-century English court consisting of judges who were appointed by the king or queen and who sat in closed session on cases involving the security of the state.

state and local government. The agencies which have political authority in individual states and local areas. All powers not established by the Constitution for the federal government are reserved for the states.

state constitution. The set of rules and laws which organize the government of a state.

state of nature. The condition of people living together in a society without government and laws.

substantive due process. Those judicial interpretations of the due process clauses of the Constitution that require that the content of laws be fair and reasonable.

suffrage. The right to vote.

testify. To make statements, or give information in court, under oath or affirmation, a solemn promise to tell the truth.

third degree. Mental or physical torture to obtain information or a confession from a prisoner.

time, place, and manner restrictions. Government regulations which place restrictions on free speech. These regulations, specifying when, where, and in what way speech is allowed, are applied when unrestricted free speech will conflict with the rights of others.

totalitarian government. A form of government in which one person or party exercises absolute control over all aspects of life and in which no opposition is allowed.

trade union. An organization of workers having the same trade formed for the purpose of improving working conditions and salaries.

unalienable (inalienable) rights. Fundamental rights of the people that may not be taken away. A phrase used in the Virginia Declaration of Rights and the Declaration of Independence.

unenumerated rights. Rights which are not specifically listed in the Constitution or Bill of Rights, but which have been recognized and protected by the courts.

unguided discretion. The freedom of juries in capital cases to impose life sentences or death sentences without any standards dictated by the court.

United Nations. An international organization comprising most of the nations of the world, formed in 1945 to promote peace, security, and economic development.

Universal Declaration of Human Rights. An international declaration of rights adopted by the United Nations in 1948.

veto. The constitutional power of the president to refuse to sign a bill passed by Congress, thereby preventing it from becoming a law. The president's veto may be overridden by a two-thirds vote of both the Senate and House of Representatives.

Virginia Declaration of Rights. The first state declaration of rights, which served as a model for other state declarations of rights and the Bill of Rights. It was adopted on June 12, 1776.

warrant. An order by a judge authorizing a police officer to make an arrest or search, or to perform some other designated act.

white supremacists. People who claim that white people are superior to other races.

writ. A written court order commanding the person receiving the writ to perform or not perform acts specified in the order.

writ of assistance. A document giving a governmental authority the power to search and seize property without restrictions.

Index

Index

Due process
    procedural   78-79, 108-110, 112, 127, 134
    substantive   78-81, 108, 137-139
Dyer, Mary 88

Education Act of 1972   73
Eighth Amendment   85, 108, 112, 129-132, 139
Emancipation Proclamation   61
England   9, 15-16, 20, 22-25, 28, 31, 44, 59, 87, 114, 125
    (see also Great Britain)
English Bill of Rights   21, 23-24, 29, 52, 98, 103, 130
Enumerated rights   82, 85, 103, 135-140
Equal Access Act   95, 107
Equal Employment Opportunities Act   73
Equal opportunity   74-75, 142, 144
Equal protection   56, 82, 84, 106 (see also Fourteenth
    Amendment)
Equal protection clause   63, 66, 70-72, 74, 76-77, 101,
    142-143
Equal protection of the laws   66, 69-74, 76-77
Equality of condition   69-70, 73
Espionage Act of 1918   96, 99
Establishment clause   87, 89-92, 95
Establishment of religion   3, 87, 89-90, 139, 146
Ex post facto laws   35, 43-45, 49, 59, 79
Exclusionary rule   113, 116-118, 122
Executive branch   141

Fair Employment Practices Commission   142
FBI   114, 117, 122
Federal system   40-41, 62, 83, 148
Federalism   38, 40-41, 83
Federalist   47-50, 52, 54, 57-58, 115, 125, 136
Federalist Party   63
Federalist, The   47-49
Feudalism   13, 15-16, 28
Fifteenth Amendment   64, 66, 68, 141
Fifth Amendment   59, 78, 84-85, 117, 119-123, 132, 139
First Amendment   3, 10, 29, 53, 58, 83, 86-87, 89-90, 92,
    95-101, 103-107, 119, 146-147
Fourteenth Amendment   29, 53, 56, 64, 66-85, 87, 90, 99,
    101, 108, 113, 124, 129, 132, 137, 141-143
Fourth Amendment   113-119
France   30, 57-58, 87, 98
Frankfuter, Felix   84
Franklin, Benjamin   28, 96, 120
Free exercise clause   87, 90, 92-93
Freedom of assembly   103, 105-106
Freedom of conscience   8-9, 14, 52-53, 78, 88-89, 92, 113,
    119-120

Freedom of expression   8, 10, 57, 96-103, 109
Freedom of religion   3, 6, 24, 39, 49, 86, 89-90, 92-93,
    107, 136
Freedom of speech   3, 10, 24, 35, 43, 59, 97-98, 139
Freedom of the press   8-9, 24, 34, 49, 52-53, 98, 104
Fulminante v. Arizona   122
Fundamental rights   23, 33, 82-84, 101, 111
Furman v. Georgia   133, 139

Gerry, Elbridge   42, 48
Gideon v. Wainwright   124, 126
Gitlow v. New York   82-83
Glorious Revolution   21, 23-24, 31
Grandfather clause   63, 67
Grayson, William   54
Great Awakening   87-88
Great Britain   21-22, 28, 30, 33, 37, 39, 44, 57, 87, 98, 104,
    109, 112, 118 (see also England)
Griswold v. Connecticut   85, 139
Guided discretion   133

Habeas corpus   21, 23-25, 30, 35, 44, 49, 79, 108, 110-112
Hamilton, Alexander   28, 45, 48, 57, 136, 148
Hancock, John   115
Hand, Learned   6, 62, 97, 111, 149
Hayes, Rutherford B.   67
Henry II, King of England   125
Henry, Patrick   48, 54, 131
Hobbes, Thomas   18
Holmes, Oliver Wendell Jr.   85, 96
Hopkins, Reverend Samuel   29
House of Representatives   49, 52-53
Huguenots   87
Hutchinson, Anne   88

Illinois   64, 98, 144
In re John Demos   127
In re Winship   85
Incorporation of rights   82-86, 90
Inherent rights   33-34
Inquisitorial system   124-126
Interest groups   9, 14, 59, 103

Jackson, Robert   114
James II, King of Great Britain   23-24
Japanese Americans   142

Picture Credits